Elementary Teacher's
DISCIPLINE
PROBLEM SOLVER

A Practical A-Z Guide for Managing Classroom Behavior Problems

Kenneth Shore, Psy.D.

JOSSEY-BASS
A Wiley Imprint
www.josseybass.com

Published by Jossey-Bass
A Wiley Imprint
989 Market Street, San Francisco, CA 94103-1741   www.josseybass.com

Jossey-Bass books and products are available through most bookstores. To contact Jossey-Bass directly, call our Customer Care Department within the U.S. at (800) 956-7739, outside the U.S. at (317) 572-3993 or fax (317) 572-4002.

Jossey-Bass also publishes its books in a variety of electronic formats. Some content that appears in print may not be available in electronic books.

Library of Congress Cataloging-in-Publication Data

Shore, Kenneth.
  Elementary teacher's discipline problem solver : a practical A-Z guide
for managing classroom behavior problems / Kenneth Shore.— 1st ed.
     p. cm.
  ISBN 0-7879-6599-5 (alk. paper)
  1. School discipline—Handbooks, manuals, etc. 2. Classroom
management—Handbooks, manuals, etc. 3. Behavior
modification—Handbooks, manuals, etc. 4. Elementary school
teaching—Handbooks, manuals, etc. I. Title.
  LB3012.S533 2003
  372.15—dc21

                                        2003015227

Printed in the United States of America
FIRST EDITION
HB Printing   10 9 8 7 6 5 4 3 2

Contents

About the Author

Kenneth Shore is a psychologist and chair of a child study team for the Hamilton, New Jersey, public schools. He is also a licensed psychologist. He received a bachelor of arts degree in psychology from the University of Rochester in 1971 and a doctor of psychology degree from Rutgers University in 1981. In 2001, he was awarded the Donald R. Peterson Prize from Rutgers University for "outstanding contributions to professional psychology."

Shore wrote *The Special Education Handbook: A Comprehensive Guide for Parents and Educators* (Teachers College Press of Columbia University, 1986), *The Parents' Public School Handbook: How to Make the Most of Your Child's Education, from Kindergarten through Middle School* (Simon & Schuster, 1994), *Special Kids Problem Solver: Ready-to-Use Interventions for Helping All Students with Academic, Behavioral and Physical Problems* (Prentice Hall, 1998), and *Keeping Kids Safe* (Prentice Hall, 2001). He has also written numerous articles for parenting magazines and professional journals. One of his articles for *Sesame Street Parents* was nominated for a national award. Shore has given talks to many professional and parent groups, appeared on numerous radio programs, and been featured on a Public Broadcasting Station television series titled *Raising Kids* and was interviewed on CNN.

He has served as a guest expert on parenting issues and learning problems on various Web sites and currently writes a weekly column for *Education World* (www.educationworld.com).

Dr. Shore has worked for the federal government in evaluating educational legislation and served as a consultant to the New York City Board of Education. He helped establish the New Jersey YM-YWHA's camp for children with learning disabilities and was instrumental in developing the North Mercer Family Consultation Center, which used family therapy approaches to help families with children experiencing severe school adjustment problems. He can be contacted by e-mail at ShoreK@aol.com.

For Rima

Introduction

Discipline is a fundamental part of teaching. Education cannot take place and learning cannot flourish in an undisciplined setting. An innovative curriculum will have minimal impact if there is no control in the classroom. Inspired lessons are of little use if students are focused on nonacademic issues. Perhaps most important, teachers who spend much of their time responding to misbehavior have little time left over to teach.

In addition to interfering with students' learning, discipline problems make the process of teaching much more frustrating. Dealing with misbehavior on a continuing basis can drain the energies of even the most enthusiastic of teachers and rob them of the potential joys of teaching. Teaching is much more satisfying and learning much more productive in a well-disciplined class.

Despite the importance of discipline in the classroom, it is often neglected during the formal training of teachers, even though there is an abundance of literature on how to discipline students effectively, as well as a range of formal classroom discipline programs. For many new teachers, the learning curve is steep when it comes to understanding how to discipline students, with the bulk of their training coming on the job. Fortunately, teachers have a variety of tools at their disposal that can help transform an out-of-control group into an orderly classroom and disruptive children into cooperative students.

This book provides some of these tools. You will find practical, concrete, and teacher-tested strategies that will enable you to gain order in your classroom while preserving your students' dignity. This is not a book about theory. Rather, it translates theory into practice, offering ready-to-use techniques that take into consideration the constraints that you face in the classroom, notably limited time and the demands of your other students.

This is not a book to be read straight through. Rather, it is a reference book to be kept handy and consulted when a vexing problem occurs and you are looking for some new strategies you can use without having to scowl or shout. Using the ideas in this book will help you maximize the time you spend teaching and minimize the time you spend disciplining. Following these practices will help you become a more effective classroom leader and manager.

The strategies described in this book are intended primarily for elementary school teachers. Both new and experienced teachers will find ideas for managing challenging classroom behaviors. Others working with children in educational settings, including principals, school psychologists, guidance counselors, learning specialists, social workers, school nurses, speech-language specialists, substitute teachers, teacher aides, and even camp personnel may also find this book helpful. In addition, parents may use the information in working with their child's teacher to solve school problems and may even find the ideas beneficial in dealing with problems at home.

The book encompasses a wide range of problems and situations that are commonly encountered in elementary classrooms. In deciding which problems to include, a broad standard was used. Rather than being limited to acting-out or disruptive behaviors, this book takes a wide-angle view, including behavioral problems that disrupt the teacher's ability to teach, interfere with the student's ability to be successful in class, or impede classmates' ability to focus on their schoolwork. For example, in addition to discussing how to respond to a child who calls out in class or has angry outbursts, this book describes strategies for dealing with students who are socially isolated, sleep in class, or have poor hygiene.

The book has a reader-friendly format. Each section tackles a different behavioral concern. The problems are listed in alphabetical order to help readers locate their particular concerns easily. For each problem, there is a brief discussion of possible motivations underlying the behavior, followed by a menu of specific and practical classroom strategies for managing the problem. The reader is also directed to related sections that may be useful in responding to that behavior through the "See Also" feature at the end of each section.

As you use this book to find ways to help your students, keep in mind that not every strategy dealing with a particular problem will be applicable to your students or your situation. Some strategies are more appropriate for younger elementary students; others are better suited for older elementary students. Some are more appropriate for severe forms of the behavior; others are better suited for milder forms. In addition, you may find that some of the strategies are incompatible with your own personal philosophy about discipline. Nonetheless, you should be able to find at least two or three ideas for each problem that suit your situation, your students' characteristics, and your teaching values.

This book is built on a number of assumptions about discipline, including the following:

1. An important part of any discipline program is prevention, namely, anticipating problems before they occur and responding in a way that keeps those problems from emerging.

2. It is essential that you consider the whole child when deciding how to discipline a student. This means trying to figure out what may be motivating his or her behavior and what this tells you about his or her psychological needs. Understanding these factors may help you determine how to respond effectively to the child.

3. Discipline problems often emerge when academic instruction is not geared to a student's ability or interest level. In considering how to respond to behavioral problems in your classroom, it is thus important to consider whether misbehaving students may be experiencing academic difficulties or frustration.

4. In choosing strategies for dealing with a particular problem, moderation should be the watchword. In your effort to help the student and gain some control, select disciplinary measures that are least disruptive to your classroom structure. The more extreme the intervention, the more likely it is to disrupt the flow of your lesson or classroom activity.

5. Discipline is not synonymous with punishment. Discipline is more than just giving students detention, putting them in time-out, or suspending them. It must also include strategies that are positive and engaging and that motivate students to behave appropriately and exercise self-control. In responding to misbehavior, you have a golden teaching opportunity. Indeed, the word *discipline* is derived from the Latin word *disciplina,* meaning instruction.

6. Disciplining students is not solely the teacher's job. It is a collaborative effort that may require the efforts of the principal, other teachers, parents, and even classmates in dealing with behavioral concerns.

In using this book, keep in mind that the strategies discussed here are not etched in stone. Feel free to adapt these ideas to the needs of your students and to your particular teaching style and values. And if you find other approaches that are effective, by all means stay the course. Discipline is very much a trial-and-error process in which you want to stick with strategies that work for you and discard those that do not.

Kenneth Shore, Psy.D.

Aggressive Behavior

Children who are aggressive are not born that way. Their education in the use of force may begin at home, where their parents may model aggressive behavior as a way of solving problems. Their children may learn from an early age that the way to get what they want is through force. They may be taught to respond to challenges with confrontation and to express themselves with their fists rather than with words. The message they receive is "might makes right."

Children also learn aggressive behavior from the media. The amount of violence they are exposed to on television is simply astounding. By the age of fourteen, a child will have seen as many as 11,000 murders on television. Research indicates that children who see violence frequently on television may become less sensitive to the pain and suffering of others and may view aggression as an acceptable way of solving problems.

Children who are aggressive in school present a substantial challenge for teachers. An aggressive student can engender a climate of fear in your classroom, creating anxiety among your students and distracting them from their schoolwork. The student who is the cause of this fear also warrants your concern. His behavior may signal that he is a troubled child and may cause him to be shunned by his peers. Moreover, his aggressive behavior in childhood may be a harbinger of later problems as an adolescent and adult.

Your task in working with an aggressive student is to help make your classroom a safe haven by furthering two goals: (1) making it clear to your students that aggressive behavior will not be tolerated and (2) helping the student develop more appropriate ways of interacting and settling disputes with his peers. In responding to the student, avoid harsh punishment or humiliation. Disciplining him severely may only fuel his anger and make him more determined to continue his aggressive behavior.

What You Can Do

1. Make it clear that aggressive behavior is unacceptable.
At the beginning of the year, when explaining your class rules, state clearly that students are

not allowed to hit or push under any circumstances. You might let them know the consequences for aggressive behavior. Reinforce this rule during the year as necessary. Encourage your students to tell you immediately if they observe any physical conflicts.

2. Make sure your students know that you will protect them.
If you observe a student physically harassing another student, take immediate action to stop it. Putting an end to this behavior is important, not only to protect the student but to send a message to your other students that you will not tolerate this behavior and will do whatever is necessary to ensure that your classroom is a safe haven.

3. Be assertive in breaking up a fight.
If two elementary school students are engaged in a fight, use a strong, loud voice to stop it. For example, you might say, "Seth and Matthew, break it up right now. Move away from each other." If that does not work, you might want to say something odd to divert their attention. For example, you might say, "Look up. The ceiling is falling." You could even think of a comment in advance. If they do not stop and you cannot separate them, have another student go to the office to request help. If a crowd of children is gathering, insist that they move away or sit down, perhaps clapping your hands to get their attention. After the incident, meet with the students so they can give you their versions of what happened and you can resolve any lingering problems. Also notify the parents.

4. Respond calmly but firmly to the student.
Speak in a firm, no-nonsense manner to stop a student's aggressive behavior, using physical restraint as a last resort. In responding to him, pay attention to your verbal as well as nonverbal language. Even if he is screaming at you, remain calm. Allow him to say what he is upset about without interrupting him and then acknowledge his feelings. Avoid crossing your arms, pointing your finger, or making threats, all of which will fuel his anger and stiffen his resistance. You might say something like the following: "I understand that you are angry, and maybe

you have reason to be upset, but hitting is not the way we deal with problems. That behavior is not acceptable. If there is something you are unhappy about, you have to use words to express it, not your hands."

5. Consider removing the student.

You may conclude that a student's aggressive behavior warrants separating him from the rest of the class, either to protect your students or to send him a strong message that what he did merits a serious consequence. You can do this by giving him a time-out in class or sending him to the office. If you give him a time-out, act quickly and firmly while saying to him, "You know the rule: no hitting. You need to go to time-out." In the time-out area, have him sit in a chair and instruct him to remain quiet. Tell him he can return to the class activity after a set number of minutes. If he leaves the chair or acts in a disruptive manner, tell him that the timer will be reset to zero and he will need to stay in time-out longer. If you decide to send him to the office, call the principal to inform her of the incident and alert her that the student is on his way. When he returns from his time-out or his trip to the office, welcome him back, perhaps reminding him of the rule about aggressive behavior, and then look for opportunities to praise him for appropriate behavior.

6. After the child cools down, talk with him privately.

Although he may expect you to react punitively, surprise him by reacting supportively. Express your confidence that he can resolve problems without being hurtful to his peers. Tell him that you think he must be upset about something to lose control as he did and that you want to understand what may be bothering him. Your effort to connect with him may encourage him to open up to you. If he does, listen attentively without interrupting him. Speaking in a calm voice, tell him that you understand why he was upset but stress that he has to find a way to express his anger with words rather than with his hands. Let him know that his behavior will cause classmates to fear him and avoid him as a result. Focus on what he can say and do differently next time to avoid responding in an aggressive manner.

7. Try to identify when and where the student is aggressive.

Look for a pattern in the incidents so you can anticipate their occurrence and take steps to avoid them. You might want to jot down some information on these incidents, noting when they occurred, what activity was going on at the time, who was the target of his aggression, what happened right before and right after the incident, and how others responded. Through this behavioral assessment, you can help determine what triggers his behavior, what reinforces it, and most important, what to do about it. For example, your assessment may tell you that a student is often aggressive while lining up to go to lunch. If so, you might ask him to be the door holder or to hold some folders as he stands in line to inhibit aggressive behavior.

8. Seek parental support.

Invite the parents of an aggressive student in for a meeting to apprise them of his behavior and obtain their perspective. Ask them if he acts similarly at home and what they think is contributing to this behavior. You may want to inquire about his exposure to violence in the media, namely, in the television shows he watches and the computer and video games he plays. If a concern, encourage the parents to limit his exposure to these violent images. Also find out what disciplinary strategies they have found successful with their child and what suggestions they have for dealing with him when he is aggressive in school. After agreeing with them on a plan for managing his behavior, bring the student in and let him know the details. Make sure he hears his parents say that they disapprove of his behavior and support your approach with him in the classroom.

9. Have the student apologize.

Although you do not want to force him to say he is sorry because this may only fuel his anger, you want to strongly encourage him to make amends with the student he hit. If he is willing to do this, it will help soothe hurt feelings and avoid future conflicts.

10. Teach your students conflict-resolution skills.

Children may resort to aggression because they lack the words or skills to solve problems with their classmates. Help them learn to resolve peer conflicts without acting aggressively by teaching them the basics of talking things out: staying calm; allowing each person to have his say without being interrupted, blamed, or put down; using "I messages" to convey feelings; and considering the other's point of view. Designate an area of your class as the "peace corner," where your students can go to settle conflicts. If two students are having a conflict, tell them to go there to talk it out and to come to you when they are finished to inform you of their solution. With young elementary students, you may want to use puppets to teach conflict-resolution skills. Puppets are effective in holding their attention and helping them see a problem from different points of view.

11. Require students involved in a conflict to fill out a behavior form.
After they have calmed down, have the students complete a form that asks them to describe what triggered the conflict, how they behaved, and how they could have handled the situation differently. Meet with the students to discuss their responses. This form provides a record of the incident that you can use when meeting with their parents and also helps them learn to reflect on and modify their behavior.

12. Send the student to a "cooling-off" place.
Tell the student that when he is feeling frustrated and on the verge of acting out, he should tell you he needs to leave the room. Then send him to an area you and he have agreed on as a cooling-off area. This might be the rear of the classroom, the library, the classroom next door (ask the teacher if this is okay), the bathroom or water fountain, the guidance counselor's office, or the main office. Suggest he bring something with him to help calm him down, for example, a book, an art activity, a toy, even a class assignment. Tell him he can return when he is feeling more in control. Be certain he understands that this is not a disciplinary measure but a way of preventing a problem. Make sure he does not abuse this privilege by leaving the classroom whenever he wants.

13. Have the student engage in activities that make aggressive behavior less likely.
When he appears tense, suggest tasks that allow him to release frustration such as drawing a picture, working with clay, taking a walk, writing

in a journal, or squeezing a ball. You may want to give him an item to carry or suggest that he put his hands in his pockets during times when he is prone to using his hands inappropriately or is feeling on the verge of an outburst.

14. Appeal to the student's desire to gain the approval of his peers.

Help him understand that when he lashes out at a classmate, he has been manipulated into acting in a way that makes him look foolish or weak to his peers. Suggest that the way to impress his peers is to show them that he can control his temper rather than be manipulated into losing his cool.

15. Connect with the student.

An aggressive student may distrust his teacher and view her in an adversarial manner. Try to gain this student's trust by listening attentively to what he says and showing respect for his thoughts and concerns. Find a few minutes every so often to talk with him about his interests and hobbies. Help him start the day on a positive note by giving him a high five or making an upbeat comment when he walks into the room. He may make better choices if he feels supported and accepted by you.

16. Obtain in-school counseling for the student.

You might ask the guidance counselor or school psychologist to counsel him. He may need guidance in resolving peer conflicts and finding alternative ways of behaving. He may also need help interpreting the behavior of his peers if he tends to perceive hostile intent when none is intended.

17. Assign the student community service.

Giving the student tasks that involve helping others may encourage him to act more sympathetically and less aggressively toward peers. You might have him do the following: serve as a buddy to a learning disabled student, organize a game for students in a lower grade during recess, record acts of kindness by students to help determine who receives school courtesy awards, or help the principal monitor younger students in the lunchroom.

Elementary Teacher's Discipline Problem Solver

18. Consider requesting an evaluation to determine special education eligibility.
If he has acted aggressively toward peers on many occasions, you may want to initiate a referral to determine whether the student warrants special education. He may need closer supervision and more individualized instruction than you can provide. If he is already classified as eligible for special education, you may want to convene a meeting of the individualized education program (IEP) team (of which you are a part) to revise his program. The team might recommend more special education help or counseling, a one-to-one aide in the regular classroom, or a behavior-improvement plan.

See Also

Angry Outbursts

Bullying

Hitting or Threatening a Teacher

Sexually Offensive Behavior

Spitting

Weapon, Possession of

Angry Outbursts

Almost every student becomes angry at some point in school. After all, anger is a normal human emotion. It is not a problem if a student becomes angry in school as long as she expresses her feelings appropriately. It is a problem, however, if she expresses that anger in a way that is hurtful to others or disruptive to your class. A student who frequently has angry outbursts can throw a classroom into turmoil.

An angry student may display her temper in a wide variety of ways. She may be withdrawn from her peers, unresponsive to the teacher, and disengaged from the learning process. Seemingly minor matters may set her off, causing her to fly off the handle with little provocation and lash out at the drop of a hat. A younger child may express her anger through a full-blown tantrum, accompanied by screaming, kicking, and throwing herself on the floor. These behaviors can be frightening to classmates and disturbing to the teacher.

Anger usually results from a build-up of frustration. Although most students can manage their frustration relatively well without going into a rage, the angry student often lacks the inner controls to keep her frustration in check and the vocabulary to express it verbally. Her anger may also be reinforced by the attention she receives as a result of her acting-out behavior.

Your challenge in working with a student whose emotional temperature often reaches the boiling point is to control your own feelings as well as the feelings of the student. You may find that an angry student may trigger feelings of anger and frustration in you. It is important that you try to maintain your composure and not say or do anything that fuels her anger or causes the problem to spiral out of control. You want to react to the student in a way that cools her down rather than fires her up.

What You Can Do

1. Model calm behavior. The most effective way to foster a calm attitude among your students is to engage in the behavior yourself. Calm begets calm. Try to maintain your composure, even in the face of stressful situations. In dealing with an angry student, avoid arguing with her, threatening her, or even raising your voice. This will only fuel her anger and risk triggering an explosion. You can convey a strong message without yelling at her or putting her down. Similarly, be aware of your body language; for example, crossing your arms might be provocative to the student. You may want to acknowledge her concern and let her know you care about her by saying something like, "I can see that what happened really upset you" or "I really want to hear what happened, but I can't understand you when you are crying or yelling."

2. Do not take her words personally.
In a fit of anger, the student may say things that make your blood boil. Try to temper your reaction by reminding yourself that her comments may have nothing to do with anything you said or did. Indeed, her anger may be unrelated to events in school and may, in fact, be due to home issues. If you fear that you may say something that will intensify the student's anger, try taking a deep breath and counting to 5 before responding to her.

3. After the student calms down, have a private, nonthreatening talk with her.
She may expect you to be angry with her and perhaps even punish her. Surprise her by reacting in a supportive manner. Tell her that she must be hurting to lose control as she did. Your effort to connect with rather than control her may encourage her to open up and tell you why she is so angry. If she does, listen to her attentively without interrupting her. Using a calm voice, let her know that it is okay for her to get angry but that she has to find a way to express her anger in a way that does not disrupt the class and cause classmates to avoid her. Ask her how else she might have responded; offer some suggestions of your own. Give her permission to come to you when angry, but stress that she has to speak in a calm, respectful manner. You may even want to suggest what she can say. Many students act out when angry because they lack the vocabulary to express their feelings.

4. Problem-solve with the student.
Let the student know that you think she is capable of controlling her temper but that the two of you must work together. Ask her what is making her angry. If she offers no response, suggest some

possibilities, including schoolwork, peer problems, and home issues, and have her tell you if you are on target. Also take a look at your interaction with her and ask yourself, as well as the student, if you might be upsetting her with comments or actions that she perceives as unfair. In trying to figure out what makes her angry, you might have her finish some incomplete sentences with her own thoughts and feelings, including

- "I get so angry when . . . "
- "Three things that make me really frustrated in school are . . . "
- "It makes me so mad when other kids . . . "
- "I hate it when adults . . . "
- "I never lose my temper when . . . "
- "What helps me calm down is . . . "

Use her responses to develop an action plan with the student to deal with the issues that are provoking her anger. You may even want to role-play with her by presenting various situations that make her angry and having her try out new ways of responding in which she expresses her feelings without being offensive or disruptive.

5. Look for a pattern in the student's outbursts. Identifying the circumstances surrounding the outbursts can help you anticipate when they might occur and take steps to prevent them. In observing these incidents, ask yourself such questions as these:

- Do they happen during a particular part of the day or in the presence of specific individuals?
- Does the student behave in a specific way to signal that an outburst is imminent?
- What happens right before the outburst?
- What is the response of others?

Answers to these questions may help you figure out what is fueling her flare-ups and what may be reinforcing them. If you can anticipate when her outbursts are likely to occur, you can talk with her prior to the activity or take other precautions. For example, if a student with a reading disability often gets upset right before she is expected to read aloud, you will want to find a way to relieve her obvious discomfort about reading in public.

6. Provide support to the academically frustrated student. It is not uncommon for a student to erupt in anger because she is frustrated by her inability to do the work or keep pace with her classmates. If you suspect one of your students is acting out for this reason, give her support and provide accommodations to lessen her frustration and increase her confidence that she can be successful with the work.

7. Intervene early. Monitor the student, and if you observe behavior that suggests an outburst is imminent, take steps to distract her. You might change the activity, have her do an errand for you, or take her aside and talk with her about a new topic. Within a few minutes, she will likely forget what she was upset about.

8. Provide the angry student with a cooling-off area. Tell her that when she feels angry and on the verge of having an outburst, she is to signal you she is leaving the room and going to a prearranged spot in the school to calm down. Inform her that she can return when she is feeling more in control. Some possible cooling-off areas are the back of the classroom, the classroom next door (ask the teacher ahead of time if this is okay), the bathroom or water fountain, the guidance counselor's office, or the main office. You might have her bring along a favorite book, a toy, an art project, or even some schoolwork. Make sure she understands that this is not a punishment but rather a way of helping her calm down. Be careful that she does not abuse this privilege as a way of leaving the classroom whenever she wants.

9. Have the student write down what happened. After she has calmed down from having an outburst, ask her to put in writing what happened. Specifically, have her write down what triggered her anger, what she did in

response, how others reacted to her outburst, how she could have handled the situation differently, and how you and others can help her avoid this problem in the future. Review her responses with her and use them as a jumping-off point for a lesson in self-control.

10. Suggest activities that allow the student to release anger. Help her find ways to vent her frustration without disrupting the class. You might, for example, have her work with clay or play dough, draw a picture, write in a journal, tear up some paper, or take a walk (supervised, of course). You might even give her a ball to keep at her desk to squeeze every time she is feeling stressed or angry. If you see her engaging in an activity to release her anger, acknowledge her effort.

11. Teach the student some relaxation techniques. An angry student is a tense student. Help her learn to relax when she is stressed out by suggesting she do one of the following (in private, if embarrassment is an issue):

- Take a deep breath by inhaling very slowly.
- Count backwards from 10 before responding.
- Tense her muscles and then slowly relax them, gradually working her way down from her head to her feet.
- Imagine that she is a balloon; take a deep breath to simulate being blown up, hold it for 2 seconds, then slowly exhale while imagining that she has a leak and the air is gradually flowing out of her. You might do this with her.

12. Reach out to the student. Angry students typically distrust teachers and perceive them in an adversarial manner. If you have a student who often has a chip on her shoulder, make a special effort to connect with her. With time, she may begin to trust you and perhaps talk with you about what is making her so angry. You might greet her at the door every day in a warm, friendly manner and find something positive to say to her. When she speaks to you, listen attentively and show respect for her thoughts and concerns. Find a few minutes every day to talk with her about her interests and her hobbies,

perhaps sharing one of your hobbies with her. You might also try these other ways to connect with the student: have lunch with her on occasion, make a home visit, call her at home after she has had a difficult day to show your concern, and contact her parents after she has had a good day to let them know.

13. Help the student resolve peer conflicts.
If the student's problem with anger is related to frequent conflicts with classmates, help mediate these disputes. Get the students together to work out their differences. Give each student a chance to speak, letting them know that interruptions and name-calling are not allowed. Have each offer her version of what happened, as you listen attentively and ask questions to clarify their views. Ask them for ideas about how to solve the problem and offer some of your own. Make sure to ask what they would do differently next time.

14. Refer the student to a school counselor.
An angry student may warrant more than a private chat with you. If so, ask the guidance counselor or school psychologist to meet with her. He will likely probe beneath the surface to understand what prompted the angry behavior and then provide guidance in solving social problems and finding alternatives to lashing out in anger. The student may also need help in interpreting the actions and comments of her peers. Children prone to anger often perceive hostile intent when none is intended. The counselor might also role-play with the student so that she can experience how it feels to be the target of anger and try out alternative responses.

15. Get her parents' perspective.
If a student exhibits a pattern of angry behavior, set up a meeting with her parents to inform them of the problem and elicit their understanding of her behavior. Ask them if they have observed similar behavior at home and what they think the source of her anger is. Find out how they handle the problem at home and what ideas they have for managing this behavior in school. You might bring the student in for part or even all of the meeting so she can see that you and the parents are in communication and in agreement about how to deal with the problem in school.

See Also

Aggressive Behavior

Argumentative Behavior

Bullying

Hitting or Threatening a Teacher

Rude/Disrespectful Behavior

Argumentative Behavior

Some children seem to enjoy arguing with teachers. They may find fault with your decisions, challenge your answers to questions, contradict your statements, and find loopholes in your directions. With many argumentative students, their intent is not just to express their point of view; they want to win the argument. If you have a student like this, you may find yourself spending an inordinate amount of time debating, justifying, and explaining at the expense of your other students.

Although you want to encourage children to think for themselves, students who constantly challenge you can be infuriating and can cause you to lose your temper. Their argumentativeness may also divert you from your lessons and even encourage classmates to engage in similar behavior. As a result, you want to deal with this behavior promptly.

Children argue not just because they have a gripe but because of what they expect to gain from arguing, namely, attention, power, and the emotional reaction of the teacher. Indeed, their intent may be to aggravate the teacher, and many have honed this to a fine art. Being able to manipulate their teacher's emotions may give them a sense of power that they are lacking in other spheres of their life.

The problem is not that students challenge their teachers. After all, an important goal of education is to help children become independent thinkers. Rather, the problem is with children who argue with their teachers in a disrespectful or inappropriate manner. Your goal in working with an argumentative student is not to stifle the expression of his opinions but to help him learn to convey them in an appropriate, cooperative, and timely manner.

What You Can Do

1. Give the student a quick lesson in communication skills.
The first two or three times he argues with you, help him see that there is another way of making his point. You might say the following: "Jordan, you don't need to

argue or speak disrespectfully to get your point across. If you state it in a pleasant, respectful manner, you have a better chance of getting what you want." You might suggest to him an alternative way of stating his opinion.

2. Don't take the bait.

The argumentative student is looking to elicit a response from you. He may be hoping you will engage him in debate or perhaps get upset with him. Give him neither. Do not argue back and forth with him, and try not to react emotionally. Instead, respond in a matter-of-fact manner, perhaps saying something like, "Zasha, I'm sorry you feel that way" or "Keith, if you're unhappy with what I said, you can see me after class." Then move on with what you were doing without giving him an audience. It is even okay to let him have the last word.

3. Have a one-on-one talk with the student.

The purpose here is not to berate him but to gently encourage him to speak in a more pleasant, less confrontational manner. Help him understand that he will be more effective in getting his message across if he speaks in a calm, respectful way. Also stress the importance of listening to what the other person is saying to understand his point of view. Tell him that his arguing can be unpleasant to listen to and that other students may avoid him if he continues to express himself in this way. You might ask him if he argues because he is angry with you and if there is something he would like you to do differently in class.

4. Help the student become more aware when he is arguing.

He may argue so often that he may not even know when he is acting this way. You might establish with him a private signal that you can use to cue him when he is being argumentative. This might be as simple as calling his name and then touching your lips with your finger.

5. Recognize the student when he communicates in a respectful manner.

Although you want to avoid engaging the student when he is arguing, you want to give him special attention when he is talking with you or someone else in a calm, mature manner. Be on the lookout for opportunities to praise him, especially situations in which he might have previously become argumentative. You might say something like, "I'm really impressed with how you told me what you wanted in a pleasant voice without arguing." In addition, if he has made his point respectfully and you conclude his argument has merit, tell him. You want to encourage independent thinking among your students.

6. Try to divert the class's attention from the student.

You may find that your other students are paying more attention to his arguments than to your lesson. Their attention may help to fuel his arguing. If so, ask your class to follow your example of ignoring the student and focusing on the task at hand.

7. Set aside time during the day to hear the student's argument.

Tell him that you are interested in hearing his concern but that class time is not the right time for this. Ask him to come see you either before or after school or right before recess to discuss the issue with you. Let him know that you will listen attentively to his argument, as long as he speaks in a calm and respectful manner, and that you expect him to extend the same courtesy to you when you present your point of view. You might also set a time limit on this discussion.

8. Tell the student to put his argument in writing.

If he is able to write, ask him to write down his thoughts and leave the note on your desk. Tell him you will get back to him within a day or two regarding his concern. Make sure to follow up with the student, even if you think his point is without merit.

9. If his argumentative behavior is disruptive to the class, consider disciplining him.

Despite your efforts to avoid giving him the attention and emotional response that he is likely seeking, he may continue to argue to the extent that it interferes with your ability to teach. If so, you may want to give him a time-out if he is a younger elementary student or keep him in after school or during recess if he is an older elementary student. Be prepared for him to argue over the discipline, but resist the impulse to respond in kind. Tell him the consequence and then move on with your lesson.

10. Allow the student to contest a grade or test score as long as he does it appropriately.

Keep this within limits, however. You do not want to permit him to challenge every item on a test.

11. Give the student a sense of importance.

Underlying his bickering behavior may be a search for power and influence. If so, try to satisfy these needs by giving him some classroom responsibilities. Some examples: being class messenger, reading the school's morning announcements, serving on the safety patrol, answering the office phone while the secretary is at lunch, and tutoring a classmate or a student in a lower grade.

See Also

Angry Outbursts

Back Talk

Complaining, Frequent

Disruptive/Uncooperative Behavior

Whining

Assembly Problems

Similar to other large-group activities, assemblies hold the potential for discipline problems. And when they occur, they can present an awkward situation for you to manage. You may feel embarrassed that one of your students is the culprit. In addition, you may feel self-conscious if you perceive that the principal and other teachers are looking to see how you handle the problem.

Your goal should be to find a way to manage the student in a way that eliminates the disruption for other students but leaves the misbehaving student's dignity intact. The point here is not to humiliate the student or force a confrontation. Rather, you want to respond in a way that does not draw attention to you or the student but nonetheless solves the problem so the other students can enjoy a disruption-free program. Although you can remove the student from the assembly if her behavior is out of control, use this as a last resort. Instead, try to find a way to curtail her misbehavior while allowing her to remain in the assembly.

What You Can Do

1. Discuss assembly protocol with your students.
Before the first assembly of the school year, take some time to talk with students about how to behave during an assembly. This is especially important with kindergartners and first graders. You might tell them that you expect them to walk to the assembly quietly and in single file, to sit with their class, to remain quiet during the activity (unless speaking is part of the activity), and to leave the assembly in a quiet, organized manner. Help your students understand that it is inconsiderate to the person presenting the assembly and to fellow students watching the program to talk while the program is going on. With younger elementary students or special education students, you may even want to practice good assembly behavior by walking to the room and sitting down quietly.

2. Have students walk to the assembly in an orderly manner.

In this way, you are setting the tone for their behavior even before they enter the assembly. They may be more likely to behave appropriately if they have walked the hallway quietly and entered the room in a calm, controlled manner.

3. Keep downtime to a minimum.

If you are in charge of the assembly program, try to get under way as soon as all the students have arrived and taken a seat. The more unstructured time students have, the more they are likely to present problems. If you are using audiovisual equipment, make sure it is set up and ready to go before the students arrive.

4. Set the tone by insisting on quiet before beginning.

Tell students that the program cannot begin until all students are quiet and seated. After they are quiet, you might have them engage in a unifying activity like singing a song before starting the program.

5. Obtain quiet by raising your hand.

If you need to silence the students or get their attention, raise your hand while forming a V shape with two fingers. Most students know that when they see this signal they are to raise their hands in a similar manner, quiet down, and look at you. If they don't, teach them.

6. Stay near your students.

Rather than stand in the rear with other teachers, sit with or stand near your class. Try to position yourself near a student who you think may have difficulty controlling herself. Your proximity may be enough to keep her under control. If necessary, circulate to make your presence known and to observe your students so you can signal any who are misbehaving.

7. Acknowledge well-behaved students.

Praise students who are behaving well, making sure to describe their behavior specifically ("I like the way that Michelle is quiet and looking at me"). Students who are talking or focusing on other things will quickly get the message.

8. Give a potentially disruptive student a job.

If you have a student who you think may misbehave during an assembly, consider giving her a task to do during the assembly. You might have her set up chairs, hand out programs, lead classes to their seats, or assist the person in charge of the assembly. This job may not only occupy the student's attention during the assembly but may boost her self-esteem so that she may feel less inclined to act in a disruptive manner.

9. Quietly signal the student.

If you anticipate that a student may have self-control problems during the assembly, work out a nonverbal signal with her that you may use to indicate that she needs to quiet down or focus on the program. Give her a choice of signals, and have her choose which she wants you to do. This list might include making eye contact with her, putting your finger to your lips, raising your eyebrows, touching her shoulder, or winking.

10. Talk with the student.

See her after the assembly. In a serious but gentle tone, describe the specific behaviors that concerned you, and explain that these behaviors made it harder for other students to enjoy the program. If she is usually well behaved, let her know you were surprised and disappointed in her behavior, but tell her that this is not like her and that you are sure she will act more appropriately at the next assembly. Get her commitment to behave well at the next assembly. If she was responsive to this discussion, thank her for the grown-up way she handled the conversation.

11. Seat the student apart from the class.

If you have asked or signaled her to quiet down and she continues to be disruptive, consider seating her away from the class and perhaps next to you so that she no longer has an audience.

12. If necessary, remove the student from the room and give her a consequence.

If the problem persists, you might remove her from the assembly altogether. Let her know what she did that led to this action, and bring her to an area of the school that is supervised (perhaps the principal's office) so you can return to your class. After the assembly, meet with the student in private and let her know that she will receive a consequence as a result of her behavior. This might be having her stay after school or miss recess, not allowing her to attend the next assembly, or calling her parents.

13. Hold a class meeting if some of your students misbehave during an assembly.
Let them know you are disappointed in their behavior, but tell them you know they are capable of acting more appropriately. Ask for their ideas about how they should behave, eliciting from them three or four simple rules to follow in an assembly. Write these rules on the board or on a poster to be placed on the wall, and ask students to raise their hands if they agree to follow them.

See Also

Bothering Classmates

Disruptive/Uncooperative Behavior

Hallway/Lining-up Problems

Talking, Excessive

Attention Deficit

Virtually every classroom has at least one student with an attention deficit. This is the student who has difficulty focusing for long periods, is easily distracted, struggles to understand directions, and is often at a loss about what to do. Even when he knows what to do, he may have trouble settling down and doing the work. Seemingly simple tasks such as remembering to take papers home or bringing a pencil to class may elude him. A child with an attention deficit may pose significant management problems for the classroom teacher and, if not managed successfully, can disrupt your classroom.

Students with attention deficits are capable of learning and are often bright, but their focusing difficulties and low frustration tolerance can impede their academic performance. In addition, they may exhibit organizational and learning problems. Indeed, about one of every three students with an attention deficit disorder exhibits a learning disability. If an attention deficit is unrecognized and accommodations are not made, significant social and behavioral difficulties can result.

Many children with attention deficits are treated with medication. Although medication may enable some students to perform better in school, bear in mind that medication does not teach. It only makes students more available for learning because they are better able to attend. In addition, even though medication may reduce some behavioral problems, it probably will not eliminate them. Thus if you have a student with an attention deficit who is taking medication, you will probably need to make some classroom accommodations.

A note of caution about medication: although you may believe that one of your students will be helped by medication, keep in mind that it is not your role to recommend it. This is a medical issue that you should encourage parents to discuss with their child's physician.

What You Can Do

1. Devise ways to grab the attention of all your students. Here are some examples:

- Flip the lights off and on a couple of times.

- Tell students that when you hold up two fingers they are to stop talking, put two fingers up in the air, and look at you.

- Say, "Stop what you are doing and look at me," while raising your hand. Tell your students that they are to follow your lead by raising their hands while not talking. Wait until all hands are raised before speaking to the class.

- Instruct your class that when you want their attention you will say, "Give me 5–4–3–2–1" and that you expect all students to be quiet and looking at you by the time you get to 1.

- Play a few notes on a piano or toy horn.

- Ring a bell and then say, "1–2–3, all eyes on me."

- Let the class know that when you want their attention, you will clap out a beat and they are to imitate your beat and then look at you when they are finished. Students will find this fun.

2. Try to understand the reason for the student's attention problem.

Children can have difficulty paying attention without having an attention deficit disorder. They may have trouble focusing in school when they are anxious, upset, not feeling well, or simply bored. Attention difficulties can also result from hearing or vision problems. Identifying the source of a student's attention problem can guide you in how to help him in the classroom.

3. Develop a signaling system to help keep the student on task. Because

the student with an attention problem is prone to drifting off in class, you will want to find some way to signal him that he needs to pay attention or get back to work. This might be as simple as walking by his desk, making eye contact with him, or pausing while you are speaking. Or it might be a private signal that you work out with him such as scratching your head, raising your eyebrows, tugging on your ear, or winking. Similarly, develop a signal that he (and other students) can use to ask for your help. You might, for example, have students attach a "help" flag to a pencil that they can stick in a piece of clay on the corner of their desk to alert you that they need your assistance.

4. Catch the student being good.

The most basic application of behavior-modification principles is to praise a student when he is displaying appropriate behavior. Because of their frequent experience with frustration and failure in school, many students with an attention deficit have a particular need for a pat on the back. Your challenge with this kind of student, especially if you have a large class, is to catch him when he is on task and then praise him immediately and genuinely. You might remind yourself to check on the student and praise him if warranted by placing a visual cue at a place you look at often (for example, a smiley face near the clock or on your lesson plan book). Another way of helping the student learn that attention to task may lead to attention from you is for you to praise other students who are highly attentive. You might go one step further by occasionally rewarding an on-task student with a material incentive or classroom privilege.

5. Minimize distractions to the student.

Give thought to where the student is seated. Try to find a spot where you can monitor him closely and help him stay focused but where there are few distractions. Although you might want to place him near your desk so you can keep a close eye on him, this is not a good location if other students are frequently coming up to you to get help. In fact, being seated near the teacher may be one of the more distracting spots in the room. If possible, avoid seating him near the pencil sharpener or window or with views of the hallway—locations that are likely to divert his attention. A better place may be next to a quiet, hard-working student. Make sure there is sufficient distance between desks. Also try to eliminate visual distractions by keeping the student's desk free of clutter and not allowing him to bring in items from home that are sure to occupy his attention.

6. Make sure you have his attention when giving directions. Use his name, and make certain he has eye contact with you when you are instructing him. Keep the directions clear, short, and specific, and do not put them in question form (for example, "Why don't you . . . ?"). If you give him a long string of instructions, he is likely to remember only part of what you say. You can highlight important information by modulating the tone and volume of your voice. Even if the student is looking right at you and appears to be attending, he may be thinking of something else; you might have him repeat the directions in his own words to ensure his understanding. If necessary, write the directions down in addition to stating them orally. With young students, you might want to capture their attention by having puppets give the instructions.

7. Place the student in a study carrel. You can also use a cardboard divider or partition to minimize distractions while the child is working independently. Make this inviting by telling him that this is his office, but place him there only for short periods and not at all if the child feels singled out or isolated from his peers.

8. Use a kitchen timer to motivate the student to complete seatwork. In this classroom version of "Beat the Clock," let the student know how much time he has to complete the task and then set the timer; 5 or 10 minutes before the timer goes off, let him know how much time is left. Make sure, however, that the student does not race through the task, giving rise to careless mistakes or sloppy performance.

9. Shorten the student's work periods. Students with attention problems have difficulty working for long stretches. You may find that a child can be more productive if he works for two or three short periods rather than one long period. Instead of having him do a task for 40 minutes straight, for example, you might have him work for 20 minutes, give him a break, and then have him work for 20 minutes more.

10. Break a task into smaller, more doable parts.
Students with attention problems may be overwhelmed by large tasks. Feeling there is little chance they can finish the task, they may give up quickly or not even attempt it. Breaking the task into more manageable parts may give the student more confidence that he can complete it successfully. As an example, rather than giving him a whole page of math problems to do, assign him two or three problems, check his performance, and then give him a few more.

11. Limit the information on your handouts.
Students' attention can be diverted, not only by the clutter in their desks but by the clutter on their paper. To minimize this problem, try simplifying the visual presentation of your handouts by limiting the amount of information on a page. You might also show the student how to fold the paper or use a piece of blank paper to cover the rest of the page to allow him to concentrate on one question or problem at a time. Similarly, you might make a window for the child out of paper or cardboard that exposes only two lines of print or one math problem. When giving a test of more than one page, consider giving the student one page at a time.

12. Vary your presentation of information.
Direct a student's attention to important information by making it stand out. When writing on the chalkboard, you might underline key words or write them in all capitals or in a different color. On handouts, you might highlight essential information or change the color, font, or type size. For students who make careless math errors, try circling the math signs or highlighting them in color.

13. Present tasks that tap the student's interests and areas of competence.
Students with attention problems will be more engaged in schoolwork if the academic activities reflect their interests and tap their areas of strength. Identify their strengths and interests (you might have the student fill out an interest inventory), and then use this information to design academic tasks that exploit their interests and skills. For example, if the

student is passionate about baseball, you might have him learn percentages by figuring out batting averages. If the student is a Girl Scout, you might present math problems using the example of selling cookies.

14. Help the student with transitions.

Students with attention problems often have difficulty adjusting to change. You can lessen this problem by letting the student know in advance of any upcoming changes. You might also keep him informed about daily activities by putting his work for the day on the board and perhaps even posting his personal schedule and responsibilities on his desk on a 4" × 6" card, perhaps numbering the tasks in priority order and suggesting times when he is to work on them.

15. If the student is on medication, monitor his behavior.

The effects of the medication are likely to be more evident in school than at home, so your observations will be crucial in helping the parents and physician assess whether it is working. It is thus important that the parents inform you when their child is starting medication and that you monitor his behavior carefully during the first few weeks and report your observations to his parents.

See Also

Calling Out

Disorganization

Forgetfulness

Hyperactivity

Listening Skills, Poor

Seatwork Problems

Back Talk

Few behaviors are more infuriating to teachers than back talk. Having a student tell you that "I don't have to do what you say" or "This class sucks" or "You don't know how to teach" can try your patience and test your ability to control your temper. Moreover, a student who speaks in such a disrespectful manner can make it difficult to conduct your lesson and undermine your authority in the eyes of your other students. This problem can grow more serious if classmates begin to emulate the behavior. In trying to resolve this problem, it is often helpful to identify what motivates the student's behavior.

Students may talk back to teachers for a variety of reasons. For many, this behavior gives them an audience and gains them attention. Some, however, are looking for more than just attention. They may be trying to push your buttons and trigger your anger. They may also be trying to divert you from your agenda, especially if you are doing or saying something they dislike. Some students may be disrespectful because they feel they have been treated unfairly and this is their way of fighting back or showing you they can't be controlled or bossed around. Students may also talk back because they think these acts of bravado will win them peer status.

It is hard to resist the temptation to give the student a stern lecture or "read her the riot act." It is also hard to resist being drawn into a power struggle in which you and the student volley angry words back and forth. Reacting in this way, however, rarely solves the problem, and it can lessen your authority with your other students if they see you losing control.

In deciding how to respond to an insolent student, keep in mind that her offensive comments often have nothing to do with anything you have said or done. In many cases, she may be venting frustration from other events in her life, and you may serve as a convenient outlet for her distress. Maintaining your composure in the face of a verbal barrage may not be easy, but it will be more effective in the long run. Scolding her, threatening her, or lecturing her may only give her what she wants and strengthen her impulse to behave disrespectfully.

What You Can Do

1. Show respect for your students.
An effective way to discourage belligerent comments is to act in a respectful manner toward your students. Foster a climate of acceptance and support, and respond to students in a kind and patient manner without talking down to them. Strenuously avoid sarcasm or put-downs of any kind. Also create opportunities to showcase their successes and highlight their talents. In disciplining a student, you can get your point across by talking in a firm manner without being rude or disrespectful.

2. Talk with the student privately.
The student may expect a stern reprimand or a long lecture. Surprise her by engaging her in a supportive conversation. Tell her that even though her words came across as disrespectful, you do not think she meant to treat you that way. You might let her know that underneath those angry words is a really nice student, although you do not always see that side of her. Tell her that students often talk that way if they are upset about something. Ask her if something is upsetting her and, in particular, if you did something to frustrate her. If she does not offer an answer, you might suggest some possible sources of distress and ask her to shake her head yes or no. Find out if there is anything you can do to lessen her frustration. Tell her that you need her cooperation in order to teach the class effectively and that you would greatly appreciate it if she treated you in a respectful manner. Tell her that you will make an effort to treat her the same way. If she is agreeable, shake on it.

3. Don't take it personally.
Although it is not easy to listen to a personal attack without reacting emotionally, it may help to remind yourself that the student's abusive comments probably have little to do with anything you said or did. It is just as likely that she is upset or hurting about other concerns and is venting her frustration at you because you are a convenient target. Appreciating this may spur you to look beyond her expression of anger to find out the source of her distress.

4. In a calm but firm manner, inform the student that her language is inappropriate.
Staying calm in the face of a verbal assault may not be

easy, but yelling at her, threatening her, or lecturing her may only give her what she wants and reinforce her impulse to act disrespectfully. If you feel yourself about to lose your temper with the student, try taking a few deep breaths. When you feel under control, tell her in a low-key but firm manner that her language is unacceptable and that you expect her to speak to you respectfully. One way of taking the wind out of her sails is to ask her to repeat what she said because you didn't hear her the first time. Whatever you do, do not give in to her demands. She must come to see that her back talk is making it harder for her to get what she wants and that she has a better chance of gaining satisfaction if she speaks to you in a pleasant, respectful manner. After giving her this message (and don't spend a lot of time delivering it), return to what you were doing without engaging her in debate or argument.

5. If the student continues to talk back, take some action.
If the student's persistent back talk disrupts your lesson and undermines your authority, consider giving her a consequence. With a younger elementary student, you may want to place her in time-out; with an older elementary student, you may want to keep her in after school or during recess. Tell her the consequence in a calm but firm manner, and then move on with your lesson. Be prepared for her to argue with you over your decision to discipline her, but stay the course and do not engage her in debate. If she still refuses to stop her disruptive behavior, give her a choice: "Martha, you can remain in class and cooperate or you can go to the principal's office. Which would you prefer?" If she opts to stay in class and cooperates, move on with your lesson. If she opts to go to the office or continues to misbehave, send her with a note of explanation. You might want to send a responsible student with her and call the office to let the principal know a student is on her way.

6. If necessary, call for help.
If the student is verbally abusive and you cannot get her to calm down, consider calling the principal and asking him to come to your room. If you think the student may become physical, avoid contact with her. Even a supportive pat on the back may trigger a physical reaction.

7. Write down what the student has said.

Make sure she sees you doing this. If she asks what you are writing down (and even if she does not), tell her that you are recording what she is saying because you want to have an accurate record of her comments to keep in her file, as well as show her parents. This may inhibit her use of offensive language.

8. Inform her parents.

If the student has been frequently or flagrantly disrespectful, contact her parents and let her know you are doing this. You might even have her call her parents from school to inform them of what she said to you; stand next to her while she makes the call. Consider inviting the parents in for a conference to share your observations and ask for their ideas about how to deal with this behavior. Work with them to develop a plan for responding to their child in school. Consider having her attend at least part of the meeting so she can see that you and the parents are in agreement about the inappropriateness of her language and the steps to be taken.

9. Help the student become more aware when she is acting disrespectfully.

The student may talk back so often that she may not even know when she is doing it. If so, establish with her a private signal that you can use to cue her when she is acting in a belligerent manner. This might be as simple as calling her name and then winking or raising your eyebrows.

10. Praise the student when she speaks respectfully.

Show the student that she can gain your attention and approval when she speaks in an appropriate, respectful manner. Be on the lookout for opportunities to praise her, especially in situations where she might have previously talked back to you. Let her know publicly (or privately if you think she will be embarrassed to be praised in front of her peers) that you are impressed with the way she spoke so respectfully and politely. Similarly, praise other students who speak to you in an appropriate manner to reinforce the message that this is a laudable behavior.

11. Try to connect with the student.
One way of doing this is to talk with the student about her interests. Find a few minutes every day to ask about her favorite hobbies, sports, television programs, or musical groups. Consider asking her parents for this information to give you a basis for talking with her. You might suggest different ways she can pursue her hobbies or even bring in a book or item from home related to one of her interests. This act of kindness and caring will likely make an impression on the student so that she will be less inclined to treat you disrespectfully.

See Also

Angry Outbursts

Calling Out

Disruptive/Uncooperative Behavior

Rude/Disrespectful Behavior

Swearing

Bathroom Problems

The bathroom is one of the few places in school that is often unsupervised. As a result, it is a frequent site of behavioral problems. These may range from writing on the wall to plugging up a toilet with paper towels to festooning a bathroom stall with unraveled toilet paper. The bathroom can also be the site of social problems, such as one student harassing another. And then there are the dawdlers—the students who spend time hanging out in the bathroom to avoid going back to class.

It is difficult for teachers to deal with problems in the bathroom because most times they are not there when the problems occur. Thus an effective way of dealing with them is to keep students from going to the bathroom when the motivation is other than physical. At the same time, you need to allow students to go to the bathroom who genuinely need to use it. Of course, it is not always easy to figure out a student's motivation, so this issue requires careful judgment on your part. And when problems do occur in the bathroom, they give you an opportunity to help your students understand the importance of showing respect for people as well as property.

What You Can Do

1. Go over your bathroom policies with your students.
At the beginning of the year, set out your rules for using the bathroom and review them as needed during the year. These rules might describe

- When students can go to the bathroom
- How many students can go at one time
- Whether they need your permission to leave the class
- Whether they need a pass and if so how to obtain one
- Whether they need to sign out and if so how to do this

You might tell your students that they should go to the bathroom during recess or lunch and that they will only be allowed to go to the bathroom during class time if it is urgent. One way of cutting down on dawdling in the bathroom is to have them go right before lunch or recess; their eagerness to get there will ensure that their bathroom visits are brief. You might also have a rule that students cannot go to the bathroom in pairs so that friends do not go together. Also talk with them about bathroom behavior. Tell them that they are expected to clean up after using the bathroom and that writing on the walls or otherwise damaging property is unacceptable. You might also inform them that you will take seriously any complaints from students that others are bothering them in the bathroom.

2. If necessary, teach students how to use the bathroom.

Young elementary students may need some guidance in this area. You may need to take them to the bathroom to show them. Emphasize the following: flushing the toilet once after using it, placing toilet paper in the toilet and paper towels in the garbage, and washing their hands after using the toilet. Also show them how to use the locks on the stall doors.

3. Have students sign out when they go to the bathroom.

It is essential that you know where your students are at all times. Monitor their whereabouts by having them write their name, destination, time left, and time returned in a sign-out book. Have a different page for each school day. Of course, you will need to adapt this procedure if your students cannot yet write or tell time. Use this sign-out book whether or not you require your students to get your permission every time they leave the room. As an alternative to the sign-out book, you might keep a 3" × 5" card for each student in a box. Instruct students to write the date and time on the card when they go to the bathroom. A simpler method of keeping track of students using the bathroom but one that does not create an ongoing record is to have them put their name on the chalkboard in a designated area or on a wipe-off board near the door and erase it when they return.

...nitor bathroom usage.   If you have students use a sign-out book or 3" × 5" cards to record when they used the bathroom, you can review these records to see if any students are leaving the room excessively. Let the class know that you will look at these records often to determine who may be abusing the bathroom privilege and, if necessary, you will call their parents to discuss this concern.

5. Check with a student's parents if he uses the bathroom excessively.

Ask the parents if there is any physical reason to explain the student's frequent use of the rest room. If they know of none but have noticed a similar pattern at home, suggest that they talk with the child's pediatrician about this problem. If they tell you that the doctor has recommended that their child be allowed to go to the bathroom whenever he needs to, find out the precise medical reason for this recommendation.

6. If you require students to get permission to use the bathroom, have them signal you.   You might suggest, for example, that they ask your permission by simply clasping their hands above their head. When you see this, you can give them a simple nod or an "Okay, go ahead" with minimal disruption to the lesson or other students.

7. Require students to carry a hall pass when they leave the room.   Have students use a permanent pass, which will save you the time and trouble of writing a pass each time a student needs to go to the bathroom. You might create this pass out of a block of wood at least the size of an eraser (make sure there are no splinters). Consider asking your custodian to make the passes for you. Designate a place to keep them, perhaps on your desk next to the sign-out book or hanging up near the door. Limit the number of passes to one for boys and one for girls. This way you can control the number of students who are out of the classroom at the same time and lessen the likelihood that they will dawdle or fool around together. Tell students that they are to see you if the pass is being used and they have a genuine bathroom emergency.

8. Check the bathroom periodically.

Although it is difficult for you to leave your classroom to monitor students' bathroom usage, ask an aide, a parent volunteer, or an especially responsible student to check on a student who is taking an unusually long time in the bathroom. In this way, you can send the message to students that the bathroom is not a place to hang out.

9. Arrange for the custodian to talk with your students about proper bathroom etiquette.

Before the custodian arrives, discuss with your class how important that person is to the running of the school. Ask him to talk about the extra work created for him when a student writes on the bathroom wall or throws wet paper towels on the ceiling or sprays water from the sink. In this way, your students can be helped to see that their actions have consequences for other people, namely the custodian and their fellow students.

10. Encourage students to tell you about problems in the bathroom.

Suggest they write you a note or see you during a break or after school. If the problem involves a classmate, you may need to problem-solve with the complaining student or get the two students together to resolve the conflict. Of course, if the student is being harassed by the classmate, this will likely call for your direct intervention with the harassing student.

11. Make the bathroom offender wait before going to the bathroom.

If you have a student who has abused the bathroom privilege, require him to get your permission before he goes, even if you do not generally require students to get permission. In addition, when he asks to go to the bathroom, tell him to see you in 5 minutes, perhaps specifying a time. If he genuinely needs to use the bathroom, he will likely ask you again, but if his motivation is to get out of class, he will likely forget about it. Another approach to use with the bathroom offender: tell him that he can go to the bathroom but the time he is gone will be deducted from his recess time.

12. Have the student help clean up the mess. If a student caused a mess in the bathroom and you are confident you know who did it, have him help clean it up. If the custodian has already done this, have the student help clean up the bathroom at another time. Let his parents know of this disciplinary measure. If the student has caused some damage in the bathroom, figure out how he can work off the cost of repairing the damage. If the damage is great enough that the parents must pay for it, encourage them to find some way for their child to work off the costs at home.

See Also

Bullying

Hallway/Lining-up Problems

Toileting Problems

Vandalism

Bothering Classmates

Students may annoy their classmates in a myriad of ways. They may poke them, pull their hair, grab something from them, trip them, push them, play with their food at lunch, interrupt them, call them names, spread rumors about them, or ridicule them. Whatever means they choose to bother other students, the incidents frequently come to your attention. This section deals with how to respond to these bothersome behaviors. It does not, however, address the issues of teasing or bullying, which are covered in separate sections. The most efficient way of dealing with this problem is to get the complaining student to stand up for himself and tell his classmate to stop. If that does not work, you may need to become involved to avoid having this small problem become a larger problem. In trying to resolve these incidents, be careful about assuming that the student being complained about is necessarily the culprit. It might be that the complaining student is motivated by a desire to get another student in trouble, or the complaint may reflect a conflict between two students, neither of whom is blame-free. Also be careful about punishing a student if you have not observed her misbehaving.

A simple appeal to the student for cooperation or a brief get-together with the two students involved may be all that is needed to resolve the problem. If you feel that the students are mature enough, you might even have them talk it out on their own and then report back to you with their solution. Of course, if you conclude that a student is genuinely bothering a blame-free student and refuses to stop, take firm steps to stop the behavior.

What You Can Do

1. Screen a student's concern before dismissing it.
Keep in mind that a complaining student may be alerting you to a problem that warrants your involvement, so do not automatically dismiss the complaint. Be especially attentive to reports suggesting that a student is being bullied, especially if you are hearing similar complaints from other students. If you are not sure

whether it is an issue requiring your involvement, tell the student you will get back to him and then keep a watchful eye on the students to observe their interactions.

2. Encourage the complaining student to assert himself. If a student tells you that another student is annoying him, encourage him to tell his classmate to stop. Suggest what he might say (for example, "You're really bothering me and I'd like you to stop") and role-play with him if necessary. Tell him that if the classmate continues after he says stop, he should see you. If he comes back to you and says he told the classmate to stop but she continued the behavior, give the offending student a consequence if you have observed her bothering the student. If you have not, get the students together to resolve the problem. Again, be careful about punishing a student whom you have not observed misbehaving; the complaining student may be trying to get a classmate in trouble.

3. Have a one-on-one talk with the student. If you observe a student annoying a classmate, take her aside and ask why she is acting that way. Do this in a calm, emotionally neutral manner so that she feels comfortable talking with you. Let her comments guide your response, which might include a simple appeal for cooperation or a conflict-resolution meeting with you and the two students. Help her understand that her behavior may cause other children to avoid her and also interfere with your teaching of a lesson.

4. Get the students together to problem-solve. The complaining student wants you to believe the other student is at fault, and he may be right. But it may also be that the complaining student is looking to get a blame-free classmate in trouble. If you are not clear about who is doing what, meet with the two students to hear both sides and work out a solution. If the accused student admits to the behavior, ask her if she realized that it was bothering another student. If she did not, she will likely be open to stopping.

5. Tell more mature students to settle the problem on their own. If a student complains about a classmate bothering him, encourage both students

to solve the problem without your help. Suggest an area of the class where they can go to talk over the problem. Tell them to see you afterwards to inform you of the resolution.

6. Provide the student with a consequence.

If you have observed a student bothering a classmate without seeming provocation, and she has continued despite your request that she stop, give her a consequence; let her know in advance that you will do this. This consequence might be loss of part or all of recess, an after-school detention, or loss of a privilege. Or you might have the student call her parents in your presence to inform them of her behavior. Be matter-of-fact and to the point in letting her know the consequence.

7. Figure out what is motivating the student.

In trying to answer this question, find time to observe the student's behavior closely (or ask the school psychologist to do an observation). Note the circumstances of her behavior, including what happens right before and after the incidents, when they usually occur, where the student is when she engages in the behavior, and whether she targets a particular student. Use this information to try to figure out what is triggering and reinforcing her behavior. It may be that she is trying to get your attention or the attention of other students, or to get back at a student or get him in trouble when he responds, or to divert attention from her academic problems. If you can identify the underlying reason for her behavior, you've got a better chance of eliminating it.

8. Move the student's desk.

If the student continues to bother her neighbors despite your requests that she stop, consider moving her desk away from other students. Another option is to put her in a study carrel that is placed on the side of the class. Tell her that if she is cooperative in her new location for a designated period, she can return to her regular seat.

9. Restrict the student's physical contact with classmates.

If the student is bothering other students as she roams around the room, limit her movement by designating a work area for her that she cannot leave without your permission. Place masking tape around her desk to make a square or rectangle, putting the tape about a foot or so beyond her desk on all four sides. Tell her that this is her office but that she must stay within the boundaries marked by the tape. Make sure that she cannot make physical contact with students from her work area.

10. Have students sit on carpet squares.

Using carpet squares during circle time will help keep restless, squirmy students in their place and discourage them from annoying their classmates.

11. Find ways to give the student positive attention.

If you conclude that a student is bothering others as a way of gaining your attention, look for opportunities to attend to her when she displays positive behavior. In particular, acknowledge her when you see her acting in a kind, respectful, or helpful manner to classmates, even if it is a small gesture. And of course praise her successes in the classroom, and look for ways she can make positive contributions through class jobs. If you are successful in doing this, she may feel less compelled to seek attention in inappropriate ways.

See Also

Aggressive Behavior

Bullying

Chair Tipping

Rude/Disrespectful Behavior

Spitting

Teasing

Bullying

Bullying—physically or psychologically intimidating another child—is a commonplace problem in schools. Surveys indicate that 15 to 20 percent of all children are bullied at some point in school. And for those who are targets of bullying, it can be one of the most painful experiences of childhood, often leaving lasting scars. Victims may experience anxiety, fear, and even depression. They may be so afraid that they beg to stay home from school.

Despite the pervasiveness and potential seriousness of bullying, it is a problem that often escapes detection by teachers. (One study found that only 4 percent of bullying episodes were observed by school staff.) Even when teachers are made aware of bullying, they sometimes turn a blind eye to it. They may view bullying as a harmless rite of passage that is often best ignored. The reality is, however, that bullying is not harmless and it must not be ignored. It is a problem that demands to be taken seriously by school staff.

As a teacher, it is critical that you be on the lookout for signs of bullying. Although you may not actually see a bullying incident (bullies are very adept at tormenting other children outside the presence of adults), you may see the results. A child who is being bullied may show some of the following characteristics:

- Anxiety while attending class
- Frequent visits to the school nurse
- Decline in academic performance
- Unusual sadness or withdrawal from peers
- Unexplained bruises

What You Can Do

1. Take action immediately if you observe or hear of bullying taking place.
Do not let it continue on the assumption that children need to learn to stand up for themselves. Bullies are often bigger and stronger than

their victims, who often lack the physical ability or verbal skill to adequately defend themselves. Allowing it to go on may result in the child being hurt physically or psychologically.

2. Take the bully aside and talk with him privately.   Give him an opportunity to explain his behavior, but expect him to downplay his actions or place the blame on the victim. If you are confident that he was engaging in bullying, let him know that further incidents will not be tolerated. Tell him that you and other staff will be monitoring his behavior very closely and that disciplinary action, including notifying his parents, will be taken if another incident occurs. (Make sure to ask other school staff, such as playground and lunchroom aides, to monitor his behavior.) After putting him on notice, try to elicit his cooperation. Tell him that you don't believe he really wants to hurt another child, and ask for his ideas about resolving the problem. You may find that a sympathetic approach elicits kinder and gentler behavior. Bullies bully for a reason, whether to gain status with or power over peers, to punish another child with whom they are angry or jealous, or to vent frustration with problems at home or in school. Try to identify what is behind the bullying and provide appropriate support.

3. Take immediate action if another incident occurs.   However, keep in mind that the purpose of your discipline is to deter aggressive actions rather than to humiliate or embarrass the child. At a minimum, insist that he return any items taken from the victim. You might want to exclude him from places or activities where he has harassed other students, remove classroom privileges, or give him detention. Notify his parents immediately of what he has done, and ask that they have a serious talk with their child about his behavior. You may want to consider having them in for a conference. Solicit their support for the steps you are taking in school. The principal may also decide the incident is serious enough that it warrants a suspension from school. On the day of his return, the student might be required to come in with his parents and sign a contract in which he agrees to refrain from engaging in any further bullying behavior. The contract should define the prohibited behaviors in a specific manner and set out consequences if he does not abide by the terms of the contract.

4. Attend to the victim.

Just as the bully warrants your attention, so too does the victim of bullying. Ask him what happened, and listen sympathetically and attentively. Let him know that he is not to blame for the bullying. Encourage him to tell you of other incidents, and reassure him that you will make every possible effort to stop it. You may also want to help him learn how to be assertive with bullies without being aggressive. Try role-playing with him, suggesting what he might do or say to project a greater air of confidence, but make sure he knows not to respond physically. Retaliating will only escalate a bully's aggression. You may want to inform the victim's parents about what happened and what actions you have taken (let the child know you will be doing this). Give the student frequent pats on the back to boost his confidence and increase his feelings of comfort. Talk with him periodically to ask if the problem is continuing; if it is, take action.

5. Survey your class anonymously about bullying.

The results may help you gauge the extent and types of bullying taking place, as well as the places where it is occurring. Of course, this can also be done on a schoolwide basis and serve as a benchmark to assess the impact of any programs intended to lessen the occurrence of bullying.

6. Hold a class meeting to discuss bullying.

With younger students, you might want to begin by reading a story suited to their age, such as the Berenstein Bears book *Trouble with the Bully*. Make it clear that bullying other children is a serious matter and that it will not be allowed in your classroom. Talk with your students about what bullying is, giving examples and asking for examples from the class. Consider writing them on the board. Also discuss how children who are bullied might feel, perhaps writing these on the board as well. Ask if any student wants to share an experience of being bullied, but do not let them talk about specific students. Also ask your students what they might do if they see another student being bullied. Encourage them to either take action to stop the bullying or report it to an adult.

7. Pay attention to students who are isolated from their peers.

They are the most likely targets for bullies. Help these students become involved with their peers by arranging for friendly and accepting students to invite them to join in classroom or playground activities. You might also arrange for students who are loners to engage in activities together. These students may need your help in learning what to say and do when interacting with peers. They may not know what to say to initiate an activity with a classmate or join in an ongoing activity.

8. Encourage children to be kind to each other.

Praise children who act in a kind or sensitive way to classmates. You might also recognize children displaying these behaviors by giving certificates or rewards at school assemblies. You can promote the kinder and gentler side of your students by offering them opportunities to help others. Perhaps the most important step you can take to help children treat each other respectfully is to model that behavior in your own interactions with your students. This means avoiding, for example, the use of sarcasm or put-downs.

9. Advocate for your school to have an anti-bullying policy.

Talk with your principal about putting a policy in place, or bring up the topic at a staff meeting. The policy might define specifically what constitutes bullying, describe its impact on individuals, discuss ways of preventing bullying, and list a gradual series of consequences.

See Also

Aggressive Behavior

Playground Problems

Racially Offensive Language

Rude/Disrespectful Behavior

Sexually Offensive Behavior

Teasing

Calling Out

Calling out is one of the more common problems that teachers encounter. Fortunately, it is also one of the easier problems to manage. A student's classroom interruptions may take different forms—from blurting out an answer without raising her hand to responding when another student has been called on to making an unsolicited comment in the middle of a lesson or discussion. A student may not even wait for the teacher to finish asking a question or a classmate to complete a comment before chiming in.

Whatever form the interruption takes, students who call out can get you and the class off track and keep you from completing your lesson. They may also prevent other students from participating. It is important to resolve this problem for another reason: if students are allowed to call out and gain your attention, classmates will be encouraged to follow their lead and call out as well.

The motivation behind this behavior is hardly complex. Students who blurt out answers are often seeking the attention of the teacher or recognition from their classmates. In short, they want to be in the spotlight. In some cases, students who call out may be trying to annoy the teacher. Other students, especially those with attention deficit disorder, may call out because they have poor impulse control. It is almost as if they can't stop themselves. They have a thought and out it pops. These children may need help in learning how to develop self-control and patience.

What You Can Do

1. Establish a "no calling out" rule.
Some students may be under the impression that calling out is okay. Make sure that your students understand that they must raise their hand and wait to be called on before answering. This might be one of the classroom rules you post. Find opportunities to reinforce the rule, especially with younger students ("I like the way Sarah has raised her

hand" or "I'm calling on Jason because his hand is up"). You might also prompt students when asking a question ("If you think you know the answer, let me know by raising your hand").

2. Instruct students who are doing seatwork or group activities how to gain your attention.
Calling out is disruptive, and having students raise their hands is not feasible if you are working with other students. You might have students who need your assistance write their name on a designated area of the chalkboard and then see them when you have time.

3. Seat a student who is prone to calling out near you.
Seat the student near where you typically stand when you are presenting a lesson. This allows you to manage her calling-out behavior more effectively by anticipating when she is about to blurt out an answer and signaling her quietly to raise her hand.

4. Ignore students who call out, and only call on those who raise their hand.
Giving attention to a student who calls out will make it more likely that she will call out in the future. Try to ignore her interruption, if possible, by continuing with your lesson and calling on a student who has raised her hand, perhaps making a comment such as, "Danielle, I like the way you're raising your hand and waiting to be called on." Call on another student, even if the interrupting student gave the right answer. Encourage your other students to ignore her comments as well. The message to the student is that she will gain more attention and have more of an opportunity to show what she knows if she raises her hand than if she calls out.

5. If ignoring is not feasible, develop a nonverbal signal to alert the student.
Work out this signal with the student. For example, you might gently put your hand on her shoulder or point to the posted rule and then call on a student who has raised his hand. If you feel the need to respond verbally, keep your comments brief and avoid expressions of emotion (for example, "Susie, we're eager to hear what you have to say, but you need to raise your hand and wait to be called on"). Do not reprimand the student or

respond with sarcasm. The key is to inform her of the appropriate behavior while minimizing the disruption to your lesson.

6. Call on the student immediately when she raises her hand.

Reinforce the connection between raising her hand and being recognized by calling on her right away, at least initially. Look for or create other opportunities for the student to gain the attention of the teacher and classmates by behaving appropriately. For example, you might let her know before class that you will be calling on her to answer a specific question that you are confident she knows, as long as she raises her hand and waits to be called on.

7. Teach the impulsive student how to hold on to her thoughts.

Impulsive students will tell you that they have to speak immediately or else they will forget what they want to say. If you have a student with this problem, suggest that she jot down a phrase or sentence to help her remember what she wanted to say. After calling on her, give her time to remember or reconstruct her thoughts.

8. Have a private discussion with the student.

State your concern about her behavior in a calm, patient manner, and ask if she is aware that she is calling out. Let her know that you are eager to hear what she has to say but that the classroom rule is that she raise her hand and wait to be called on before she can answer. Tell her that her calling out disrupts your lesson and deprives other students of a chance to participate in class. Ask her if she has any ideas for dealing with this problem. Tell her that you expect her to change her behavior, and express confidence in her ability to do so. Let her know, however, that if she continues to call out and disrupt your lessons, she will be given a consequence.

9. If the problem persists, consider a classroom consequence.

Give the student one or two warnings before providing a consequence. This might be, for example, missing part or all of recess or staying after school. If her calling out is severely disrupting the flow of your lessons, consider removing her from her seat and placing her away from the rest of the class. Tell her that she can listen to the lesson but cannot participate. Let her know that she can return to her seat when she is ready to contribute properly.

10. Teach the student to self-monitor.

Have the student keep track of the times she calls out as a way of raising her awareness of her behavior. One way of doing this is to tape to her desk a 3" × 5" card that is divided into the days of the week (Monday through Friday). Have her put a check in the appropriate box each time she calls out. Review the card with her at the end of the week to see if she has made progress. If so, reward her with either praise or a classroom privilege.

11. Develop a behavior-modification system for the student.

Provide the student with classroom privileges or material rewards if she shows evidence of calling out less. An easy way to do this is to divide a 3" × 5" card into ten boxes and tape it to the student's desk. Set a timer for 30 minutes at the beginning of the day. If the student does not call out within the 30-minute period, put your initials in a box and reset the timer. If she does call out, reset the timer immediately but do not initial the card. When all ten boxes are initialed, provide the student with an agreed-upon reward or privilege. Adjust the length of the period and the number of boxes needed to obtain a reward with the age of the student and the severity of the problem.

12. Set aside a specific time every day to talk with students.

Some students feel the need to talk with you in the middle of an activity. Let your students know a specific time when they can talk to you about any concerns. Suggest that they write a note to themselves if they are concerned about forgetting what they want to say.

13. Role-play with your class.

If blurting out answers is a classwide problem, you might talk with your students about this problem and, as part of the discussion, role-play with them. Have a student play the part of the teacher and a couple of others play the part of students who call out. Ask the students how they feel when their classmates call out, and elicit suggestions from them to discourage students from calling out, including possible classroom consequences.

14. Develop a classwide behavior-modification system. If calling out answers is a frequent problem in your class, consider setting up a reward system with all your students. Establish a goal of a maximum number of call-outs allowed per day or per week. Keep track of them by putting a check on the board every time a student calls out, but otherwise ignore the interruption. If the number of call-outs is below the maximum allowed for the day or week, provide the class with a reward that you and the class have previously established. If the reward is appealing to the students, you will find that students will discourage their classmates from calling out.

See Also

Disruptive/Uncooperative Behavior

Hyperactivity

Talking, Excessive

Chair Tipping

Few things are more unsettling for a teacher in the midst of instruction than to observe a student leaning back in his chair. It is hard to focus on the lesson when a child is teetering on the brink of falling over. This is not an unrealistic concern; chair tippers can easily tip too far, fall back, and hit their head.

Part of the reason students lean back in their seats is that their chairs are typically not very comfortable. They are hard, and students are often asked to sit in them for long periods. Leaning back may be their way of stretching and getting some exercise.

Many chair tippers are not even aware of their behavior, which makes this a hard habit to break. This is not, however, a behavior that you can ignore because of the real risk that the student could fall. In trying to break this habit, you need to help the student become more aware when he is tipping his chair and then take measures to ensure he stops.

What You Can Do

1. Establish a "no tipping" policy.
Be clear with your students that chair tipping is not allowed in your class. Explain that if they lean back, they can easily fall over and hit their head. If you know of a student whose chair has tipped over, let your class know this. Tell them the possible consequences in your class for chair tipping, which might include having their chair taken away or having to stay in for recess.

2. Give the student opportunities to move around periodically.
Some students tip their chair because it is their way of moving around or stretching without getting out of their seat. If you have a student who is frequently tipping his chair, and you conclude he needs to release excess energy, as many do, allow him to get out of his chair more often. You might give him some classroom chores or even allow him to work standing up, perhaps by leaning against a wall, as he writes on a clipboard or reads a book.

3. Address chair tipping immediately.
If one of your students is rocking back in his chair, do not ignore this. This is not a behavior that students do to elicit their teacher's attention. Because it is a potential safety concern, it warrants your immediate attention. Your first response should be to simply tell the student to stop. A simple statement such as "Andrew, all four legs on the floor, please" may suffice.

4. If the student continues, remove his chair and have him stand.
Have him stand until he is confident he can sit without tipping his chair. Or you might take away his chair for the remainder of the lesson. If he seems excited about the idea of standing, ignore him; he will eventually tire of it. Tell the student that removing the chair is not a matter of punishment but a matter of safety, namely, that you do not want him to fall back and risk hitting his head.

5. Get help from your students.
Let your students know that you cannot always see students who are rocking back in their chair. Ask them to help you out by giving gentle reminders to classmates who are tipping their chair.

6. Consider disciplinary measures.
You might have the persistent chair tipper stay in for recess or an after-school detention.

7. Praise "no tipping" behavior.
Recognize the student who is prone to chair tipping when you see him sitting properly. Similarly, find occasions to praise other students who are doing the same. In this way, you are conveying to the chair tippers in your class that sitting appropriately is an effective way of gaining your attention.

See Also

Hyperactivity

Cheating

Although cheating is more of a problem in middle and high school, it is not uncommon with elementary school students. The pressures that older children often feel to do well in school and that may give rise to cheating can also affect younger children. Elementary school teachers play an important role in instilling the importance of honesty in school and helping students learn to take pride in their own work.

In finding appropriate consequences to cheating, teachers need to think not just about punishing the student but about correcting the behavior. Simply punishing students for cheating without attending to the underlying reasons for the behavior often has the effect of making students more crafty and careful cheaters. Correcting the behavior may require finding out why a student cheats and then addressing those needs. At the same time, teachers need to be aware that in responding to a student who cheats, they are sending an important message to their other students about the consequences of cheating. Failure to confront a student who cheats may lead the cheater's classmates to think they can cheat with impunity.

With younger children, it is important to make sure that they understand what it means to cheat, especially if they have little experience working independently. If they are used to working in groups where sharing information is expected, they may not appreciate that it is inappropriate to copy the work of others when working on their own.

In trying to deter cheating, be aware that children can be very inventive in devising ways to cheat. For example, they may use hand signals to convey answers, write key information on notes taped to the bottom of their desks, use a watch calculator to figure out math answers, write information on their hands or arms, or look at classmates' test papers as they walk to the teacher's desk to ask a question.

What You Can Do

1. Have a class meeting about cheating.

Discuss this issue early in the year before the problem emerges. Talk with your students about how it feels to earn a good grade by studying hard, compared with how it feels to earn a good grade by getting the answers from someone else. Ask them why they think students feel the need to cheat and how they would feel if they found out one of their idols had cheated. Elicit their ideas about some of the possible consequences of cheating. Offer your own views, perhaps indicating that the lessons they learn are more important than the grades they receive. Tell them that students who copy answers from a classmate may be getting the wrong answers. Inform them that if they are having problems with a subject, you expect them to let you know and you will give them extra help. At the same time, let them know your policy about cheating and the classroom consequences.

2. Organize the room so as to minimize cheating.

You might have students move their desks farther apart while taking tests. Some teachers even have students place simple barriers (perhaps made of file folders) on their desks during tests so their neighbors cannot see their papers.

3. Review your rules before administering a test.

For example, you might tell your students to clear their desks of all materials, face forward during the test, keep their eyes on their own paper, and remain seated and silent until the test is over. You might also remind them of the consequences for cheating. Consider posting these rules in the classroom.

4. Give your students multiple versions of the same test.

Developing different versions of a test is easy with a computer. This doesn't involve adding new questions to the alternate versions but rather changing the order of the questions on the original test. Letting students know that you are doing this will deter them from cheating. You don't even have to create different versions to achieve this effect. You might just label the tests Version A, Version B, and Version C or have the test run off on two or three different-colored papers without changing the order of the questions to make students believe there are different forms of the test.

5. Have your students show their work or answer open-ended questions.

Tests that require students to explain their answers, whether by showing the steps used to solve a math problem or the reasoning behind their answer, are hard to copy. These tests have the added advantage of allowing you to give partial credit for using a correct process or demonstrating some understanding.

6. Observe your students from the back of the room.

Students are less likely to glance at their neighbor's test if they do not know where you are looking. Occasionally, circulate around the room, passing students in an unpredictable pattern but making sure to pass those who are prone to cheating.

7. Deal with the issue of cheating without the assistance of your students.

Keep in mind that the problem of cheating is for you to handle, not your students. Do not ask for their help in identifying classmates who cheat. This will only cause conflict and disharmony in your class.

8. Lessen the academic pressure.

Children who cheat are likely acting out of fear that they cannot compete with their peers. Incidents of cheating in your class may call for you to decrease the pressures the students are feeling, which may lessen their impulse to cheat. Some ways to evaluate students that might minimize these pressures are as follows:

- Consider effort, classroom participation, and homework completion in determining grade.
- Allow students to retake tests.
- Arrange group projects.
- Review portfolios in which students select the items to be included.
- Assign oral presentations.
- Give oral tests.
- Use open-book tests.

9. Talk with the student privately. If you are confident the student was cheating, talk with her after class but do not embarrass her publicly. In considering what to say, remind yourself that her cheating reflects her desire to do better in school. Adopt a calm but serious demeanor while avoiding expressions of anger. Accusing her of cheating will likely elicit a denial. Also avoid trying to trick her into an admission of cheating. Instead, describe what you saw, and let her know that you are concerned about and disappointed in her behavior. Try to find out what prompted her to cheat, with particular attention to academic weaknesses, poor study habits, feelings of academic anxiety, and parental pressure to succeed. Then let her know the consequences for cheating as a result of this incident and in the future (see next item).

10. Provide consequences for the student who cheats. In deciding what, if any, consequences to give to a student who has cheated, consider her age and sensitivity level and whether this has happened before. With a young elementary student, you might simply let her know that copying from another student's paper is not permitted and perhaps move her desk away from those of other students and allow her to continue. With an older student, you might go over to her, quietly take her test away, and ask her to see you after class. In talking with her, you might let her know what you observed and then inform her that she will have to retake the test (if necessary, in a private setting) and that you will average her second test score with a zero or F on the first test. Let her know that if this behavior happens again she will receive an automatic zero or F without a chance for a retake. If a student is caught copying an assignment from a classmate, you might follow a similar approach: have the student redo the assignment and average the grade on the second assignment with a zero or F on the first.

11. Find out why the student is cheating, and provide appropriate support. Simply giving the student a consequence for cheating may not address the underlying problem. Find out what is motivating her to cheat. She may be feeling intense pressure to do well in school, or she may lack confidence in her ability to succeed, or she may be feeling a combination of the two. As a result of your inquiries, you may want to give her academic support, which might take the form of working with her after school to improve subject-area skills or study skills, prodding her to ask questions in class or during a test, arranging for a peer tutor, or encouraging parents to provide assistance at home. You might also give the class a review sheet prior to the test. If you conclude that the cheating reflects a lack of confidence or self-esteem, find opportunities to praise the student, highlight her accomplishments, and foster her success with academic tasks.

12. Consider informing the student's parents.

You may want to inform the parents of their child's cheating, especially if it has happened more than once. In speaking with them, focus on trying to find ways to correct the behavior more than punish the student. If the cheating reflects the student's academic weaknesses or lack of confidence, encourage the parents to provide additional assistance in completing homework and preparing for classroom tests.

13. Monitor a student closely who has cheated previously.

If a student has a history of cheating, you might seat her near your desk and away from other students. Wherever she is seated, try to wander by her desk frequently during a test. If necessary, have her take the test in a private setting with adult supervision (for example, in a resource center). Give the student permission to ask questions if she is confused about the test instructions or a particular question or problem.

See Also

Motivation, Lack of

Seatwork Problems

Class Trip Problems

Class trips can provide students with unique learning experiences, giving them an opportunity to see firsthand what they are studying. Unfortunately, they also give students a new forum in which to display disciplinary problems. These problems can be minimized with some advance planning.

What You Can Do

1. Visit the site ahead of time. A site visit will help you identify potential problems and plan for them. If you are unable to visit, talk with a representative of the site and ask what specific rules you should emphasize to your students (for example, whether they can touch the exhibits) and whether there are any special circumstances that may present problems for students.

2. Try to arrange the trip in the morning. Children are likely to be more alert, focused, and cooperative before lunch.

3. Establish ground rules for the trip. Let your students know that they are representatives (better yet, tell them they are ambassadors) for their school and that you expect them to be on their best behavior. Inform them that the regular school rules are in effect during the trip. In addition, outline a few rules specific to the field trip (for example, no talking while a tour guide is speaking). Also talk with them about what to do if they get lost. You might have each student sign a form spelling out the rules for the trip and the consequences for violating them and asking for their agreement to comply with them.

4. Review bus rules with students. Bear in mind that some students may not take a bus to school so they may not be familiar with rules on the bus. Make sure they understand bus protocol relating to seating arrangements, getting out of their seat, talking, using the windows, and exiting the bus.

5. Talk with a problem-prone student before the trip.
If you have a student who is likely to present behavioral difficulties on the trip, take him aside and ask for his cooperation. Review with him the rules and the consequences for violating them, and let him know you expect him to follow them. Remind him that class trips are privileges and students who misbehave run the risk of losing that privilege in the future. Ask him if there are any changes you can make to ensure he will cooperate.

6. Prepare your students for the trip.
Begin by letting them know the activities of the day, including the arrangements for lunch, and inform them of any events that may be distressing to them (for example, loud noises). Talk about what they will see, perhaps sharing some literature about the place they are visiting or directing them to its Web site. Giving students this information will make the trip more meaningful. They may also be less likely to fool around because they will be more understanding of what they are seeing.

7. Give students activities to do while on the trip.
These activities might include taking notes on what they hear or drawing a picture of what they see. You might also give them a list of items to look for and check off when they see them. In addition, you might give them a series of questions before they go on the trip and tell them they will be asked to discuss or write about them when they return. Encourage them to pose questions of their own to the guide. These tasks may help them focus on what they are seeing and lessen the chance they will misbehave.

8. Establish a signal to get students' attention.
At some point during the class trip, you may need to quiet the students down and get them to focus on you. You might do this by raising your hand, with fingers forming a V shape. Tell them they are to raise their hand when they see you raising yours and be silent.

9. Avoid disruptive combinations when grouping students.
Assign trouble-prone students to chaperones with good management skills or assign them to

your group, but avoid grouping students together who have a history of problems when they are together. If you are especially concerned about a student's behavior, consider asking his parent to serve as a chaperone and then place him in his parent's group. Meet with the chaperones briefly to discuss with them the rules for the trip and how they should handle it if a student misbehaves.

10. Assign each student a buddy.
Assignments will help ensure that students stay with the group. Tell them that they must stay with their partner both on and off the bus. You might let students choose their own partners, but if you see some problematic combinations, don't hesitate to make changes.

11. Bring a cell phone with you.
A cell phone provides you with immediate access to the school if there is a problem. It also gives you a way to contact a student's parents if he is presenting a problem. You might even have the student make the call. Consider letting your students know that you have a cell phone and that if they misbehave you may have them call their parents to inform them.

See Also

Disruptive/Uncooperative Behavior

Complaining, Frequent

Some students seem to find fault with almost everything. They may gripe about the amount of homework, the food in the lunchroom, their seat in the classroom, and the comments of other students. For these chronic complainers, not much seems to be going right. Their cup is decidedly half-empty rather than half-full.

Although you want to discourage these students from complaining as a way of seeking your attention, you do not want to discourage them from voicing legitimate grievances or concerns. There is nothing inherently wrong with a student lodging a complaint. Indeed, you want your students to let you know if they are unhappy with some aspect of the classroom. Their complaints may even help by prompting you to modify a classroom activity or practice. So even though you want your students to bring up legitimate concerns, you do not want them complaining in an inappropriate manner or so often that it interferes with your ability to conduct your lesson.

What You Can Do

1. Talk with your class.   In talking with your students about your classroom procedures, let them know it is okay if they come to you with concerns or problems, but encourage them to try to resolve the problem on their own first. If they come to you with a complaint, suggest that they also have some ideas for dealing with it. If you have a complaint box in the classroom, tell them how to use it.

2. If the student has a legitimate complaint, try to resolve it.   If the student brings to your attention a genuine problem that is presenting difficulties for her or her classmates, work with her to find a solution. If, however, her complaint is beyond your control or without merit (for example, "It's not fair that we get math homework every night"), you might help her understand this by responding in the following way: "I'm sorry you feel that way, but this is what I think is best for the class and I'm going to stick with it." Then return to what you were doing without engaging in further conversation with the student.

3. Encourage the student to look on the bright side.
In response to a complaint, try redirecting the student's attention to something positive about the situation. For example, if she complains about the food in school, you might ask her to name her three favorite meals served in the cafeteria. Also listen to what she is saying to peers, and find time to talk with her about activities that she speaks positively about and seems to enjoy.

4. Talk privately with the chronic complainer.
Take the student aside, and let her know that the two of you need to work together to help her learn to complain less frequently. (With a young elementary student, make sure she understands what you mean by a complaint.) Let her know that she is of course allowed to come to you with concerns but that she needs to make sure the problem is really bothering her and is one you can help solve. Help her understand that if she complains very often, adults may not take her concerns seriously and classmates may find it annoying and start to avoid her.

5. If the student makes frequent, unreasonable complaints, ignore them.
If after your discussion with her the student continues to make complaints that do not allow for or warrant a solution (for example, "I hate it when we have a substitute for gym"), do not pay attention to her negative comments. Avoid responding to her, making eye contact with her, or even making a face. Rather, continue what you were doing.

6. Praise the student when she is making an effort to solve a problem.
Just as you want to ignore her when she is complaining unceasingly, you want to praise her when she is trying to solve a problem rather than complaining about it.

7. Look for patterns.
Observing when the student complains and whom she complains to may tell you why she is complaining so often. If she is griping frequently to peers, this may be her way of gaining status with them. But if she complains mostly to you and your response is often to listen to and comfort her, this may be her way of gaining your attention. If she often complains right before a particular activity, her grievances may suggest she is having problems in that setting, although she may not be comfortable telling you that directly.

8. Establish a complaint quota.
If you have a student who is a relentless complainer, tell her that she is limited to two or three complaints per day. Let her know that you will respond to those complaints but not to any others, so she will need to think carefully before making a complaint. Try to stick to this plan, although of course you will not want to ignore serious complaints, even if she has exceeded the quota.

9. Signal the student when she complains.
Chronically complaining students may not be aware of how frequently they make negative comments. Set up a private, nonverbal signal with the student that you can use in class to alert her when she is complaining. You might say her name to get her attention and then signal her by, for example, raising your eyebrows, pulling your ear, or giving her a wink. This will help her become more aware of her behavior.

10. Tell the student to write down her complaint and put it in the classroom complaint box.
Make sure all your students know about this procedure. Tell them that if they are unhappy about some aspect of the class, they should write it down, sign the piece of paper, and put it in the box. Encourage them to suggest a solution for the problem. If time allows, try to look at and respond to the complaints by the end of the day, dealing with those that are most pressing first. This box will help minimize disruptions to your lessons and allow students to voice concerns they are not comfortable expressing to you in person. Make it clear to your students that they can see you in person if a problem needs your immediate attention.

11. Monitor the student's complaints.   Keep track of the number of times the student complains each day. Use the results to demonstrate to her how often she complains and to determine if she is making progress in decreasing this behavior. If she is old enough, you might even have her monitor her own behavior by recording on a 3" × 5" card each time you signal her that she has made a complaint. This act of self-monitoring will make her more aware of this behavior and less likely to engage in it.

See Also

Argumentative Behavior

Dependent Behavior

Pouting

Tattling

Whining

Crying, Frequent

Children may cry in school for various reasons. They may be genuinely distressed by something that happened to them in school or at home. Or they may cry because they're afraid that something upsetting *will* happen to them. Or they may become teary-eyed out of frustration with an issue they are struggling with in the present.

For some children, however, crying is less a reaction to something happening to them and more an effort to get a reaction from someone else—typically, attention or sympathy. They may have learned that crying is an effective way to gain others' attention, which they have difficulty gaining in more appropriate ways. Children may also cry to manipulate others into giving them what they want, such as an easing of discipline or a decrease in academic expectations.

Some children are temperamentally more prone to crying than others. For these children, stressful situations such as being disciplined may elicit an emotional reaction. Being yelled at or even getting their name on the board can seem like the end of the world to them. They may not be used to being corrected by someone other than their parents and may come to believe that the teacher dislikes them. Other classroom situations may also trigger tears from the sensitive child, such as giving a wrong answer, having no one to play with on the playground, being called a name, or not being chosen to be line leader.

Crying episodes, whatever the cause, can distract your other students and interfere with your lessons. In addition, the student who is crying may lose out on valuable teaching time. In determining how to respond to the student, it is of course important to figure out why he is crying. In particular, you want to determine if he is crying because he is genuinely distressed by something that happened to him or because he wants to get your attention or because he is trying to manipulate your reaction to him.

Although sometimes a child's reason for crying is a blend of all three reasons, usually one reason will stand out. If a student rarely cries, his crying is likely due to genuine distress and calls for you to try to ease the specific problem. If, however, you conclude that he is trying to get your attention or manipulate you, you may want to discourage his crying by ignoring it or not giving in.

In responding to a child who is crying, keep in mind that crying is not necessarily a behavior problem that needs to be controlled. Indeed, a child may be crying for very understandable reasons, and crying may be an appropriate response to a distressing situation (for example, his parents getting a divorce or his dog dying). Simply getting him to stop crying does not make the hurt go away. Rather, you need to figure out why he is crying and try to address the underlying problem rather than just put your energies into controlling the crying.

A common problem that teachers of young elementary students see is the child who cries after his parent drops him off at school. He may weep uncontrollably and be hard to comfort. Most students with separation anxiety eventually adjust as they begin to feel secure in the setting, trusting of their teacher, and comfortable with their classmates.

What You Can Do

1. Comfort the genuinely distressed child.

If you conclude he is upset about something and not crying to get his way or gain your attention, respond in a soothing manner. Dignify his distress by letting him know it is okay to cry, but tell him that you would like to help him. Ask him why he is upset. If he has difficulty putting into words why he is distressed, suggest some possible reasons and tell him to shake his head yes or no. Ask if he is upset by things his classmates are saying or doing or by something at home.

2. Try to figure out what triggers his crying episodes.

Talk with other adults who are involved with him in school to see if he cries at certain times of the day. Make note of where he is and what he is doing when he cries. Does he cry when his parents leave in the morning? During tests? While eating lunch? On the playground? When disciplined? When asked to leave the room for speech therapy? When he has difficulty doing the work? Also note what happens when he cries. Do you rush over to him and provide sympathy? Do you back off from making demands of him or disciplining him? Do his classmates try to comfort him? Answers to these questions will help you identify what may trigger and maintain his crying and what you can do to help him.

3. Provide support in identified areas of need.

Your detective work may help you determine what is prompting the student's crying and how you can help him. If he is crying because he is frustrated academically, find ways to give him help in his areas of weakness. If he is crying because other children are teasing him or excluding him from activities, take steps to improve his peer interaction skills and integrate him into peer activities. If he is crying because he does not have anyone to sit with on the bus, try to find a partner for him. The goal here is not to control his crying but to solve the problem that gave rise to the crying.

4. Talk with his parents.

If a student cries often in your class, ask his parents to come in for a conference. Describe his behavior to them, and offer your thoughts about what is triggering his crying. Ask them if he is quick to cry at home and if there are any family issues that may be upsetting him. Tell them how you would like to handle his crying in school, and get their reaction to this plan. Keep them posted about his progress.

5. If you conclude he is crying to get your attention, try to ignore him.

If you are confident he is not hurt or genuinely distressed but rather is crying to gain your attention or get his way, try not to respond to him and certainly do not give him what he wants. His crying may intensify, but try to stay the course. At the same time, give him immediate and positive attention when he stops crying. If he starts to cry again, inform him that you do not want to be with him when he is acting this way, and then move away from him.

6. If the attention-seeking student continues to cry, consider removing him.

Ignoring a crying child is not a viable option if he is distracting other students or interfering with your ability to teach. If this is the case, consider sending him to a quiet area of the classroom or to the guidance counselor or principal. Explain to him that he cannot remain with the other students if his crying is disturbing them but that he can return when he has stopped crying. If he is sent to a quiet area of the room, ignore him while he is crying and encourage students to do the same. Keep an eye on him, however, and as soon as he stops crying go over to him.

7. Discipline the student in a matter-of-fact manner.
If he tends to get upset or cry when disciplined, don't back off on giving him the consequences you think are warranted, but do it using a soft voice and a calm demeanor. Make it clear that you are displeased with his behavior but not with him. Explain in brief terms why his behavior is inappropriate and how it causes a problem for you and his classmates. Let him know you are confident he can act more appropriately in the future.

8. Hold the student accountable for completing his work.
If he falls behind in his work because of his crying episodes, expect him to finish it, even if he hands it in late or has to complete it in school or at home. If he gets the idea that he can get out of doing his work if he cries, he may be more inclined to have crying episodes.

9. If the student cries when his parents drop him off, weather the storm.
Make sure to have some pleasurable activity for him to engage in after his parents leave. You may be surprised at how quickly he calms down. As he appears more comfortable in school, give the parents a call to reassure them that their child is adjusting better. Although you may need some support from a classroom aide or the principal if his crying disrupts the class, strenuously avoid the impulse to call his parents to have them pick him up. That will only make the next day that much harder.

10. If the student is crying because he misses his parents, ease his distress but do not send him home.
You might lessen his anxiety by encouraging him to carry a security item during the day that connects him with home, such as a picture of his family or a favorite book or toy. If

necessary to calm him down, consider having him call his mother or father at a set time every day, gradually cutting it down to two or three times per week and eventually none at all. Use this strategy with caution; calls home can upset children and make them more determined to go home.

11. Prepare the student for a change of routine.

If the student becomes upset and tends to cry when the class or school routine is altered, let him know ahead of time about changes that may set him off (for example, a shortened day, an assembly, a substitute teacher, an indoor recess). New situations can also throw him for a loop, especially if they involve meeting new people. Discuss with him what he will be seeing or doing so he feels more prepared and in control.

12. Talk with the student prior to an activity.

If he is prone to misbehaving and crying when disciplined, you might avoid a crying episode by talking with him right before the activity. Tell him the behaviors you expect of him, and ask for his commitment to behave in this way. You might ask him to suggest a reasonable consequence if he misbehaves, or tell him the consequence and ask for his agreement. If he cries when disciplined, remind him that he said he would behave properly and suggested (or at least agreed to) the consequence.

13. Provide the student with counseling.

If the student is distressed about a personal concern, have the guidance counselor or school psychologist talk with him. Inform the parents of this arrangement.

See Also

Bullying

Dependent Behavior

Pouting

Self-Esteem, Low

Teasing

Whining

Dependent Behavior

The dependent student has a problem with trust, but the person she has trouble trusting is herself. She is reluctant to think for herself, make decisions for herself, even talk for herself. Instead of looking inward for answers, she may look to you for support and assistance at every turn—so much so that she may become your constant companion. She may spend more time at your desk than her own, as she bombards you with a blizzard of questions or just clings to your side.

The dependent student is surely seeking attention, but she may be seeking more. Feeling helpless and perhaps possessing a "what's-the-use" mindset, she may have concluded that it is pointless to try because she will fail anyway. As a result, she may expect you to not only think for her but to do her schoolwork for her as well. She may even resist learning so she can maintain that connection and closeness with you.

Dependency can create a problem for both teacher and student. The dependent child can command so much of your attention that you have little time left for other students. But the time you spend with a dependent child is not always helpful. Indeed, her excessive reliance on you and others can stifle her social development by limiting her involvement with peers and thus minimizing opportunities to develop essential social skills.

The student's dependency can also keep her from learning to think independently and act responsibly. This is especially likely if you and her parents accede to her desire for dependence by doing her thinking, making her decisions, solving her problems, and shielding her from every obstacle that comes her way. The result will be a child who lacks confidence in herself and her ability to relate with others.

Your goal in working with a dependent student is to help her become more self-reliant and more trusting in her own judgment. This requires that you communicate your expectations to her and set firm limits on your interaction, giving her attention in ways that foster her independence and avoiding interacting with her in ways that foster her dependence.

What You Can Do

1. Identify the reason for the student's clinginess.
Some children may be temperamentally shy and clingy; others may be acting that way in reaction to something. If you have noticed a change in the student's behavior, in that she has become more dependent on you and less willing to act on her own, you will want to talk with her and her parents to see if something is upsetting her. It may be, for example, that she is having trouble adjusting to the beginning of school, that she is distressed about a problem at home, that another child is picking on her, or that she is feeling overwhelmed by the work. If you can figure out the reason for her behavior, you can respond to her much more effectively.

2. Convey your expectations to the student.
Have a private conference with her, and be clear about the behavior you expect. Let her know that you want her to try her hardest to solve problems or figure things out on her own. If she does that and still needs assistance, tell her to ask a classmate for help. Only when she has tried to figure things out on her own and asked a classmate for help can she come to you for assistance—unless it is an emergency; in that case, she can see you immediately. Tell her that if she continues to come to you all the time with questions or requests for assistance, you will have little time left to help other students. Let her know that you think she can figure out the answers to many of her questions by herself; at the same time, reassure her that if she makes a mistake it is no big deal. You may want to give her some specific restrictions about her asking of questions; some options are offered next.

3. Discourage her from bombarding you with questions.
Children who are insecure in their abilities often look for reassurance by questioning their teacher at every turn. Here are some ways to reduce their questions to a reasonable number. You may want to use these strategies for your entire class.

- Instruct the student to ask herself, before asking you a question, whether she needs the question answered to complete the assignment. If not, then she is not to ask the question.

- Tell your students that there will be certain times when you will be busy and not available to answer questions. You might signal them of this by, for example, putting a notation on the board or a hair scrunchy on your wrist.

- Tell the student to "Ask three, then me." Explain that this means that if she has a question, she is to ask three classmates before she can come to you.

- Tell the student to put her question in writing and hand it to you. Having her write it down may make her think seriously about the question. In doing so, she may conclude that the question is not important or may figure out the answer on her own.

- Tell the student that she must work for 5 minutes on the task before she can ask a question. If she has a question during this period, she may solve the problem on her own or decide that the question is not relevant.

- You might limit the student to a set number of questions she can ask per day, perhaps giving her that number of poker chips every day and requiring her to give you a chip every time she asks a question. If she has used her chips for the day, she is not allowed to ask you any more questions. She must turn in her remaining chips at the end of the day, but they will earn her points that she can exchange at the end of the week for a prize or privilege.

4. Encourage the student to trust her own judgments.
She may be insecure about her own abilities and thus may look to others for feedback and approval at every step. Try to lessen her reliance on others by building confidence in her own judgment and ability to solve problems. Avoid doing things for her that she can do on her own. If she asks you a question, ask her for her ideas and then find a way to support what she says. If she struggles to answer a question, give her some hints and lead her along but try to get her to figure out the answer. If she is having a conflict with another student, you might tell both students that they must resolve the problem by themselves. If she makes a decision, try to put a positive spin on that decision, even if it requires modification. For example, if she chooses a book for a book report that is

much too hard for her, help her find a book on the same topic that is more within her ability ("Ashley, you chose a really interesting topic to read about. I have a book in mind on just that topic that I think you'll like.").

5. Try to ignore the student when she acts in a clingy, dependent manner.

Although this may not be easy if she is grasping your arm, do not look at or talk with her. Try to move away, if necessary, by gently undoing her grasp. Continue with your lesson, and give attention and praise to students who are behaving appropriately. The idea is to help the student understand that appropriate behavior will be responded to and clingy behavior will be ignored. As soon as she begins to act in a mature, independent manner, pay attention to her and acknowledge her behavior with a positive comment.

6. Praise the student when she acts independently.
You want to respond to her so that she gains more attention when she behaves independently than when she behaves dependently. Make sure to acknowledge her appropriate behavior in situations where she had acted in a clingy, dependent manner in the past. You might want to praise her for behaviors that you take for granted with other students (for example, "Jennifer, I'm really pleased with how you hung up your coat yourself") or for making an effort to solve a problem herself, even if the result is unsuccessful ("Jennifer, I like the way you tried to sound out the word by yourself. Keep up the good work."). If she behaves independently in a particularly noteworthy way, you might make a big deal of this by giving her a special reward or privilege (for example, having lunch with you). As she begins to demonstrate more independent behavior, you can gradually lessen the frequency of your praise.

7. Give the student special attention.
A clingy child is looking to gain your attention. Try to spend some one-on-one time with her a few times a week when you can engage in an activity of her choice, such as playing a game, reading a book to her, or talking with her about a hobby. Even 5 minutes of your undivided attention will be very satisfying to her. You might want to make this special attention from you contingent on her exhibiting non-clingy, independent behavior. For example, if your one-on-one time takes place at

the end of the day, you might tell her that she can spend time with you if she has behaved appropriately during the day. Tell her the specific behaviors that you want to see and that will earn the special attention.

8. Signal the student when she is acting in a clingy, dependent manner.

Meet with her privately, and work out an inconspicuous signal, such as winking or raising your eyebrows, that you will use to alert her that she needs to be acting more independently. If necessary, define for her what you mean by acting independently. You might need to say her name first to get her attention before giving her the signal.

9. Assign the student a classroom buddy.

If you have a student who is excessively reliant on you, pair her up with a mature, responsible classmate and instruct the student to see her buddy when she is confused about directions or needs help. As an alternative, you might group students at tables, with tablemates expected to help each other when questions arise.

10. Give the student a sense of importance.

You may be able to enhance her sense of responsibility and independence by having her take on a valued classroom job. Moreover, giving her tasks that involve helping others will encourage her to focus on the needs of others and not just her own. Let her know that her assignment is very important and that you are giving her this responsibility because you are confident she can carry it out well. Some possible assignments: serving as class messenger, being a buddy to a classmate who speaks little English, taking care of the class pet, serving on the safety patrol, taking a new student on a tour of the school, and answering the school phone while the secretary is at lunch.

11. Help the dependent child adjust to new situations.

The dependent child is often insecure when placed in new situations. She may react by withdrawing or taking more time than most to warm up to the new activity. Help prepare her for the change by letting her know what the new situation will be like and what the rules and expectations are. Listen attentively to her concerns and try to resolve them in advance. You might also have her rehearse an unfamiliar activity (for example, if she is going to do an oral report, have her do a dry run with you or her parents) to give her confidence when she has to do the real thing.

12. Orchestrate social interactions with her peers.
Although the clingy child may spend more time with you than with her peers, her lack of social interaction is likely due more to anxiety than lack of interest. She probably wants to interact with her classmates, but staying by your side is often the safer, more comfortable choice. Put on your social director's hat, and try integrating the student in peer activities. You might ask a couple of friendly and easygoing students to ask her to play during recess or join them during lunch. If you pair up students in class, assign her a kind and congenial partner. Also encourage her parents to arrange play dates with classmates, perhaps suggesting specific children, and sign her up for community activities in her areas of interest.

See Also

Crying, Frequent

Forgetfulness

Pouting

Shyness

Whining

Disorganization

The ability of a student to be organized is one of the key building blocks of school success. Elementary school teachers often find that they are spending too little time teaching their students academic skills and too much time helping them get organized. These problems cut across all ability levels. Some of your students may have well-developed academic skills but get failing grades when it comes to organizational skills. Keeping your students on track can prove very time-consuming.

A student's organizational problems can take various forms, including forgetting to bring the necessary materials to class, losing papers, producing hard-to-follow written work, having problems getting started with a project or report, using time inefficiently, or not completing seatwork. Even such simple tasks as bringing a pencil to class may elude the disorganized student. He may be overwhelmed by having to keep various times, dates, and assignments in his head and may even have difficulty remembering his school schedule.

Homework is probably the biggest challenge for the disorganized student—and his teacher. The student may neglect to write down the assignment and later on forget what to do. Or he may write it down but record it incorrectly. Or he may write it down correctly but fail to bring the needed materials home. Or he may complete it but forget to bring it to school on the day it is due. Getting the disorganized student to turn in homework on time can exasperate the most experienced of teachers.

It is important that elementary teachers, particularly those in the upper grades, focus on organizational skills because they will be essential in middle school, where students will be expected to keep track of their assignments and school responsibilities with little teacher assistance. Fortunately, organizational skills can be taught.

What You Can Do

1. Designate a place in your classroom for students to turn in their seatwork.

Having students turn in their work as soon as they complete it will lessen their chance of misplacing it. Make the system simple to use. You might designate a box, crate, file divider, or file drawer for this purpose, with individual student folders arranged alphabetically. Or you might have folders for each assignment that are color-coded to decrease the chance of misfiling. You might also have students check off, on a conveniently placed sheet, that they have turned in the assignment.

2. Have students organize their papers in folders.

Students might have a folder for completed work, a folder for work to be done, and a folder for parent information. Or they might have different folders for each subject. By keeping these folders in their desks and color-coding them, they can access their work quickly. You can help students avoid being overwhelmed by loose papers by having them bring completed work home on a specific day of the week. Let parents know of this procedure so they can help their child sort through the papers.

3. Encourage responsibility for bringing materials to class.

Review with your students the materials that you expect them to bring to school every day. Do spot checks periodically. If a student forgets to bring the proper materials, loan him what he needs, but you might require him to give you some "collateral" that must be returned when he gives back the borrowed materials. If forgetting becomes a pattern, contact his parents or give him a school consequence. A neat trick for the student who is constantly losing his pencil: have him put a piece of Velcro on his desk as well as on his pencil. You might also keep a "pencil stubs" box on your desk or near the pencil sharpener so students who forget a pencil do not need to disrupt the class.

4. Give the student clear and simple directions.

State directions with a minimum of words. If you go over every detail, the student may miss the key points. You might have him repeat the directions to you so you are confident he understands them. If you are explaining a complex task, give him one or two instructions at a time. You might also demonstrate it to him and then have him do it while you observe.

5. Provide the disorganized student with a classroom buddy.

This buddy should be a mature, responsible classmate who can help the student with classroom tasks when you are unavailable. A variation of this is to group students at tables and expect them to help each other when questions arise.

6. Simplify the student's schedule.

Try to schedule the student's activities so that he does the same activity at the same time every week. Even though working this out is not easy, as you are often at the mercy of other staff members' schedules, this will make the student's day much less confusing.

7. Require older elementary students to use a three-ring binder.

Students as early as third grade can adapt to using a three-ring binder with subject dividers and a pouch for pens and pencils. Suggest they get a binder with pockets or three-hole-punched folders, and have them label one pocket or folder as "To Bring Home" for homework to be done and notes for parents and another as "To Bring to School" for completed homework and notes from parents. You might also have them place a monthly calendar in their binders on which they can indicate tests, projects, and important school activities. Punch holes in the handouts you give to students so they can put them in their binder easily.

8. Meet briefly with the student before he goes home.

Use this time to make sure he has the proper materials and has written down his homework correctly.

9. Teach the student memory aids.

Teach the child the acronym PANTS to remind him what he needs to bring to and from school every day (P = Parent information, A = Assignments, N = Notebook, T = Textbooks, and S = Student, namely himself). Show him how to make a checklist of school tasks and his schedule that he can tape to his desk or binder. With a younger student, have him draw pictures rather than use words as reminders. If he has a watch with an alarm, have him set it to go off at the time of a schedule change (for example, when he needs to go to a remedial program).

10. Provide the student with a container for small items.
Items such as pencils, pens, erasers, and scissors can be easily lost in a desk or backpack. In trying to find them, a student may disrupt the class as he rummages through his desk. You can help him solve this problem by having him place the items in a case, such as a plastic zippered pouch kept in his binder or a box or resealable plastic bag kept in his desk.

See Also

Attention Deficit

Forgetfulness

Homework Problems

Messiness

Seatwork Problems

Disruptive/Uncooperative Behavior

The disruptive student may be referred to in a variety of ways. He may be called uncooperative, disobedient, acting out, noncompliant, oppositional, defiant, troubled, even emotionally disturbed. What most teachers call him, however, is frustrating. The disruptive student makes the job of the teacher far more difficult and can take considerable time away from instruction. Disruptions can also take a toll on the rest of the class. Studies show and teachers know that students make greater academic gains in a setting with few disruptions.

The uncooperative student may disturb your class in a myriad of ways. He may make noises, giggle uncontrollably, call out answers, refuse to follow your directives, get out of his seat, sharpen his pencil in the middle of a lesson, talk frequently with his friends, make wisecracks, clown around, make fun of other students, and throw objects. What these behaviors share in common is that they disturb the class, making it difficult for you to teach and difficult for your students to learn.

It is critical that you find ways to minimize any behaviors that disrupt the flow of your lessons and impede your students' ability to focus on those lessons. This section offers a variety of strategies to manage a disruptive student. These strategies include ways of preventing behavior problems as well as dealing with them when they do occur. In deciding which measures to use, give preference to positive over negative strategies. Keep in mind that your goal is not just to stop the student from misbehaving but to foster self-control.

What You Can Do

1. Increase your leverage with the student by treating him with respect.
He will be less likely to disrupt your class and more likely to cooperate if he senses you care about him. Similarly, he will be more receptive

to your disciplinary efforts if he feels he has been treated in a respectful manner. Build a bond with him by praising him, highlighting his accomplishments, joking around with him, and finding a few minutes every so often to talk with him about his interests. When he walks in at the start of the day, give him a warm greeting or a high five. Pay close attention to your tone of voice and body language when talking with him. Give him an opportunity to share his feelings and concerns with you, and listen attentively when he does. If he misbehaves and you take him to task, do not belittle or humiliate him, especially in front of his peers. This will only incite his anger and perpetuate his disruptive behavior.

2. Tell the student clearly, firmly, but unemotionally to stop his disruptive behavior.

When giving a directive, try to be near the student without getting in his face and make sure you have eye contact. After directing him to stop the behavior, turn away and continue with your lesson. This decreases the chance of a confrontation and allows him to save face. When said in this way, he will come to respect your authority and understand you mean business. This approach is far more effective than vague or indirect comments such as, "How many times do I have to ask you to stop that?" or "Give some thought to . . . . " Also avoid lecturing or belittling him. Vary your degree of firmness depending on the student, his history of misbehavior, and his sensitivity level. Some students may call for gentle reminders; others may need firm, no-nonsense statements. If he continues to misbehave, use the broken-record technique of repeating your instruction a maximum of three times. If he brings up secondary issues, briefly acknowledge his concerns, but refocus him on what he needs to do (for example, "I know that you feel that I'm being unfair, but I need you to stop making noise in class right now").

3. Acknowledge positive behavior.

In this way, you send a message to the student that he is more likely to get your attention through positive rather than negative behavior. In praising him, describe the behavior to the class (for example, "I am so impressed with how Jimmy raised his hand to answer rather than calling out"). If you think the public acknowledgment would be embarrassing to the student, give the praise in private. Find some behavior to praise with a problem-prone student, even if it means highlighting a behavior that is ordinary for most students. Praise him as soon as the behavior occurs, if possible, and avoid adding a negative comment such as, "Why can't you act this way all the time?" Look for different ways to acknowledge the student other than praise: sending a note home to his parents or phoning them in his presence, allowing him to overhear you making positive comments about him to another individual, giving him a good-behavior award, or selecting him as your student-of-the-month due to improved behavior.

4. Try to ignore minimally disruptive behavior.

You cannot respond every time a student misbehaves. Nor should you try. Focus on misbehaviors that interfere with your ability to teach or your students' ability to learn. For example, a student who gives you an angry look, laughs at inappropriate times, or mutters under his breath is better left alone. Also try to avoid responding to mild misbehaviors that are designed to gain your attention. This means not giving the student eye contact, not talking with him, not even being in his presence if you can avoid it. As soon as he begins to behave appropriately, however, try to give him some attention and comment positively on his behavior.

5. Elicit the student's cooperation.

When the student is in a reasonable mood, meet with him privately and, in a calm manner, tell him specifically what he is doing that is disruptive and how it is disturbing you and his classmates. Use "I statements" to help him understand its impact on you (for example, "I find it very frustrating to try to teach when you are making loud noises"). Ask him why he is behaving that way and whether he understands that this behavior is not acceptable in your class. You might tell him that his behavior is more like that of a younger child; this may spur him to change because many children want to be seen as acting like an older child. Allow him to voice his concerns about any aspect of your class or peer issues. Ask for his suggestions about what you can do to lessen the problem. End the discussion by expressing your confidence that he can stop the disruptive behaviors and learn to cooperate, perhaps even letting him know that you would like him to be a leader in class and show other students how to behave. Then have him summarize in his own words what he is going to do differently. Let him know you will meet with him again after a short period to review his progress.

6. Involve parents in resolving the problem.
If the student continues to disrupt your class despite your disciplinary efforts, contact his parents and invite them in for a meeting. Describe your concerns with their child's behavior, and ask if they can help you understand the reasons for his behavior. Ask them to express to their child their support for your rules and to convey to him clearly and directly how they expect him to behave—and not behave—in your classroom. If feasible, bring the student into the meeting so he can hear that his teacher and parents are of one mind about the importance of his following your rules and respecting your authority. Talk with the parents after one week, and periodically after that, to review the student's progress. Make sure the student knows that you and his parents will be in communication. Another way to use the parents' leverage is to invite one of them in to observe their child or even sit beside him in class. If the parents are able to come in, let the student know this. The mere mention of his parents coming in for an observation may be sufficient to correct his behavior and may even deter misbehavior by other students who will not want their parents coming to school either.

7. Look for a pattern to the behavior and modify the environment accordingly.
Keep mental or written notes about the student's disruptive behavior, and try to discern a pattern. Once you have identified factors that contribute to the problem, take steps to modify them. In identifying these factors, consider the following questions:

- Is the student more difficult on some days than others?
- Is he more likely to act out in certain situations, in certain subjects, or at certain times of the day?
- Does he tend to misbehave when he experiences academic difficulties?
- Does he misbehave more when he is sitting near certain students?
- Is he more cooperative when he is sitting near particular students?
- Is his disruptive behavior being reinforced by the reactions of his classmates?

Elementary Teacher's Discipline Problem Solver

Answering these and other questions will help you figure out whether to modify aspects of the classroom environment that trigger or reinforce his disruptive behavior. For example, if you observe that the student often misbehaves the first thing in the morning, make sure to have appealing activities for him at the beginning of the school day. Or if you notice that his classmates give him an audience when he fools around, you will want to instruct them to ignore his behavior.

8. Check with last year's teacher.

Ask the teacher whether the student misbehaved in class. If so, find out the nature of his misbehavior, what seemed to trigger the problems, and what strategies were effective in dealing with him. Also take a look at his school file for information about previous behavioral patterns.

9. Bolster the student academically, if necessary.

Consider the possibility that his misbehavior may be linked to academic frustration. He may often be confused about what to do or overwhelmed by the difficulty of the work. If so, find ways to support him by helping him feel that he is a capable learner and giving him assistance, perhaps through after-school help, parent support, or a buddy in class. You might need to adjust the level of his work and closely monitor his understanding of directions. Breaking an academic task into smaller, more doable parts can help a student feel less overwhelmed. Also consider the possibility that his misbehavior is related to boredom because the work is far too easy for him. If so, consider giving him more challenging or stimulating work.

10. Avoid a power struggle with the student.

Misbehaving students are expert at drawing teachers into battle. Resist the invitation. You cannot have a tug-of-war if one person drops the rope. Although it is easy to lose patience and become angry with a student who is disrupting your class, this may only stiffen his resistance and reinforce his misbehavior. Try pausing momentarily before reacting to him to avoid losing your temper. When you feel the impulse to raise your voice, try lowering it while insisting firmly but quietly what the class rule is and what he needs to do. If a consequence is warranted, carry it out in a calm, unemotional way. After the incident is over, wipe the slate clean and do not hold a grudge. One way of avoiding a power struggle is to provide the student with a choice of options that are acceptable to you so the student feels a sense of control (for example, "Megan, it's time to clean up. Would you like to collect the scissors or the markers?").

11. Redirect the misbehaving student to another activity.

With some disruptive students, particularly those in the early elementary grades, it is better to gently guide them to another activity than to confront them or give them a consequence. You might divert a student's attention by asking him a question, letting him assist you, having him do a class chore, or sending him out to the water fountain. The student's energy is thus refocused on a useful activity and away from the misbehavior and a likely confrontation.

12. Discourage misbehavior by staying close to the student.

The student will be less likely to act out when you are near him, so consider placing his desk near yours or standing close to him when he is prone to misbehave. If you are unable to be near him, call out his name and catch his eye when he is acting out to let him know you expect him to behave appropriately. You might also have him bring his chair near you when he is disrupting those around him. Tell him he is to sit there quietly until you allow him to return to his seat. Or tell him he can go back to his seat when he feels ready to behave properly.

13. Cue the student that he is being disruptive.

Establish with the student a subtle way to alert him that he is misbehaving and you want him to stop. In this way, you can inform him of his behavior without interrupting your lesson or embarrassing him in front of his peers. Ask him for suggestions about possible signals. Some examples: making eye contact, scratching your nose, raising your eyebrows, touching your lips, winking your eye, pointing to a posted rule, or touching him on the shoulder. You may need to say his name softly to get his attention prior to signaling him. Of course, if he continues to disrupt class despite your repeated signals, take some stronger action.

14. Enlist the help of classmates.

A disruptive student often alienates his classmates. As a result, they may avoid and even shun him, which may only perpetuate his misbehaviors. If you see this pattern occurring, arrange for the student to be called out of the room and have a candid conversation with the rest of the class. Tell them that you are aware that the student can be very annoying, but help them understand that he is only trying to get their attention and is probably hurt by their rejection. Ask their cooperation in helping him change by ignoring his annoying behaviors, not making nasty comments to him, and reaching out to him in a friendly way. Elicit their suggestions, and offer some of your own, about what they could say or do to reach out to him. You might tell them some positive things about him that they may not know. Also meet privately with the student and point out to him the specific behaviors that are causing his classmates to reject him. Accentuate his positive qualities and suggest some things he can say or do to connect with his classmates.

15. Make notes on his disruptive behavior.

Wander by his desk as you are recording this information so he can see you doing this. If he asks what you are writing down (and even if he does not), tell him that you are making notes on the way he is acting so you have an accurate record of his misbehavior to show both the principal and his parents.

16. Require a misbehaving student to fill out a behavior-improvement form.

Students are often more candid about their feelings when they write than when they speak. Have the student complete a form that asks him to describe his behavior and say why he behaved that way, how he could have behaved differently, how his behavior affected other students, and what will happen to him if this behavior continues. Tailor the form to the age of your students. Take some time to discuss the responses with the student, and then send a copy home for parents to review and sign, keeping the original for your records. This form provides a record of his behavior problems that you can use when meeting with his parents and helps him learn to reflect on and monitor his behavior. A variation of this is to create a behavior book by placing a page for each of your students in a three-ring binder. When a student misbehaves, instruct him to enter the requested information on his page, after which you review his responses and decide whether to give him a consequence.

17. Keep track of the student's behavior or, better yet, have the student do it.

You may be surprised how simply monitoring the frequency of a behavior and giving this feedback to the student can spur him to change. This process is even more effective if the student monitors his own behavior—a process called self-monitoring. Children as young as seven or eight can do this and are typically honest in evaluating their behavior. Choose a behavior that is easy to observe (for example, yelling out without raising his hand), and instruct the student to put a check on a 3" × 5" card taped to his desk every time he exhibits the behavior. As an alternative, he might tally the number of times you have given him a silent signal to alert him about his behavior. Still another alternative is to set a timer to go off every 15 minutes or so and instruct the student to put a check on the card for every 15-minute period in which he exhibited the behavior. Whatever system you use, review the student's performance with him at the end of the day and compare it with the previous day's tally. Talk with him about what he did well and what he needs to do differently. You can use the results as the basis for a behavior-modification program in which you reward him for attaining a certain prearranged goal.

18. Provide consequences to the student on a gradual basis.

If the student continues to disrupt your class despite your efforts to win his cooperation, consider giving him a negative consequence that is proportional to the severity of his misbehavior. Let him know in advance what these consequences will be and, if he misbehaves, follow through with them in a timely, consistent, and matter-of-fact manner. Some examples of consequences: loss of recess, after-school detention, loss of a class privilege, or the student's phoning his parents or writing them a letter to explain his behavior. You might establish a gradual hierarchy of consequences. For example, the first consequence might be a loss of 10 minutes of recess; the second, a loss of half the recess; and the third, a loss of the entire recess. After that, his misbehavior might result in a call home or a visit to the principal's office in addition to the loss of recess. Do not punish the entire class for the actions of the student, although you may want to reward the whole class for his positive behavior. The former strategy will cause classmates to be angry with him, whereas the latter will cause them to be encouraging him.

19. Remove a highly disruptive student from class.

This is a last-resort measure to be used when the student continues to disrupt the class despite your disciplinary efforts and you and the other students need some relief. You can do this by giving him a time-out or sending him to the principal's office. A student given time-out sits apart from other students, either in your class or in another room, for a short period and is not allowed to engage in any activity. Some teachers call this sitting in the "thinking chair." The technique is most commonly used with young children and to help angry or acting-out students settle down. You might have a time-out area in your class (perhaps a chair in the back of the room), but make sure the student is visible and is not placed in an enjoyable location. If the student continues to be disruptive while sitting in the chair, he should be made to stay longer. If you opt to send the student to the office, one way of doing this without having a confrontation with the student is to write a note saying, "This student is disrupting my class and would not stop. Please keep him in the office until I can see you." Put the note in a sealed envelope and ask for a volunteer to take the letter, making sure to select the disruptive student for the task. Tell him to wait for a response before leaving the office. Let the principal know in advance that you may use this approach.

20. Develop a simple behavior contract with the student.

Meet with the student and work out a written contract in which he agrees to behave in a certain manner in exchange for a reward or privilege that you provide. The contract should describe one or more specific behavioral goals ("Alex will not call out an answer more than two times a day"), the way the behavior will be measured ("The teacher will put a check mark on the right side of the chalkboard under the heading 'Calling Out' every time Alex calls out an answer without raising his hand"), the precise reward ("Alex may choose an item from the class treasure box if he has met the behavioral goal for the day. If he meets this goal every day of the week, he will receive a good behavior certificate that he can take home, as well as the privilege of being line leader one day the following week."), and the time when the contract will be reviewed ("The teacher and Alex will review his performance at the end of the school day"). The contract should be written in a brief and simple manner, but the terms should be defined precisely and concretely. Make sure that the student is involved in developing the contract so he has a sense of ownership of the agreement. Once completed, you and the student should sign the contract.

21. Reward the student for appropriate behavior.

Set a timer for 15 minutes, and when it goes off, give the student points or chips toward a reward if he has not displayed disruptive behavior during that time interval. Continue this throughout the day. Gradually increase the length of the interval. Inform the student of the details of this plan and let him have some say in determining the reward. If you have a timer on your watch, you might want to use that to time the intervals.

22. Use Canters' Assertive Discipline Program.

This is a formal program developed by Lee and Marlene Canter and described more fully in their book *Succeeding with Difficult Students*. Begin by establishing and posting four or five rules for class behavior. Explain these rules to your students, and then describe the rewards for complying and the consequences for not complying. When a student violates one of these rules, place his name on the board; for a subsequent violation, place a check next to his name. When he has two checks by his name, give him the prearranged consequence. If he meets the established standard for compliance (for example, three days without his name on the board), provide a reward. You can of course alter any aspect of this approach to suit your own preferences.

23. Discipline by lottery.

This is an effective disciplinary strategy that you can use with your entire class. Give students lottery tickets that you have designed when they behave in a way that you deem desirable; of course, praise them as well. Be generous in giving out tickets, especially with students who are trouble-prone. Have the students write their names on the tickets they receive. At the end of the day (or class if you are a specials teacher), collect all the tickets and place them in a bowl or bag and select one ticket randomly. Give the winner a choice of a prize or privilege. The students will quickly catch on that the more tickets they receive, the greater their chance of winning, so this may serve as an incentive to behave well.

24. Request a classroom aide to help manage a highly disruptive student. Your principal may be open to trying to find an aide to assist you in the classroom. Or if the student is a special education student, the IEP team may decide that an aide is needed to meet his educational needs. If an aide is assigned to your class, give her explicit instructions about her role in dealing with the disruptive student as well as your other students. You want to make sure that she responds to the student in a manner that is consistent with your own approach.

See Also

Aggressive Behavior

Calling Out

Hyperactivity

Making Noises

Talking, Excessive

Forgetfulness

Some students practice forgetfulness with an almost religious zeal. Their memory lapses may extend to all aspects of school, from copying down assignments to bringing in lunch money, from remembering their daily schedule to getting permission slips signed. If you have many students who are memory challenged, you can find yourself spending considerable time tending to their needs at the expense of your classroom lessons. In addition, classmates may become annoyed by students who are constantly asking to borrow materials.

Remembering school responsibilities is an essential part of being a student. Fortunately, for most students it is also a skill that can be learned. Many students can be helped to remember more effectively through memory aids and classroom accommodations. Others require an absence of aid, namely, they need to learn from their mistakes without being bailed out by the teacher. Put another way, they need to experience the natural consequences of their forgetfulness.

What You Can Do

1. Allow students to borrow items on the condition that they return them.

Set up a loaner box containing classroom supplies such as pens, pencils, rulers, erasers, and paper. Let students borrow these items, but have them sign a checkout sheet. Insist that the items be returned at the end of the day, and have students note their returns on the sheet. If a student has a history of not returning a borrowed item, you might have her leave a personal item to ensure its return. (One teacher has her students leave a shoe to be sure she gets the item back.) You might assign a student the responsibility of loaning these items out and keeping a record of the loans. Give her the title of Supply Manager. Using this loaner book will allow you to focus on your lesson without being interrupted by a forgetful student.

Elementary Teacher's Discipline Problem Solver

2. Talk with the student, using a matter-of-fact manner and a problem-solving approach.

Meet with the student during an activity she enjoys, such as recess, rather than during instructional time. Let her know that part of being a responsible, independent student is to keep track of classroom rules, routines, assignments, and materials. Then address the specific area in which she is having problems. Describe how her forgetfulness will cause difficulties for her, but let her know that this is a solvable problem if the two of you work together. Have her explain her typical pattern so you can see where the problem is and offer some solutions.

3. Acknowledge the student when she remembers.

Praise the student when she remembers what she is supposed to do or bring (for example, "Tamika, you did a good job today of remembering to feed the pet").

4. Avoid bailing out the student.

If you continually bail her out when she forgets, the student will have little incentive to remember. So help her learn responsibility by letting her experience the natural consequences of forgetting. For example, if she forgets to bring in her instrument, she can't play in the band concert. If she forgets to bring in her book report on the day it is due, she will be marked down. If she forgets to bring in a signed permission slip allowing her to be on the safety patrol despite repeated requests, she cannot participate. Hopefully, the student will come to see that she is missing out on activities because of what she has forgotten to do rather than what someone else has done to her. Allow some latitude, however. You do not want to keep her from going on a class trip because she forgot to bring a permission slip back by the due date.

5. Assign the student a classroom partner.

Ask the partner to help the student by reminding her, if necessary, of classroom rules and routines and making sure she takes home the materials she needs.

6. Give her some memory aids.

Teach the student the acronym PANTS to remind her what she needs to bring to and from school every day (P = Parent information, A = Assignments, N = Notebook, T = Textbooks, and S = Student, namely herself). You might also have her make a list of end-of-the-day school tasks that she tapes to her desk or binder.

7. Give the student a second set of books for home.
Consider doing this with a student who consistently forgets to bring her books home. This way she has no excuse for not doing her homework. Although you may be bailing out the student by doing this, it may be worth violating this principle if it allows her to do her assignments.

8. Use a signal or single word to jog the student's memory.
If a student tends to forget class routines or rules, remind her with an agreed-upon gesture or phrase. Or ask her a question to trigger her memory: "Jessica, where are you supposed to put your homework?" or "Sarah, what is the classroom rule about using the bathroom?"

9. Have students sign a sheet indicating that they received information.
If a student has previously claimed that she did not receive information, you might avoid this problem in the future by having her sign that she received information such as a permission form, a study sheet, or a project description. This way, if she claims not to have received it, you can show her and her parents evidence that she did. In addition, having her sign may make her more serious about remembering.

10. Send a reminder note to a student's parents.
If a student is prone to forgetting about upcoming events or deadlines such as tests, projects, book reports, field trips, or special school activities, send a note home with the student informing her parents of this information. You might extend the practice to the entire class by sending a notice to all parents with this information. Send this notice the same time each week or month so parents come to expect it. You might attach permission forms to the notice.

See Also

Attention Deficit

Dependent Behavior

Disorganization

Listening Skills, Poor

Friends, Lack of

Few things are more painful to children than to have no friends. Just about all children need to feel a connection with their peers. For those on the social fringe, school brings frequent reminders of their status of being unwanted—being chosen last for a team, having trouble finding a partner for an activity, having few classmates to invite to their birthday party, or not having anyone to play with during recess.

Beyond its effect on a child's self-esteem, isolation from peers can have a marked impact on his school adjustment. He may have difficulty focusing on schoolwork as his attention drifts to social concerns. In addition, having limited relationships with peers denies him a valuable learning experience. It is through these relationships that he learns the skills of developing and maintaining friendships. It is not surprising then that children who are isolated from their peers tend to have social problems later on.

Children can be friendless for very different reasons. A child may lack awareness of the basic skills of peer interaction and thus may not know what to say or do around his classmates. Rather than run the risk of trying to connect with a classmate and failing, he may withdraw from his peers and opt to spend time alone. Staying to himself is often the less painful option.

Some children are isolated from classmates for a far different reason: their behaviors may turn off other students. They may cut in line, talk too much, interrupt conversations, make fun of others, or butt in during games. Not surprisingly, these students have trouble making and keeping friends.

Friendship skills come more easily to some children than others, but fortunately they are skills that can be, and should be, taught. If you have a student who is socially immature, you may need to give him coaching in social skills. In addition, you may need to put on your social director's hat and try to orchestrate successful peer interactions. Through these activities, the student may gain valuable social skills, and his classmates may come to see him in a more appealing light.

What You Can Do

1. Have a class meeting about friendship issues.

Put two headings on the board: "What Friends Do" and "What Friends Don't Do." Ask your students to give examples for each list, prompting them when necessary to make sure certain characteristics are included. Use their contributions as the basis for a discussion about what makes a good friend. Help them understand how children may feel when they are left out of activities. Underlying your comments should be the message that you expect them to show concern for their classmates. You might even establish a rule in your classroom that students are responsible for making sure no classmate plays or eats alone unless he wants to.

2. Try to figure out why the child is isolated.

Find time to observe him in different settings such as lunch, recess, and gym. Or get a report from staff in those settings. Also talk with last year's teacher as well as his parents. You might even talk discreetly with an observant and trustworthy student. The information you gather may help you determine if the student's difficulties in connecting with peers are related to shyness, bossiness, aggressive behavior, appearance, or hygiene issues.

3. Raise the student's social intelligence.

When peer conflicts occur, help the student take a close-up look at what happened and how he can improve. After dealing with the immediate incident, take the student aside and help him understand what happened by asking some questions: "Why do you think the student reacted to you that way? How do you think he felt? What could you have said or done differently?" In this way, you can help the student become more observant of his behavior, more aware of alternative ways of acting, and less impulsive in responding.

4. Coach the student in social skills.

Talk with him privately, and give specific guidance about social situations he is likely to encounter. With young children, you may need to start with very basic skills such as making eye contact, joining in activities, or asking others to play. Suggest some "door openers" (for example, "Would you like to play a game with me?" or "Do you want to be my partner?"). If he is comfortable, role-play with him some common social situations (for example, asking if he can join in a soccer game during recess). Also give him ideas for things to talk about with classmates during recess or after school. And, of course, make sure to lavish praise on him (privately, if you think he will be embarrassed by public recognition) when you see him demonstrating good social skills.

5. Arrange social interactions with classmates.

This may call for you to again put on your social director's hat and orchestrate the child's involvement with his peers. Find activities in which he can interact with other students successfully and can be with peers who are likely to be accepting. For example, you might ask a couple of kind and mature students to ask him to play during recess or join them at their lunch table. Or you might split the class into four or five groups for an academic activity, perhaps having them meet outside of school to complete the project. This may help him foster relationships with classmates. If you have students pair up in class, assign him to a student who is likely to relate well with him.

6. Organize a group of classmates to reach out to the student.

Carefully select a group of four or five students, and meet with them privately to ask them to make a special effort to involve the student in their activities. Talk with the group about what kinds of activities they could do with him, eliciting their ideas and giving some of your own, based on your knowledge of the student. As one example, you might ask each student to phone him once a week. Encourage them to invite him to the movies, to an after-school activity, or to walk to school with them. The more you can build a peer-support system for the student, the more he will feel a sense of belonging to the class. Ask the class members to respond positively and naturally when the student speaks with them.

7. Help the child befriend another student.

You might play the role of matchmaker by identifying a classmate with similar interests and an accepting manner who might become a friend to the isolated student. Look for opportunities to pair them up by placing them in the same group for an academic or social activity or assigning them to be partners during a field trip or classroom activity.

8. Encourage the parents to foster peer relationships.

The parents play an important role here, so encourage them to help their child develop friendships by arranging social contacts with classmates. You may want to suggest to them particular children to call. Give them ideas for how to structure the visit to enhance its success, including inviting only one child at a time and providing an appealing activity for the first visit. Also suggest that they involve their child in community activities that he has an interest in and is likely to do well in.

9. Start a lunch club.

If you have students who are isolated from other children and are playing or eating by themselves, consider grouping these students together during lunch and recess. Tell them the only requirement for being a member of this club is that they be kind to each other. You might have them choose an organizing activity for the group (for example, playing board games or doing art projects). You may find that friendships begin to develop and that lunch, previously a dreaded part of the day, is now a time they look forward to.

10. Help the student feel important through his classroom contributions.

A student who has few friends is likely experiencing a lack of self-esteem. Try to enhance his sense of self-worth by assigning him classroom jobs or finding ways he can help others. Tell him that you are giving him this responsibility because you are confident he can carry it out well. You might, for example, have him be a classroom messenger, hand out papers, read the school's morning announcements, or tutor a student in a lower grade.

11. Help classmates recognize the child's strengths and talents.

Talk with the student or his parents to find out his interests, hobbies, and talents. Find a way to bring these to the attention of the class in a natural way. If he is a good math student, ask him to show the class how to do a challenging math problem. If he is a baseball card collector, have him bring in his collection and talk about it. If he is an ESL student, have him talk to the class in his first language and have a staff member familiar with the language translate. If he excels on the computer, have him become the class troubleshooter. This may allow other students to see him in a new light.

12. Intervene immediately if the student is being ridiculed.

Take the offending students aside, and help them understand how hurtful ridicule and rejection can be. Adopt a serious, stern tone in telling them that this behavior is unacceptable in your class and that you will monitor closely to make sure it has stopped. If it does not stop, contact their parents or take disciplinary action. At the same time, consider teaching the victim of the teasing some steps he can take and things he can say if he is ridiculed.

13. Pay special attention to playground issues.

This setting gives you a good opportunity to both observe a student's friendship problems and do something about them. You may see students going off on their own to play a game, leaving him isolated and alone. If he is not able or willing to join in, suggest other ways he can participate by, for example, keeping score, being timekeeper, or turning the jump rope. To avoid the distress associated with always being chosen last by peers for a team or activity, you might make the assignments yourself or have students count off and have even members on one team and odd on another. If you are not responsible for supervising the playground, speak with the playground monitor about the student's isolation and suggest ways for integrating him in activities.

See Also

Hygiene, Poor

Playground Problems

Self-Esteem, Low

Shyness

Special-Needs Students

Teasing

Gum Chewing

Students may engage in behaviors that are hardly serious problems but can nonetheless take time away from the instructional process. Gum chewing is one such behavior. Teachers may find that they are spending too much time telling students to throw away their gum or debating students who claim they are not chewing gum. Although students need to comply with the school or classroom policy for gum chewing, you want to make sure that your efforts to elicit compliance interfere minimally with your classroom lessons.

Educators have differing opinions about whether students should be allowed to chew gum in school. Some maintain that it is a waste of valuable time for teachers to monitor this behavior and discipline students for violations of school policy. Others believe that gum chewing should be prohibited because it can impede the learning process. They contend that gum chewing can be noisy and distracting to other students, can interfere with students' ability to express themselves, and can cause an unsightly mess if students stick their stale gum on classroom furniture.

What You Can Do

1. Find out what your school policy is.
School districts may take different positions on the issue of gum chewing. Some prohibit it altogether; others leave it to the discretion of individual teachers. Talk with your principal, or check your code of conduct to find out your school's policy. If the school forbids gum chewing, let your students know this at the beginning of the year when explaining your class rules.

2. If left to your discretion, make a decision and explain it to the class.
In formulating a gum-chewing policy, you may want to get input from your students. If you are considering allowing students to chew gum, ask them what restrictions they think are reasonable. Once you make a decision, make your policy clear to your class and spell out your reasons. Your students will be

more likely to follow the rule if they understand your rationale. If you have decided not to allow gum chewing, you might say, for example, that it can be noisy and bothersome to other students. If students bring up that other teachers allow it, simply state that this is your rule and that this is what you think is best for the class. You might reinforce the rule by posting it in a prominent place (for example, a picture of a piece of gum with a bold line drawn through it).

3. If you allow gum chewing, set some conditions.

You might decide to allow gum chewing as long as it does not interfere in any way with your ability to teach or students' ability to concentrate. Tell your students that this means that they may chew gum as long as they do it silently and dispose of it appropriately. If you hear gum chewing, inform them you will ask the person chewing gum to spit it out. Also tell them that they must pick up any gum wrappers and are not to stick gum on any furniture. If you find that students are not following your "no noise" and "no mess" policies, you can decide to prohibit gum chewing altogether. But if students are complying with your rules, the frustration of having to stop the class and deal with gum chewers will be minimized.

4. Deal with a gum-chewing student quickly.

If you or the school prohibits gum chewing, find a way to respond to gum chewers in a way that is minimally disruptive to your lesson. Consider the following ideas:

- Tell the student to throw the gum away while adding a brief explanation ("Sarah, get rid of the gum by wrapping it up and throwing it out. Chewing gum can be distracting to other students.")

- Look at the student and simply say, "Gum, please."

- Say the student's name, point to your mouth or the posted rule, and then point to the wastebasket.

- Bring the wastebasket to the student and point to it.

Whatever approach you use, keep an eye on the student to make sure she follows your instruction.

5. If the problem continues, give the student a consequence.
Don't make a big deal if the student is caught chewing gum once or twice, but if it happens more often, consider having the student stay in for recess or after-school detention. There is probably no need to contact parents unless this becomes a constant problem.

6. Take firm action in response to inappropriate gum deposits.
If a student has stuck gum under her desk, make her remove it. If she does it a second time, you might have her stay after school and remove gum from under all the desks with a paint scraper or clean the desks.

7. Don't challenge a student if she denies chewing gum.
When confronted about chewing gum, a student may claim that she is not chewing gum or is just chewing paper. Don't make an issue of this unless you are absolutely certain. There is no point in having this escalate into a power struggle or a confrontation if you are unsure. If you spot a student chewing gum, you might avoid dealing with her directly by simply saying to the class, "I would like anyone chewing gum to please get rid of it now."

8. Allow gum chewing on special occasions.
If gum chewing is not allowed in your class, you might consider allowing it on special occasions, for example, during parties or while watching movies. If your students find chewing gum helps them cope with stressful situations, you might allow gum chewing during tests as long as students are quiet and do not distract their classmates.

9. Ignore students who pretend to be chewing gum, to a point.
If this reaches the point that the student's playfulness is becoming time-consuming to deal with, you might have her pay you back in time lost by staying after school or staying in during recess for a brief period.

See Also

Disruptive/Uncooperative Behavior

Making Noises

Hallway/Lining-up Problems

Behavior problems often take place while students are lining up to leave the classroom or walking the halls. In their eagerness to be first in line or get to the next activity, they may run to the door while knocking into other students, push their way to the front, or cut in line. They may argue over who is the line leader, who stands next to whom, and who gets to hold the door. Problems may continue as they leave the room. While walking the halls, they may chatter incessantly, disrupting nearby classes.

Although a variety of strategies are available to teachers to manage these problems, it is not always easy to know when problems are occurring. Students may sometimes walk the hallways unsupervised. And even when you are there, it is tough to observe every problem. So you need to keep a watchful eye when your students are in the hallway and other unstructured areas. This is not the time to relax your behavioral standards or lessen your effort to maintain discipline.

What You Can Do

1. Explain your rules and then have them practice.
Tell your students that when lining up in class they are to walk quietly to the front of the class and face the door with their hands to their side. Emphasize that they are not to butt in line, push, or shove. Upon leaving the room, they are to walk in a straight line and keep their distance from the student in front of them. You might tell them that if they can touch the student just ahead when walking the halls, they are too close. Inform them of your rule regarding talking while in the hallway; some teachers allow quiet conversation, whereas others insist on silence. You will want to practice these behaviors if you have young elementary students. You will no doubt need to remind your students of these rules periodically.

2. Give students advance notice when they are about to leave the room.

Alert them that they should begin to put their books and other materials away because they will be leaving class in a few minutes. Make sure they have enough time to do this without feeling rushed. This is especially important for students who are disorganized and have difficulty with transitions. Students who feel rushed may knock into other students as they hurry back to their seat or run to the door.

3. Have students line up in an orderly manner.

If you don't have a system for lining up, you can face chaos as your students butt in line to stand next to their friend or push aside classmates so they can be line leader. The following are some ways you can minimize the chaos:

- Have students line up by rows or tables.
- Have girls line up first and then boys, or vice versa.
- Have students who are sitting quietly line up first.
- Have students line up according to personal characteristics. For example, you might have students line up first whose first name has a specific letter or whose birthday is in a particular month.
- Assign students a day of the week, from Monday to Friday. On Tuesdays, students assigned that day would line up first.

Once your students have lined up, take a quick look and separate those who are likely to fool around with each other. Also, if they walk in double file, place students who are problem-prone with well-behaved partners.

4. Play a game with students while they are lined up.

If they are already lined up but can't leave because your class has not yet been called, try playing a game with them. With older students, you might have each student name a state, beginning with the first student in line. With younger students, you might have them count by 2's.

5. Don't leave the room until students are lined up properly. If students leave the room in an orderly manner, they are more likely to walk the halls the same way, so tell them they cannot go until they are quiet. Once the class is settled, tell the line leader she can leave, instructing her where to stop. Remain in the room until the last student has left, and then, from the end of the line, monitor the class as it walks the hall. If a student strays from the line or is too loud, making eye contact with her or saying her name may be sufficient to keep her in line. If it is not, remove her from the line and have her walk next to you. If you need to talk to your students while in the hall, use a soft voice so you model quiet behavior; of course, do not disrupt other classes.

6. Tell the line leader to stop if the class is noisy. Let the class know she will be doing this. Once the talking stops, she can start walking again. Your students may be frustrated by the delay, so this will serve as an incentive for them to quiet down.

7. Have students start over if they misbehave. If they are very noisy while lining up or are pushing and shoving, have them return to their seats to try again. Similarly, if students are noisy or disruptive in the hallway, have them return to the classroom and start anew. You can do this with the entire class or with individual students. Although this is a time-consuming consequence, your students will eventually get the idea because of their frustration with the delay in getting somewhere they likely want to go, such as lunch or recess.

8. Set up hallway checkpoints. Identify two or three checkpoints in the hall (for example, hallway intersections), and tell the line leader to stop at those points. This gives you a chance to make sure the students are under control. If the class has to go up or down stairs, make that one of the checkpoints. This way, you can observe as students negotiate the stairs. You might also put down markers leading to the lunchroom, showing students where to walk.

9. Praise or reward the well-behaved student. A simple comment such as, "I like the way Yvonne is standing in line" or "I see that Victor is walking in a straight line and is quiet" sends a message to other students about how to behave and can spur them to act properly. You might also consider rewarding individual students or the class as a whole for lining up or walking the halls properly, especially if they have had trouble doing this. The reward might take the form of increased recess time, a party at the end of the month, or a special snack at the end of the week.

10. Tell students they are role models for younger children.

If you have older elementary students, impress upon them that they have an important job, namely, to show younger students in the school how to behave while walking the halls. You may be surprised how seriously they take this responsibility. Conversely, you might tell your younger students that they should try to impress the older students with how well behaved they can be in the hallway.

11. Give the trouble-prone student a job.

The job might be holding the door open or closing the door and turning off the lights. This job will not only give her a sense of importance but may keep her from getting in trouble while in line. Allow her to do this job as long as she behaves properly while lining up and walking the halls. She may want this job enough that it serves as an incentive to act properly.

12. Require individual students to carry a pass while walking the hall.

Have them use a permanent pass, which will save you the time and trouble of writing passes each time a student leaves class. You might keep the passes on your desk or hang them on the door or wall. Limit the number of passes to two or three so you can control the number of students who are out of the class at the same time and lessen the likelihood that they will dawdle. Tell students that they are not to hang out in the halls but should return promptly.

13. Use the hallway as a disciplinary measure on a selective basis.

If you place a student in the hallway to lessen the disruption in your class, be aware that she may find being out there more enjoyable than being in class, especially if other children are wandering by. In addition, be careful whom you place in the hallway; some students will use this opportunity to wander the school. And most important, don't forget she is there.

14. Stand by your door while students are changing classes.
This is often a time when problems occur, so keep a watchful eye as students navigate the hallway.

15. Separate the lockers of students who have conflicts.
If your school has lockers in the hallway, make sure that students who do not get along have lockers that are not near each other.

See Also

Assembly Problems

Bathroom Problems

Disruptive/Uncooperative Behavior

Lunchroom Problems

Talking, Excessive

Hitting or Threatening a Teacher

A student hitting a teacher is a serious incident that merits a serious response. Although this problem occurs very infrequently, when it does occur it can dramatically alter the climate of the class and leave its imprint on the teacher and the students. Being struck or threatened by a student can undermine the teacher's authority, especially if she loses control in reacting to him, and can frighten the other students. You have an opportunity through your handling of the situation to demonstrate your authority and control and to restore a sense of security and calm among your students.

In deciding how to respond, you need to consider the nature of the incident, the student's age, and his intent. There is a marked difference between a six-year-old child who, in the course of having a tantrum, flails his arms and accidentally hits the teacher and an eleven-year-old child who strikes a teacher with the intent of hurting her. The latter situation clearly calls for a more serious response.

The same reasoning applies to a student threatening a teacher. All threats deserve a response, but some are more serious than others. There is a substantial difference between a first grader who says in a fit of anger, "You make me so angry I feel like hitting you" and a fifth grader who says, "I know where I can get a gun, and I just may get it and do something bad to you." Clearly, the latter comment merits a more vigorous response than the former.

In responding to a child who has struck a teacher, the first and foremost goal is to ensure that he does not act this way again. This calls for impressing upon the student the seriousness of his behavior and providing consequences that reinforce this message. It is also important to attend to his emotional needs. Behind his display of bravado is likely a child who is hurting.

What You Can Do

1. Respond to a student's threats, even if he is unlikely to carry them out.

Students who are angry may make threatening comments to their teacher as a way of venting frustration and exercising power. Even if you are certain he will not follow through, talk with him about the inappropriateness of his comments. Help him understand that what he said could be taken as a threat (with younger students, explain what you mean by "threat") and might cause him serious problems. If this is the first time he has made these kinds of comments in your class, you might let him know that you will not tell his parents and the principal this time but you will if it happens again. Tell him that it is okay to be angry with somebody and to even express this anger verbally, but he has to do it in a way that does not threaten or hurt another person. Ask him what he might have said differently in this particular case. You might want to give him some suggestions.

2. Inform the principal immediately if a student makes what you perceive to be a serious threat.

In judging the seriousness of a threat, consider the student's age, his history of aggressive behavior, and his ability to follow through with the threat. The school district may have a policy for how to handle threats toward teachers. At a minimum, this will involve contacting the parents. Depending on the nature of the threat, the principal may also opt to inform the police, which will put the student on notice that threatening a teacher is a serious issue. In talking with the parents, the principal should ask about their child's history of violent or aggressive acts outside of school and his access to weapons. If there is a gun in the house, the principal may want to inquire whether the child is aware of the gun, whether it is locked away and inaccessible to him, whether the bullets are located in a separate place from the gun, and whether the gun has a trigger lock. Consider asking the principal what security measures can be taken at school to help you feel more at ease.

3. Distract a volatile student.

Things can quickly spiral out of control if the student hits you, so put your energy into preventing this from happening. If you fear he may strike you, keep your distance from him but try to distract him from what is making him so mad. You might acknowledge his anger and then try to shift the topic: "Danny, I know you are feeling angry with me. I want to hear why you're so upset, but first there is something I want to say to you." At that point, you might ask him about his favorite hobby or sports

Elementary Teacher's Discipline Problem Solver

team or tell him a joke or funny story; the idea is to say anything that will soften him up and distract him from what was making him angry. After he has cooled down, you can have a calmer discussion with him about what was upsetting him.

4. Convey to the student the seriousness of his behavior. Respond firmly if a student hits you, but maintain your composure. Tell him in a stern, no-nonsense voice that violence toward anyone in your classroom is unacceptable and that he is never to do that again. Do not scream at him, do not call him names, do not belittle him. This will only antagonize him further and make him more determined to find ways to upset you. Bear in mind that his goal may be to get you to lose your cool. Do not give him this satisfaction. At the same time, let him know that you will be informing his parents and the principal of what he did. You may want to reinforce your verbal message with a consequence such as time-out.

5. Use physical restraint sparingly. If a student is out of control and you fear he may hit anyone who comes close to him, tell your students to move away from him; you should do the same. Avoid physical contact, even of the supportive variety. A reassuring tap on his shoulder may be misinterpreted and trigger a physical response. You only want to step in and restrain him physically if he is at risk of hurting another student or himself or if he is damaging property. Make sure you use the least force necessary to accomplish this goal.

6. Give the student a time-out. If a young elementary student hits you while having a tantrum, you might convey to him the seriousness of his behavior by isolating him from the class. Act quickly and firmly while saying to him, "You know the rule: you cannot hit anybody in this class, including me. You need to go to time-out." Send him to the designated area for a set period, and tell him to sit quietly and not get up until you give him permission. During this period, do not have any contact with him, and tell your students to do the same. If he misbehaves while in time-out, tell him that the timer will be reset to zero and he will need to stay there longer. After he has completed the

time-out, welcome him back to the class, once again reminding him of the rule about hitting, and then look for opportunities to praise him for appropriate behavior.

7. Inform the principal if a student hits you.
After telling the student in a stern manner that he cannot hit you, let the principal know of the incident by calling her on the intercom or taking the student to the office. When you get there, have the student tell the principal what he did.

8. Confer with the parents.
If a student has been aggressive toward you, inform his parents. Insist on a face-to-face meeting rather than a phone call. You may want to have the principal present at this meeting. After describing his behavior, elicit the parents' perspective, including whether he is aggressive at home and what might be triggering his outbursts. Obtain their suggestion for preventing this behavior and for responding if he behaves similarly again. After gaining their agreement to a plan for managing his behavior, bring the student in so he can hear that you and his parents are of one mind about his behavior and how it will be dealt with in school. With an older elementary student who has struck you, talk with the principal about having a police officer present to reinforce the seriousness of the incident, and help the student understand the real-world consequences of his aggressive behavior.

9. Write down in his presence a description of the incident.
Tell the student you are doing this so that you have an accurate record of his behavior when you speak with the principal and his parents. If the student is in an upper-elementary grade, you might add that you also need a record of what happened in case you need to discuss the incident with the police.

10. Talk with the student after the incident.
Using a calm voice, tell him that it is very upsetting to you that someone you care about would hit you. You might let him know that you do not think he meant to hurt you. Ask him if he behaved that way because he was upset about something. If he is not forthcoming, suggest some possible reasons for his anger. Ask him if there is something he wants you to do differently in the classroom. Then talk about

what *he* needs to do differently; most important is using nonthreatening words, rather than his hands, to express his anger. Also talk with him about going to a cooling-off area when he is angry. Impress upon him the seriousness of hitting a teacher, and let him know that the principal, his parents, and perhaps even the police officer—the three P's—will be contacted if it happens again. Tell him that if he feels on the verge of hitting a teacher in the future, he should remember the three P's.

11. Ask other teachers to be on call.

This is a useful strategy if the principal is unavailable or her office is far away from your classroom. If you have a student with a history of aggressive behavior, ask a teacher whose classroom is close to yours to be available to help you if the student loses control or becomes physically unmanageable. If this happens, ask a responsible student to go tell the nearby teacher you need help. Although you may never need to call on this teacher, having a backup will help allay your anxieties and give you some peace of mind.

12. If concerned for your safety, request the student's removal from your class.

You may have concerns for your physical well-being if one of your current students has previously hit or threatened you. If so, talk with your principal and ask that the student be transferred out of your class on a permanent basis. Make the point that your ability to teach will be compromised if you feel uncomfortable and unsafe in his presence. The principal may opt to move him to another class or seek to have him placed in a special education program where he can obtain greater supervision.

13. Move on after the incident.

If a student has hit you, you will likely remember this incident for a long time, and your anger may take a while to subside. Although you will want to be vigilant with this student to avoid a similar problem in the future, you will also want to try to move beyond the incident and not hold a grudge. It is important that you try to find ways to connect with him and even praise him when he handles a situation well that previously he might have responded to in an aggressive manner.

See Also

Aggressive Behavior

Angry Outbursts

Bullying

Weapon, Possession of

Homework Problems

Homework is a frequent source of tension between teachers and students. For most teachers, homework is an integral part of their instructional program. It is not only a way to reinforce academic skills but an opportunity to teach children to be independent learners. For some students, however, homework is something else—an unpleasant burden to be avoided, forgotten, or raced through.

The task for the teacher is to encourage students to take homework seriously and turn it in on time without spending much time dealing with homework stragglers. When your students are not completing homework, they are missing out on an important teaching tool. Their failure to do homework also denies you a chance to find out if they understand your lessons and need further help. Although homework is of course the responsibility of your students, and you want to make sure to reinforce this idea in various ways, parents are also a key resource in your effort to ensure homework compliance.

What You Can Do

1. Spell out your homework policy.
Establish a predictable homework pattern (for example, math assignments on Mondays and Wednesdays and reading assignments on Tuesdays and Thursdays). During the first week, explain the pattern to your students and tell them that you expect homework to be completed on time and done neatly. Let them know how homework is graded and the consequences for not completing an assignment or turning it in late. Also tell them that they are required to write down the assignments. Allow them to decide how—but not whether—they will do this. They might use an assignment pad, a daily planner, or a page of their notebook for this purpose. Make time to check your students' assignment-recording methods.

2. Communicate your homework policy to parents.
Send a letter home during the first week explaining the purpose of homework, how often and when it

will be assigned, how much time you expect students to spend per night on homework, and what resources are available if their child is having difficulty with an assignment. In your letter, you might also suggest that parents do the following:

- Establish a routine with your child as to where and when homework will be done, and try to stick to it.

- Encourage your child to do homework in a quiet, uncluttered, well-lit setting that is free of distractions and family traffic.

- Make sure your child is writing down assignments regularly in her notebook or on a pad.

- Have your child do the harder assignments first when she is most alert.

- Give your child a breather while doing homework by building in study breaks.

- Consider establishing a rule that homework be finished before she is allowed to watch TV during the evening.

- Note long-term assignment due dates on a calendar—or better yet, have your child do it.

3. Hold your students accountable for completing homework.

Convey to your students the importance of not only completing homework but turning it in on time by giving them a consequence when they fail to do that. Here are some possible responses:

- Take points off or lower the grade for an assignment turned in late.

- Give a detention for a set number of missed assignments.

- Have the student stay in during recess to complete an assignment.

- Call the parent—or better yet, have the student call the parent in your presence—to say she has missed a number of assignments.

4. Make the assignment crystal-clear.

Write the homework assignment on the board in the same place and same format every day, and leave it there for the remainder of the day. Be clear about the nature of the assignment, the due date, and the expected length, and give your students time to write all that down. Ask them if they have any questions about the homework.

5. Make your homework assignments available by telephone or the Internet.

Your school may already have a policy of recording assignments on a telephone message system or the Internet. If not, talk with your principal about looking into such a program or check out the Web site, TeacherWeb.com, which allows you to post homework assignments, announcements, and other educational material on your own classroom's bulletin board. This technology allows students who are absent to keep up with homework and prevents students from claiming they did not know what the homework was. You might also send e-mail messages listing daily assignments to parents with on-line addresses so they can monitor their child's homework.

6. Have students begin homework at the end of class.

Starting the work in class allows students to ask questions about the assignment and enables you to identify problems they are having in understanding the directions or completing the work. Pay special attention to the students who typically struggle with homework by checking to see that they understand what to do and that the difficulty level is appropriate.

7. Check homework on a regular basis.

Students will be more likely to do assignments if they know you will check it. You might collect the assignments from students individually, which gives you a chance to praise those who turned their homework in on time and talk with those who did not. If a student did not hand in the assignment, listen to her excuse but make it clear that she has to make it up. Get a commitment from her when she will turn it in, noting this date in your grade book in the child's presence so she knows you expect her to comply.

8. Reward students who have completed all assignments with an end-of-the-week activity.

Schedule an appealing activity for Friday afternoon for students who have completed all homework and seatwork. Students who have work that is not completed must spend that period catching up on the assignments in a separate area of the classroom or, if feasible, in another room with adult supervision.

9. Provide classwide incentives for homework completion.
You can of course devise behavior-modification programs to spur a student to complete homework, but be careful that she does not learn to do homework only when there is a reward forthcoming. As an alternative, provide a reward for homework completion to the entire class. One way of doing this is to write on the board a letter of a word or phrase (for example, "WAY TO GO") for each day the entire class turns in homework (except students who are absent). You might have a different word or phrase each time and not tell your students what it is; this will pique their curiosity. When the word or phrase is spelled, give a reward or privilege to the entire class.

10. Establish an assignment folder for absent students.
Keep a folder on your desk with assignments dating back a week or so that students can check to get missed assignments. Have a separate sheet for each day's assignments, and instruct students who were absent to sign the sheet to indicate they obtained the assignments for that day. This promotes independence on the part of your students and lessens the burden on you to give missed assignments to absent students.

11. Do not give homework as punishment.
Using homework as punishment will only intensify any negative feelings students already have about it.

12. Talk with the student who struggles with homework.
Ask the student questions to try to get to the root of the problem. Here are some examples:

- Are you copying down the assignments?
- Are you remembering to bring home the proper materials?
- Do you understand the directions?
- Is the homework too hard?

- Do you have too little time to do the work because of your schedule of outside activities?

- Is the time you are spending talking on the phone, watching TV, or playing video games interfering with your completion of homework?

- Are you completing homework but forgetting to bring it in?

Using a problem-solving approach, work with the student (and parents if necessary) to develop a specific plan to correct the problem, and follow up periodically to see how she is doing.

13. Create an assignment checklist for the student.

Make a list on a 3" × 5" card of homework-related tasks that she needs to do at the end of the day, including writing assignments in her assignment pad, figuring out which books and papers to bring home, and putting these materials in her backpack. Tape this list to her backpack or her desk. Check with her at the end of the day to make sure she has done these tasks, or ask another staff member such as an aide or guidance counselor to do this with her.

14. Check the student's assignment pad, and ask parents to do the same.

Require a student who struggles with homework to bring her assignment pad to you at the end of the day so you can review its accuracy and initial it. Ask her parents to review her assignment pad daily and initial it when they have made sure the assignments have been completed and placed in her backpack. You and the parents might also make notes to each other on the assignment pad.

15. Adapt the homework to the student's needs.

If the assignment appears overwhelming for her, consider shortening it. For example, you might have her do only the odd-numbered problems or have her write a two-paragraph rather than a four-paragraph composition. As her confidence and skills improve, you can increase the length of the assignment. If the student's skills are well below the level of her classmates, consider giving her a different assignment altogether. If the act of writing is especially hard for the student, allow her to do the assignment on a computer. If motivation is a factor in the student's homework resistance, design the assignment to reflect her interests and strengths.

16. Have the student complete a missing homework form.
Require students who fail to bring in homework to complete a form for every missed assignment and give it to you. The form might have the following questions on it:

- Did you understand the assignment?
- Why did you not turn in the assignment?
- What is your plan to make up the assignment?
- What can you do to make sure you do not miss any more assignments?

The answers to these questions may guide you in whether you need to follow up with the student. In addition, the mere act of filling out the form may be sufficient to deter students from missing assignments.

17. Assign the student a homework partner.
This classmate can help make sure the student has recorded the assignments correctly and packed the right materials at the end of the day. If her homework buddy is willing, encourage the student to call her buddy at home if she needs to check on the homework assignment.

18. Make the student a homework aide.
Assign to the student who is having trouble getting her homework done the job of collecting homework and making a list of students who did not turn it in. She may be more motivated to complete the assignment because she will not want to have to put her name on this list.

19. Help the student develop a timetable for long-term assignments.
The student who has trouble keeping up with daily assignments will probably have even more trouble with long-term assignments. She may leave things to the last minute, panic when she realizes how much she has to do in so little time,

and give up out of a feeling of hopelessness. Help her feel more in control by working with her to set up a timetable for the various tasks involved in the project; then check with her to make sure she has completed these tasks by the assigned dates. For example, if she is assigned a book report, help her set dates by which she will find a book, finish reading the book, write the draft, and write the final report.

See Also

Cheating

Forgetfulness

Listening Skills, Poor

Motivation, Lack of

Seatwork Problems

Hygiene, Poor

One of the more sensitive issues that you may face as a teacher is dealing with a student with poor hygiene. This is not an issue that you can easily ignore, especially if it is giving rise to ridicule and rejection from peers. If the child does not learn good hygiene by the time he leaves elementary school, he is likely in for a rough time in middle school.

Poor hygiene can take various forms, such as having disheveled hair, wearing dirty clothes, and having bad breath. Perhaps no hygiene problem causes more difficulties for students than body odor. Students with BO are likely to be shunned by their peers, giving rise to feelings of unhappiness and low self-esteem. Because of this potentially significant impact, you cannot sidestep hygiene issues with your students. Rather, you must deal with these issues with honesty and directness but with sensitivity and concern for students' emotional well-being.

What You Can Do

1. Make hygiene a regular part of your health curriculum.
Conduct a hygiene lesson with your class at the beginning of the school year, and reinforce these issues during the course of the year. Teaching materials on hygiene are available, including curricula, videos, and books. You might check with the kindergarten teacher or school nurse, who is used to dealing with these issues and may have some tips on teaching hygiene to your students. The following are some potential behaviors you want to promote with your students: taking a shower or bath, washing their hair, brushing their teeth, wearing clean clothes, maintaining sufficient personal space when talking with another person, washing their hands after using the bathroom, covering their mouth when they cough, and using a tissue to wipe their nose. If you are not comfortable discussing these issues with your class, you might ask the school nurse to conduct this lesson.

2. Invite a local dentist to talk to your class.
The dentist can instruct your students in proper dental hygiene, including how and when to brush their teeth, and may even bring along free toothbrushes to hand out to your class.

3. Have a private talk with the student with poor hygiene.
Help the student understand that poor hygiene can cause him to get sick and can lead other children to avoid him. Talk with him about the basics of good hygiene, and then zero in on his particular areas of need. This calls for you to be honest but also demands that you be sensitive and nonjudgmental. Approach this talk the way you might if you were teaching the student an academic skill: in a matter-of-fact way, find out what behaviors he does not exhibit, and then impart the information and motivation he needs to do them. You may need to give him very specific instructions in hygiene behaviors that we take for granted in most children.

4. Ask the nurse to speak with the student.
If you are uncomfortable talking with the student about these issues, ask the nurse to meet with him. She has no doubt discussed these concerns with many children and likely understands the sensitivity that is called for. If the student has a trusting relationship with another adult in the school, such as the guidance counselor, you might ask her to talk with the student instead. Whoever talks with the student, let her know the student's specific hygiene concerns.

5. Monitor the student's hygiene.
Provide the student with a checklist of hygiene activities that he needs to do on a daily basis, and have him put it in his notebook or backpack. The list might include the following: taking a shower or bath, washing his hair, brushing his teeth, combing his hair, and putting on clean clothes. Tell him that these tasks are part of his homework assignment. For the first couple of weeks, meet with him in private for a few minutes every morning to review how well he did his homework. Praise him for any evidence of good hygiene, and give instruction where needed. If you don't have the time to meet with him every morning, perhaps another school staff member such as the nurse, an aide, or a guidance counselor can do this.

6. Praise the student privately.

Find opportunities to praise him when he is demonstrating good hygiene, but do this in private. Acknowledging this behavior in the presence of other students may be embarrassing for him.

7. Contact the student's parents.

If the hygiene problems persist, consider calling the student's parents. Let him know you will be doing this, but reassure him that this is an effort to help him, not get him in trouble. Although poor hygiene is a sensitive issue to discuss with parents, who may feel defensive no matter how tactful you are in your presentation, it is important to be direct and honest with them. Tell them the specific hygiene problem their child is having, and let them know its effects on his peer relationships. Ask them how they might help with this problem. They may tell you that he has resisted their efforts to get him to practice good hygiene. This may provide an opening for you to join forces with the parents to help lessen this resistance.

8. Have some hygiene items handy

In talking with a student with hygiene problems, you may find that he does not have some hygiene items at home. For occasions like these, keep some of these items in your desk, such as brushes, combs, packs of tissue, soap, shampoo, deodorant, toothbrushes, and toothpaste. You may be able to obtain sample-sized hygiene products inexpensively at a pharmacy or supermarket. Let the student know that he can take what he needs from your drawer as long as he assures you that he will make use of them. Check to make sure he knows how to use them. If not, spend a few minutes with him privately and show him.

9. Work out a private signal to cue a student who is picking his nose.

Few behaviors turn peers off more quickly than a student who picks his nose. If you have a child who is a frequent nose picker, meet with him privately and tell him that he needs to use a tissue instead. Give him a pack of tissues to keep in his desk. Let him know that other children will find this behavior unpleasant and may avoid him as a result. Work out with him a subtle, nonverbal signal to alert him when he is picking his nose and to encourage him to use a tissue. You might need to use his name before giving him a signal to get his attention. If your signal fails to get him to stop, ask him to come up to your desk to see you. Tell him what he was doing, and remind him that he needs to use a tissue. Ask him if wants to go to the bathroom.

10. Address hygiene issues in the student's IEP.

If the student is a special education student, suggest that hygiene issues be included in the IEP's goals and objectives. In doing this, you will help to build consensus with parents and other school staff that hygiene is an important educational concern for this student.

See Also

Friends, Lack of

Teasing

Toileting Problems

Hyperactivity

A hyperactive student is not hard to recognize. He is the student who is constantly on the move, bouncing from one activity to another and rarely completing any task. Even if he is sitting in his seat, he is anything but still as he fidgets, wiggles, twists, and turns. He is a "mover and shaker" in the literal sense of the words. A hyperactive student can usually be found anywhere and everywhere, except in his seat.

It would be nice if teachers could simply turn off a switch with hyperactive students to calm their behavior, but there are no easy answers with these children. Indeed, teaching a hyperactive student can be one of the most challenging management problems that teachers face. It can also be one of the most exasperating, especially if he is disrupting your ability to teach and your other students' ability to learn.

As a result of the hyperactive student's often disruptive behavior, he frequently finds himself in trouble in class. And he is not always sure why. He may feel misunderstood by his teacher and believe that he is being treated unfairly. He may also feel rejected by his peers and become socially isolated in the classroom. These experiences may take their toll on his self-esteem and self-confidence as he comes to view himself in a negative manner.

The challenge in working with hyperactive children is to balance their needs with the needs of your other students. You want to create an optimal learning environment for the hyperactive student, mindful of the issues of peer rejection and low self-esteem. At the same time, you want to minimize the disruption to your other students. This requires considerable structure, support, and consistency. It also demands your patience and restraint in the face of often difficult and frustrating behavior.

What You Can Do

1. Incorporate exercise into your students' daily schedule.
This is a good practice to follow with all your students, not just with those who are

hyperactive. Most children will get restless if seated for long periods. You can give your students a chance to vent this excess energy by having them engage in occasional exercise after a long lesson. This can be as simple as having the class stand and stretch or playing a game of Simon Says. You might also incorporate physical activity into academic tasks by, for example, having students go up to the board to do math problems.

2. Identify the source of the student's high activity level.
Although his hyperactivity may stem from an attention deficit disorder that has a physiological basis, it may also result from other causes. It may be, for example, that the work is too hard for the student, causing him to be frustrated, or too easy, causing him to be bored. Also check whether the student is confused about the directions or lacks the materials needed to complete the task. In addition, consider whether his high activity level reflects agitation or distress.

3. Talk with the student privately.
Help him take a close-up look at his behavior and its impact on others. Describe his behavior to him, and then let him know that his moving around is interfering with your ability to teach and other students' ability to learn. You might tell him that other children may be bothered by his behavior and avoid him as a result. It is important that the hyperactive child hear this information because he may be genuinely unaware of the nature of his behavior and its effect on others. But don't stop there. Work with the student, using a supportive, nonpunitive tone, to develop a plan to improve his behavior. Make suggestions to him and ask for his own ideas about what can be done differently in class. He is more likely to buy into a plan if he has had some input in designing it.

4. Praise or reward the student for calm behavior.
Acknowledge the student when you observe him sitting in his seat in a quiet, nondisruptive manner. This might be a simple statement of praise ("Billy, I really like the way you sat quietly and attentively during the assembly") or a reward of some kind. You might also praise or reward other students for similar behavior as a way of conveying to your more active students that they will be recognized for calm

behavior. Consider setting up a behavior-modification program for a hyperactive student. One simple method is to set a timer to go off at varying intervals. If the student is seated when the timer goes off, give him a token or sticker while describing the behavior for which he is being rewarded. Allow him to exchange a set number of tokens or stickers for classroom privileges or material items.

5. Relax your classroom standards.

You may need to adjust your classroom practices when teaching a hyperactive student. In particular, you may have to rethink your assumption that all students must be seated at their desks, facing forward, feet on the floor, and back straight. For example, you might allow a hyperactive student to stand up near his desk, walk around with a clipboard, or read while standing as long as he does not disrupt other students. Some teachers have even let their more active students work in the hall (under their watchful eye) so they can get up and walk around when they are feeling antsy. You might even permit a student to work on the floor if he is more productive and attentive there than when sitting at his desk.

6. Give the student a break.

A hyperactive student tends to get restless sooner than other students. If so, give him a breather. For example, you might have him work for 20 minutes on a math assignment, then take a break for 5 minutes, and then begin work on a reading task. Have the student engage in some movement during the break by, for example, going to the bathroom or getting a drink of water.

7. Provide opportunities for the student to release excess energy.

Allow the student to redirect his seemingly boundless energy by engaging in constructive activities rather than moving around aimlessly. In this way, he learns to be responsible and contribute to the class while releasing energy that might otherwise disturb other students. Feeling a sense of belonging is especially important to the hyperactive student. The following are some examples of activities that you might ask him to do:

- Decorate a bulletin board.

- Collect or distribute papers.

- Feed the animals in your classroom.

- Take lunch money or attendance information to the office.

- Take a message to another teacher.

- Erase the chalkboard.

- Make signs for the classroom.

- Water the plants.

- Collect books from students.

You might treat these tasks as privileges and have the student earn the right to do them by, for example, staying in his seat for a set period.

8. Allow the student to manipulate objects at his desk.

Some hyperactive students are able to play with small items and still stay on task and remain in their seat. Indeed, doing so may actually help them pay attention. Consider letting an active student play with such items as a paper clip or a pipe cleaner as long as he can remain on task. Or you might let him squeeze a stress ball to release tension while sitting in his seat. Another stress reliever is to have him place an elastic exercise band under his desk and press his legs against it while sitting at his desk.

9. Set up a workspace for the student.

Establish physical parameters for him by placing masking tape around his desk to make a square or rectangle, putting the tape about a foot or so beyond the desk on all four sides. Tell him that this is his office and that he can stand up or move around as long as he stays within the boundaries of his workspace but that he can't leave the space without your permission. This will give him a feeling of freedom but will also help him learn some self-control. With time, you may want to make the space smaller by bringing in the tape. A variation of this approach is to give the student two desks to use that are placed in the back of the room but on opposite sides and separated by two pieces of masking tape that form a lane between the two desks. The student is allowed to use either desk but must always be seated at one of the desks or traveling between them as long as he stays within the lane.

10. Have students sit on carpet squares during circle time. This will help keep fidgety, squirmy students in their place and lessen the chance they will bother other students.

11. Establish a signal to cue a student that he is out of his seat. Just as you might with a student with an attention problem, arrange a subtle signal with a hyperactive student to alert him that he needs to return to his seat. This might be a wink of your eye, a touch on your shoulder, or a pull on your ear. You may need to quietly say his name to get his attention. If necessary, follow up the signal with a verbal reminder to the student to return to his seat. If he is having a tough time staying in his seat, you might want to establish a signal that tells him to go to a prearranged place in the classroom where he is more likely to be calm and attentive.

12. Ticket, please. If the student gets out of his seat often to do such things as sharpen his pencil or ask you a question, you might give him a limited number of tickets and require that he give you one when he wants to leave his seat. When he runs out of tickets, he is not allowed to leave his seat. If he does, take away 3 minutes from his recess every time he leaves his seat. This will help teach him self-control while lessening his out-of-seat behavior.

13. Provide consequences if the student is highly disruptive. Making accommodations for a hyperactive student does not mean that he is allowed to behave as he wishes. If his behavior begins to disrupt the class and interfere with students' ability to concentrate, let him know that his behavior is unacceptable, and tell him precisely what you expect of him. If he continues to disrupt the class after you have spoken to him, consider giving him a time-out, having him stay for detention, or withdrawing a privilege. If you opt to give him a consequence, do it immediately for maximum effect. As frustrated

as you may be by the student's behavior, talk with him in a serious, low-key manner without humiliating him. Firmness is called for, not anger.

14. Provide comfortable seating.
You might place beanbag chairs or cushions in the corner of the room. Although many of your students may enjoy this area, a hyperactive student may find it especially appealing because he can sit longer and focus better in comfortable seats. You might hold this out as a reward for a hyperactive student if he sits at his desk for a set length of time.

15. Help your students understand a hyperactive classmate's behavior.
This is especially important because your students may have developed negative feelings toward the student. Talk with them when the student is not present, and help them understand that he has a problem controlling his activity level. Let them know that many of the student's annoying behaviors, such as bumping into them or interrupting them, are not intentional. Similarly, help them understand the student's need for classroom accommodations, explaining that he has special needs that are different from those of other students. You might suggest that they let him know in a nice way when his behavior is bothering them.

16. Consider using an aide to help manage the student's behavior.
If the student becomes disruptive in class, you might ask the aide to take him for a walk in the hall or to the gym to play a game or get some exercise. She may also help manage him during unstructured activities such as recess, lunch, and passing in the hallway. In addition, the aide can be used to chart or monitor his behavior as part of a behavior-modification program.

17. Arrange for the student to wear a weighted vest.
This is a vest with extra weight that has been used to help distractible or hyperactive students calm down and relax. Some teachers have also used moist neck rolls with hyperactive children. When worn around the neck, they can provide weight, heat, and tactile stimulation that may lessen stress and calm the student. If your school has an occupational therapist, ask her if these items are appropriate and available for your student.

18. Play soft music. You may find that playing soothing music, including classical music, can have a calming effect on your students and may even improve their ability to focus.

See Also

Attention Deficit

Calling Out

Chair Tipping

Disorganization

Hallway/Lining-up Problems

Lateness

Students may be late to school for reasons that are not under their control. Their school bus may have been slowed by bad weather, or their parents may have been delayed driving them to school. In many cases, however, students are late because of choices they have made. Younger children may not always appreciate the importance of getting to school on time. Even students who know they must be in their seat when the bell rings may be late for other reasons.

For some, their lateness may reflect anxiety about school, either about academic or social concerns. It may be that they are finding the work overwhelming or that another child is picking on them. Other children may wander in a few minutes after the bell rings because they like the attention they receive making a grand entrance, especially if it results in a few minutes of one-on-one time with the teacher. For still other children, their lateness may be their way of irritating you due to feelings of anger or hurt.

If you have a consistently late-arriving student, try to identify the pattern. Although you will of course want to talk with the student and her parents, you might also want to check with her previous teacher and review her previous report cards to find out if lateness was a problem in past years. Also consider whether her lateness is part of a larger pattern of disorganization and difficulties with time issues. Students who are late to school may also be delayed in returning homework or permission slips or have problems keeping track of their materials.

What You Can Do

1. Model punctual behavior.
Begin class promptly, and make sure your students are on time for school activities such as assemblies, lunch, and special classes. In this way, you will be setting a standard of punctuality for your students, and they are likely to take notice.

2. Clarify your expectations regarding the start of the school day.

Your students, especially if they are young, may not realize they are arriving late to school or appreciate the importance of being on time. If so, tell them. Make sure they understand what time they are expected to be in school, and tell them that you expect them to be seated at their desks at that time.

3. Do not allow late students to disrupt your lesson.

Tell your students at the beginning of school that if they arrive late they are to enter quietly, take their seat, and try to catch on to what is happening. Give the tardy student minimal attention when she arrives, and do not make sarcastic comments or reprimand her for being late. If she enters in a noisy manner or comes to see you in the middle of a lesson, ask her to take a seat and tell her you will see her later. Other ways to minimize disruption are to seat her close to the door so she can enter class quietly and to pass out papers to her at the beginning of class (if she is not there, put them on her desk), so you do not need to do this when she arrives.

4. Require older elementary students to fill out a late form.

Tell your class that any student who arrives late is to enter class quietly, pick up a late form, complete it, and return it to a place you designate. On the form, ask students to indicate the date they were late, the time they arrived, and the reason for their lateness. At the bottom of the form, have this statement: "I will do my best to be on time for class in the future." Ask the student to sign it. Review this form during the day, and if necessary meet with the student to talk about her lateness. In addition to reinforcing the importance of arriving on time, this form also provides you with a record of your students' tardiness and helps you identify patterns of lateness. As an alternative to this approach, have tardy students sign a late sign-in book with the date and time.

5. Have a talk with the late-arriving student.

Take the student aside and, in a matter-of-fact manner, explain how being tardy can interfere with her learning as well as your instruction. Ask her why she was late. She may have a legitimate explanation. If, however, you conclude that she is responsible at least in part for her lateness, then work with her and perhaps her parents to find a remedy. Ask what she can do differently to ensure she gets to school on time. After the two of you agree on a plan, get her to commit to this plan in writing or with a handshake. Let her know that you will follow up with her to check on her progress.

6. If a pattern of lateness develops, talk with the parents.

It may be that they are unaware their child is coming to school late. Or they may be aware but are having trouble getting her off to school on time. Either way, it is important that you talk with them. Review with them when students are expected to be in the classroom, emphasizing that your instruction begins soon after the bell rings. Help them understand the academic difficulties posed for their child when she arrives late. You might ask them about their child's morning pattern and suggest some ways she might change the routine to get out of the house earlier. For example, if she is often late because she takes time gathering her materials in the morning, suggest she set out her clothes, pack her backpack, and get lunch money the night before.

7. Provide a consequence for tardiness, but recognize her punctuality.

You might have the student stay in for recess or after-school detention for a set number of lates, but make sure to only count those lates for which she had some responsibility. Impose this consequence in a matter-of-fact manner without showing signs of anger. Also acknowledge the student when she is punctual ("Marissa, I'm really pleased to see you were on time this morning"). You might even work out a reward system for the student with a history of being late. For example, tell her she can earn a privilege that you know she likes if she is on time for school every day of the week.

8. Grab the student's attention with a most unusual note.

You may have fun and find it effective to place a note by her chair. It might go something like this: "Dear Marissa, I was cold and lonely this morning when you came to school late. It would really 'chair' me up if you could get to school on time. Sincerely, Your Seat."

9. Make the beginning of class interesting.

This may entice the dawdlers to get to school on time. Start your class soon after the bell rings, but rather than engage in mundane tasks such as collecting lunch money or taking attendance, begin the day with a brief but fun task such as a puzzle, a joke, a brain teaser, an educational game, or a Shel Silverstein poem. You might even place a fun task on their desk for them to begin as soon as they enter class. Give your students a choice of these "bell ringers" by having them vote on what they like. You might also greet each of the students in a cheerful manner as they arrive, giving special attention to the student with a history of being late (as long as she is on time).

10. Give the student a job she likes at the beginning of the day.

For example, you might make her responsible for taking the lunch money to the office or collecting homework.

See Also

Disorganization

Forgetfulness

School Phobia/Separation Anxiety

Leaving Class

A student may leave class without permission for three basic reasons: (1) he is upset about something going on in class; (2) he is trying to go somewhere else that is more appealing; or (3) he is trying to gain your attention. Often his motivation for leaving is a combination of these reasons.

Of course, your first priority when a child leaves class is to drop everything and find him. Most times he will not go far. On the rare occasion when he cannot be found immediately, it can be a frightening experience for you and panic may set in. Your concern for the student may prompt you to lecture him sternly that he is not to do that again. This is not always effective, however. Some students are determined to leave the room, and all your powers of persuasion and even threats of consequences may not be sufficient to get them to stop.

In dealing with this problem, try to figure out the child's reason for leaving class. You might talk with his parents, talk with his previous teacher, and talk with the student. You may get the most information, however, from observing carefully the occasions when he does leave the room. Take note of when he leaves (for example, if he leaves soon after arriving at school, he may be having separation problems), what was happening before he left (for example, if students were choosing teams on the playground and he was not picked, he may be feeling left out), and where he goes (for example, if he goes to see his sister in another class, he may be feeling in need of emotional support).

What You Can Do

1. Bring him back immediately but give him minimal attention. Although you cannot avoid paying attention to a child who has left class without permission, give him as little attention as possible once you do find him. Do not welcome him back with a hug, do not give him a sympathetic ear, do not lecture him. You can do this later. For now, get him involved in a classroom activity that he likes. The point is to avoid letting him believe that a way of getting your immediate attention and sympathy is to leave the room.

2. Alert the principal immediately if you can't find the student within a few minutes.

You might call the office on the intercom or send a student to inform the principal, but try to stay calm and not alarm your other students.

3. Talk with the student later.

Using a serious, stern tone, make it clear that leaving class is not allowed unless he is with an adult or has your permission. If he left the building, tell him this is unsafe and you do not want anything to happen to him. Ask him why he left class and where he was going. Although some children may have trouble explaining this, others will tell you directly. Tell him if it happens again you will take strong action such as calling his parents or having him stay in for recess.

4. If the student left class because he was upset, talk with him to find out what was upsetting him.

Was he upset about something that you or a classmate said or did? Was he feeling left out by other students? Was he upset because the work is too difficult? Was he frustrated by a particular activity? If the student is not able or willing to express what was upsetting him, suggest some possible reasons and ask him to nod if you got it right. Once you identify the source of his distress, work with him to remedy the problem.

5. If the student left class because he wanted attention, find ways to show him appreciation.

If he announces to you that he is leaving class and then giggles as you run after him, it is a safe bet that he is leaving to elicit your attention. If so, give him positive attention in class at other times by, for example, calling on him more in class, giving him a class job, highlighting his work in the presence of his peers, and praising him for positive behavior.

6. If the student left class because he was seeking adventure, try to stimulate him in other ways.

If you sense the student is bored by the activities you are doing in class, try to adapt your instruction to reflect his particular interests and abilities. If you sense he was leaving class and wandering the halls because he was curious about the school and eager to explore, find some time to take him on a tour of the school to satisfy his curiosity.

Elementary Teacher's Discipline Problem Solver

7. Set up an area of the classroom the student can go to if he is upset or bored.

This area would of course be available to all students. Make it an enticing area with comfortable seating such as a beanbag chair. In designing the area, ask the student for his ideas about what he would like to put there, such as books, art materials, games, or audiotapes. Encourage him to bring items from home.

8. Make it difficult for the student to leave class.

Make sure the classroom door is always closed, and seat him far away from the door. You might also position yourself near the door to prevent him from leaving, especially during unstructured activities when it is easier for him to leave unobserved.

9. Ask other children to alert you if a student leaves the class.

Rather than single out one student, tell all your students to let you know if any of their classmates leave class. Another way of being alerted that a child is leaving class is to attach a bell to the door that rings when it is opened.

10. Alert other staff in the building.

Make the principal, faculty, and other school staff aware that a particular student is prone to leaving the classroom. Tell them to return him to your class if they see him wandering the halls.

11. Help the insecure student feel at home.

Some students walk out of class because of difficulty separating from their parents. If this is the case with one of your students, you can help him feel more secure in the classroom by encouraging him to bring in to school a favorite doll, teddy bear, toy, or book. You might also suggest that he bring in a picture of his family to keep in his knapsack.

12. If a student leaves class often, request an aide.

If you can identify the time of day when he is most likely to bolt, the principal may be willing to assign an aide to your class during that time.

13. Allow the student to leave class with supervision or your knowledge. It

may be that his leaving class is due to his need to take a break or release some pent-up energy. If you can identify when he is most likely to leave class, try to arrange for someone to take a brief walk with him in the school around that time. Or if you feel you can trust him to leave the room without an adult, you might have him go get a drink or do an errand that requires him to leave class.

See Also

Class Trip Problems

Hyperactivity

School Phobia/School Anxiety

Listening Skills, Poor

Good listening ability is an essential learning tool. Indeed, the majority of what children learn in elementary school is acquired through the auditory channel. Some students, however, have a problem in their ability to listen. They may have what is called an auditory processing problem, namely, a difficulty in understanding spoken language.

A student who has problems processing auditory information typically hears normally. She hears the sounds accurately, but her brain may have difficulty making sense of what her ear is telling it. Just as a child with a reading disability typically has good visual acuity but a problem interpreting visual symbols, a child with poor listening skills usually has good hearing but difficulty interpreting auditory information.

A student with poor listening skills may struggle in school, especially if the listening conditions are less than optimal. She may frequently ask you to repeat questions or directions. Or she may stare at you blankly or respond with "what" or "huh" or an irrelevant response. Or she may respond immediately, only to then do the wrong thing. She may have particular difficulty when the message is long, complicated, or spoken rapidly, or when there is a lot of background noise. If the problem is extreme, the student may act out in class because of intense frustration and a lack of understanding of what to do.

Teachers can promote good listening skills by varying the way they communicate and making subtle changes in the classroom setting. Simply telling the student with poor listening skills to listen or pay attention is usually not sufficient. The following strategies may help you deal more effectively with a student with poor listening skills but may also help foster understanding with your entire class.

What You Can Do

1. Consider possible reasons for a student's listening problem.
Listening difficulties may signal the presence of another problem. Investigate whether

the child has an ear infection, a hearing problem, or an attention deficit. Also consider whether she may be bored, distressed, or oppositional. If you suspect the possibility of a hearing problem, ask the nurse to screen her hearing. Keep in mind, however, that this screening is a limited and superficial diagnostic tool, so she will require testing by an audiologist to definitively rule out a hearing problem. You may also want to request an evaluation from your school's speech-language specialist to further pinpoint her difficulties.

2. Seat the student so as to maximize understanding.
Place the child near where you typically stand and away from the hallway door or window. In this way, she will be better able to understand your instructions and less vulnerable to distraction. Avoid standing in front of the window on a sunny day while talking to your class because it will be harder for students to see your face clearly.

3. Minimize distractions.
The student's attention may be diverted by noises from the pencil sharpener, reading groups, shuffling of chairs, students moving around class, and classroom conversation. Even mild noises such as the hum of a heater may distract the student. Although you cannot eliminate all distractions, you may be able to lessen them by seating the student away from major sources of noise and keeping classroom chatter to a minimum. Suggest to her that she consider using earplugs or a study carrel to block out distractions.

4. Make sure you have the student's attention before speaking with her.
This is especially important when you are giving assignments or directions or introducing new ideas. If necessary, alert the student that you are about to begin speaking by gently tapping her on the shoulder or calling her name. Face her and make sure she has eye contact with you. Varying your tone and volume helps to maintain the student's attention.

5. Speak slowly and distinctly, and use simple vocabulary.
Make directions and questions simple, brief, and concrete. Do not give the student more than one or two directions at a time, and have her complete those directions before

giving her more. If you need to repeat directions, rephrase what you said rather than repeat them word for word. Emphasize key words, and try to use vocabulary consistently to lessen confusion. Present directions in the order tasks are to be done, and introduce each direction with words to facilitate understanding such as *first, next,* or *last.* You will need to walk a fine line here. Although you want to speak in a way that allows the student to process what you are saying, at the same time you want to avoid the appearance of talking down to her.

6. Monitor her understanding.
Check her understanding periodically by having her repeat your directions or asking her questions to assess her grasp of what you have said. Make sure that she really understands and is not just parroting what she has heard. If she has not understood, repeat what you said but simplify the vocabulary, syntax, and grammar. You might assign another student to regularly check her understanding of directions and assignments.

7. Show patience with the student who confuses easily.
Becoming frustrated with a student who has difficulty grasping what you say will only compound her problem by increasing her anxiety and decreasing her ability to focus. Be understanding of her difficulty, and allow her to take occasional breaks from schoolwork to get a drink of water, go to the bathroom, pass out papers, or serve as a messenger. Students with poor listening skills must put forth more effort than their classmates to attend and listen in class and can become easily fatigued.

8. Encourage the student to let you know when she is confused.
The student may be reluctant to ask you for clarification for fear of your reaction. Let her know that you expect her to tell you when she is unclear about directions or assignments. Make sure, however, that she does not take advantage of this by not paying attention when she first hears your instructions.

9. Increase your "wait time" with the student.
The student may take somewhat longer to process information presented orally. If so, wait a little longer for a response than you normally might after asking her a question.

10. Reinforce what you are saying with gestures.

Gestures and facial expressions can help a student grasp your message as long as they reinforce the essential part of your message. For example, if you want students to give four examples of an adjective, hold up four fingers.

11. Supplement orally presented information with written information.

This is particularly helpful if you are giving multistep directions. The student with listening problems may remember the first or last step but lose the others. Write down the directions on the board or provide a handout with the information. Prior to giving a lesson to your class, consider distributing outlines to your students, or list the topics and key points on the board. You may also help students retain what you say through the use of visual aids.

12. Prepare the student when shifting to a new topic.

When moving from one subject to another, make it clear that you are changing topics by saying, for example, "That ends our discussion of (name of topic). Now let's move on to talk about (name of new topic)." In discussing the new topic, begin by summarizing the main points. When finished with your lesson, review the main ideas and perhaps previously learned material.

13. Enhance the student's recall.

Here are some ways to help her remember what you have said:

- Speak in short sentences and talk relatively slowly.
- Repeat what you have said or have her repeat it to you.
- Have her write down the information.
- When posing questions in class, give her three or four possible answers to choose from, or ask questions with a number of correct answers.

14. Refer the student for speech and language therapy.

Although speech-language specialists typically see students with speech articulation or expressive language problems, they may also work with students with poor listening skills. In an effort to increase a student's understanding of spoken language, the speech-language specialist may give her exercises to improve her ability to comprehend directions of increasing length and complexity, to discriminate sounds, and to listen effectively with background noise. Training these skills in isolation, however, may not help as much as giving the student and teacher strategies to use in the classroom setting, as well as teaching the student functional language skills (for example, vocabulary, grammar, and conversational ability).

See Also

Attention Deficit

Forgetfulness

Seatwork Problems

Special-Needs Students

Lunchroom Problems

There are few tasks teachers dislike more than lunchroom duty. The lunchroom is probably the rowdiest place in school, and sometimes the noise can be downright unbearable. This setting often presents more challenging management problems than the classroom. Students may see lunch as a time to release pent-up energy. In addition, they may feel that the rules that apply in the classroom do not apply in the cafeteria. As a result, it is not unusual for lunchrooms to get out of control.

Schools need to walk a fine line in managing students' behavior in the lunchroom. On the one hand, lunch should be a time for students to relax and unwind as well as chat with their classmates. This is not a time to require their silence. On the other hand, they must still show respect for their fellow students and keep noise at a moderate level. This demands a modicum of structure and a few basic rules. Failure to enforce rules in the lunchroom is an invitation to chaos.

What You Can Do

1. Establish a lunchroom code of conduct.
Let your students know that you understand their need for a break from classroom rules during lunch, but emphasize that they must still follow some basic rules in the lunchroom out of respect for their fellow students. Tell them in clear terms the specific behaviors that are expected of them. These might include rules about lining up, emptying their trays, cleaning their table, not running, not shouting, and not throwing food. Consider posting these rules in a prominent place in the lunchroom. State them clearly and simply, and do not have more than five rules. You might invite lunchroom personnel to this meeting to reinforce their importance. Also let your students know of any reward system used in the lunchroom, as well as the consequences for poor behavior.

2. If problems emerge, have a class meeting.

Brainstorm with your students about what they can do to improve, making sure to elicit their suggestions. Ask for a show of hands, or better yet a written statement, of students who agree to follow the plan. They will be more likely to cooperate if they have had some say in the solution and committed themselves to following it.

3. Have students practice lunchroom behavior.

Younger students or special education students may need some practice in lunchroom protocol. If so, have them role-play such skills as walking to the lunchroom, waiting in line, carrying a tray, taking a seat, and clearing their tray.

4. Have students walk to the lunchroom in an orderly fashion.

If they enter the lunchroom in a controlled manner, they may be more likely to behave appropriately while eating lunch.

5. Assign lunchroom monitors to groups.

Rather than have monitors responsible for supervising all the students in the lunchroom, they might be given responsibility for specific groups. In this way, they can get to know the students they are supervising better and manage them more effectively.

6. Communicate with the lunch monitors.

Ask them to let you know of any of your students who have misbehaved in lunch so you can take appropriate action.

7. Praise or reward individual students.

Compliment students who are behaving well and following the lunchroom rules. You might even reward them with tokens that can be exchanged for prizes or privileges. If you sense they are not comfortable being praised or rewarded publicly, acknowledge them in private.

8. Reward well-behaving tables.

By rewarding tables of students rather than individuals, you can prompt students to encourage their tablemates to behave well to obtain the rewards. You can do this in various ways. You might allow the quietest table to get lunch first or have the table that behaved best during lunch go to recess before other tables. Or you might develop a more formal system in which each table earns points for such behaviors as keeping their voices down or lining up properly. Keep track of the points each table has earned on a chart on the lunchroom wall. When a table earns a set number of points (or has the most points at the end of the week), you might give its members a reward such as a special dessert. Once they receive their reward, their points are wiped out and they can begin accumulating new points.

9. Conduct a lunchroom raffle.

Give tickets to students who are behaving appropriately in the lunchroom, with each student eligible to receive a maximum of three tickets per lunch. Have them write their names on the tickets and place them in a box. At the end of lunch or the school day, draw a ticket from the box and reward the student who has the winning ticket with a prize or a special privilege.

10. Quiet students by raising your hand.

Use the old standby to silence students or get their attention. Raise your hand with two fingers extended to form a V shape. Tell the students that when they see this signal they are to raise their hands, quiet down, and look at you. If necessary, you might first get their attention by, for example, blowing a whistle.

11. Give the student a gentle reminder, and if he continues to misbehave provide a warning and then a consequence.

Let him know what he is doing and what he needs to do differently ("Matthew, you're making too much noise. I need you to speak more quietly."). This may be sufficient to elicit his cooperation, at least for a short time. If he misbehaves again, give him a warning ("Matthew, I have already spoken to you about your yelling. If I have to talk to you again about this, there will be a consequence."). Make good on your word if he misbehaves a third time, perhaps by having him miss part or all of recess or assigning him to a separate table for the rest of the week.

12. Place misbehaving students at a separate table.

If a student continues to misbehave despite your efforts to obtain his cooperation, consider having him eat lunch at a separate table or in another room that has adult supervision for a set period of time, perhaps a week.

13. Provide fun activities after lunch.

By keeping students occupied with activities that they enjoy, you can lessen the chance of having problems. Consider putting out some quiet games, books, or art activities. Some other possibilities: have someone lead students in a song or have them come up to a microphone to tell jokes or riddles. If you provide a large-group activity, tell students that it cannot begin until there is quiet in the lunchroom.

14. Play music in the lunchroom.

Consider putting on background music while students are eating, but make sure it is music that has a calming rather than a stimulating effect. You might suggest that students bring in some of their favorite CD's to play, but make sure the music is suitable.

See Also

Disruptive/Uncooperative Behavior

Talking, Excessive

Lying

Just about all children lie at some point. Younger elementary students tell tales more than older elementary students. In part, this is due to older children being more skilled at recognizing lies and more likely to criticize classmates who exaggerate the truth or fabricate stories. All elementary teachers, however, will encounter this problem at one time or another.

Although preschoolers may not understand that lying is wrong, most school-aged children know the truth about lying. Even so, the line between honesty and dishonesty can be ambiguous. Is it a lie to tell a friend that you like her haircut when you don't? Is it a lie to tell a bully that you don't know where a potential victim is when you do? Is it a lie to embellish a story to make it funnier? As these examples illustrate, lying can be a tricky issue for teachers to handle.

An occasional lie by a student is not reason for serious concern. Teachers should be more concerned, however, if a student lies frequently. Students who lie often may become skilled at this behavior. Their lying may become habitual to the point that they come to lie with little concern for the consequences, which may be considerable for them. Frequent lying can cause classmates to mistrust the student. It may also lead to their shunning or rejecting her in school, which may in turn give rise to academic or behavioral problems. Compulsive lying may also accompany other problems, including cheating and stealing.

Children lie for various reasons. They may want to

- Avoid the consequences of telling the truth, namely, disappointment, blame, or punishment.

- Cover up a mistake or a failure to do something.

- Avoid hurting someone's feelings.

- Avoid dealing with an anxiety-provoking situation.

- Gain attention from others.

- Obtain power or independence.
- Elevate their status with peers.
- Obtain a material benefit.
- Gain special treatment.

Some instances of lying are of greater concern than others. Do not be concerned if a child lies to avoid hurting a classmate's feelings or occasionally embellishes a story. In determining whether the lying warrants your involvement, consider how frequently the child lies, the nature and context of the lie, the reactions of her classmates, and other behaviors the child is displaying. Avoid disciplining the student, however, if you are not certain she has told a lie.

What You Can Do

1. Show your students that you value honesty.
Children's impulse to lie may be fostered by observing others lying. Although it is impossible to keep your students from being exposed to dishonesty, make a point of modeling honest behavior yourself. Let your students see you interacting in an open, honest manner with colleagues. You can show your commitment to honesty by acknowledging when you made a mistake or apologizing if you did something wrong.

2. Respond to mistakes in a constructive, not a critical, manner.
If a student expects that you will react to her mistakes by blaming her or getting angry, she will be more inclined to hide them through lying. If instead you react to her mistakes in a calm, constructive, solution-focused manner, she will be more likely to be truthful.

3. Acknowledge a student for being truthful.
If a student admits making a mistake or acknowledges her responsibility in causing a problem, let her know you are pleased she had the courage to speak the truth. Although you may want to give the child a consequence for her misdeed, consider going easy in

light of her honesty. Let her know that you are lessening the consequence because of her truthfulness. Giving her a harsh punishment or yelling at her may only encourage her not to tell the truth the next time.

4. Do not treat a young child's fantasies as lies.

Some kindergartners or first graders may fabricate stories as a way of expressing things they want. They may believe these fantasies because they have not completely learned to distinguish fantasy from reality. Although you may want to help the student learn the difference between fantasy and reality, do not treat this as an instance of lying.

5. Address the lie.

If you observe a child lying, even occasionally, don't ignore it unless it is a harmless "white lie" or an embellishment of a story. Lies that go unchallenged will make the student feel she can get away with lying and may encourage her to tell bigger lies on other occasions. A child who lies without being challenged may become a skilled, even compulsive, liar. It is also important to intervene quickly, as lying can give rise to social problems.

6. React calmly to a student who has lied.

Even though it is important to confront lying as soon as you observe it, it is also important not to overreact to this behavior. Reminding yourself how common lying is may allow you to react calmly. You might let the student know you are disappointed in her behavior, but if you react in an angry, critical manner, you may only encourage her to lie more skillfully in the future. The child who lies but is found out and reprimanded harshly learns to lie better so that she is not found out next time. In addition to avoiding expressions of anger, avoid conducting an inquisition to determine conclusively whether the student had told a lie. In doing this, you are giving this issue more attention than it is worth and perhaps encouraging the student to add to her lies.

7. Meet with the student in private.

In responding to a lie, focus on the behavior rather than the student. Let her know that she made a mistake and that you hope she will act differently next time, but do not call her a liar or otherwise make her feel like a bad person for having lied. Help her understand the consequences of lying, namely that a child who lies often is unlikely to be trusted by classmates and may be rejected by them. Let the student know that if she lies often, you and her classmates won't know when she is telling the truth and may assume that she is lying. You might even tell her the story of "The Boy Who Cried Wolf." Help her understand that lying typically does not make the problem go away and that others may even pick up when she is lying.

8. Attend to what underlies the lying.

In responding to a lie, it is often helpful to focus on the emotional need that gave rise to the lie. The nature of the student's lie may give you clues about her underlying emotional need, which may suggest ways of intervening. For example, if you observe a child frequently lying to her classmates about her achievements, it is likely that she feels insecure with peers and is trying to gain status with them. If so, look for ways for the child to gain peer attention by highlighting her actual accomplishments. If a student tells a classmate that she has a lot of friends in another class when you know this is not true, the child is conveying her feelings of social isolation, suggesting an avenue for teacher intervention. If you conclude the child is lying to cover up inappropriate behavior for fear of being punished or reprimanded, help her learn to engage in appropriate behaviors by focusing on solutions rather than assigning blame.

9. Use punishment sparingly.

A gentle talk with the student may be more effective than a punitive approach in deterring future lying. There may be situations, however, in which you feel punishment is warranted. If so, accompany the punishment with an explanation of why lying is wrong and what the consequences of lying are. You might consider lessening the punishment if she acknowledges her dishonesty.

See Also

Cheating

Self-Esteem, Low

Making Noises

Students have a wide variety of ways to make noise in class. They may hum a tune, grind their pencil in the pencil sharpener, roll their pen across the desk, tap their hand, crack their knuckles, or click their tongue. These noises can drive teachers and other students to distraction. Although an effective response may be to ignore the noises, that is not always possible if they are interfering with your lesson or your students' ability to concentrate.

What You Can Do

1. Make sure the student is aware he is making noise.

It is not uncommon for students to tap their fingers or click their tongue without knowing they are doing this. If you have a student who seems unaware he is making noise, take him aside and let him know precisely what he is doing that is distracting others. Tell him that if he makes noise in the future, you will give him an agreed-upon nonverbal signal (for example, touching your finger to your lips, raising your eyebrows, or pulling your ear) to signal him that he is making noise and needs to stop. Do not stop class to reprimand him. The idea is to give him a reminder without interrupting the flow of your lesson.

2. Move in the direction of the student.

If he is making noise while you are teaching, walk toward him while continuing to present your lesson. Stand there for a minute or two, perhaps making eye contact with him. Your presence may be sufficient to get him to stop.

3. Place the student in a study carrel.

If your efforts to get him to stop making noise are ineffective and his behavior is distracting your other students, consider separating him from the class to lessen the noise. Suggest he use a study carrel that is placed on the side of the class. Make this appealing by telling him that this is his office, but only put him there for short periods and not at all if he feels isolated from his classmates.

4. Identify when the student is most likely to make noise.
You may observe that the noises emerge at certain times of the day, for example, during a particular class, while taking a test, or while doing seatwork. Learning when he is making noise may lead you to consider why he is doing it. He may be making noise because he finds the work boring or tedious, is confused about what to do, is having trouble with the work, or has difficulty focusing for a sustained period. Identifying the source of the noise may suggest the need to adjust the level of the work, the length of the activity, or the way you present the information.

5. Provide the student with positive attention.
If you conclude that he is making noise as a way of gaining your attention, look for opportunities to pay attention to him when he displays positive behavior or has an academic success. In this way, he may feel less compelled to seek attention in inappropriate ways.

See Also

Disruptive/Uncooperative Behavior

Gum Chewing

Talking, Excessive

Tourette's Syndrome

Masturbation

Children may learn at a very early age that they can experience pleasure by touching different parts of their body. In the process of exploring their body, they may discover that touching their genitals makes them feel good and gives them comfort. It is not unusual for children to masturbate even before they begin attending school. By the time they enter kindergarten, however, most have learned a sense of discretion and will only engage in this behavior in private, if at all. Some children, however, are slow in learning this lesson and may touch their genitals in public, including in school.

Although masturbation does not pose any health risks to the child, it can suggest the presence of a larger problem, especially if he is engaging in this behavior often. In particular, frequent masturbation may suggest that he is experiencing stress and is using it as a way of comforting himself and reducing the tension. If so, it is important to identify the source of his stress and find ways to alleviate it.

In rare cases, a child's masturbation, if accompanied by other behaviors, may suggest that he has been the victim of sexual abuse. These other behaviors include immature or babyish behavior, withdrawal from peers, uncharacteristic sadness, frequent crying episodes, and unusual irritability, anger, or aggression. If you suspect the possibility of sexual abuse, talk with your principal and make sure the parents are informed so they can seek professional guidance. Because of the extreme delicacy of this issue, you need to deal with this concern with the utmost care and sensitivity.

Although masturbation is not inherently harmful to the child, the reaction of adults may be. In dealing with a student who is masturbating in class, avoid overreacting. Acting disgusted or appalled by the behavior may cause him to think that something is terribly wrong with him and may actually increase the behavior in his effort to obtain some comfort. The incident could even provide you with an opportunity to teach him about socially appropriate behavior. Rather than punishing him, berating him, or labeling his behavior as bad, dirty, or sinful and thus making him feel ashamed of what he has done, you want to help him understand that it is not his behavior that is a problem but rather where he engaged in the behavior. In short, you want to help him understand that masturbation is a private activity that should not be done in public, including school. Although your words are important in tempering the student's reaction, so too is your accompanying tone.

What You Can Do

1. Don't ignore the behavior.
As much as you might want to overlook the student's touching of his genitals because of your own discomfort in dealing with it, this is a behavior that you do not want to ignore, especially if other children have noticed it. Classmates may react in different ways: some may be disturbed, others may perceive him as strange or different, and still others may tease him. Try to resolve the problem promptly without adding to the student's embarrassment.

2. Consider whether the student has a physical problem.
It may be that he is touching himself in the genital area because he needs to urinate or has an irritation or infection or because his clothing is uncomfortable. If so, he may not be trying to stimulate himself but rather to lessen an irritation. If he appears to have a physical problem that is persisting, let his parents know of your concerns and suggest they consult his pediatrician.

3. Inform the parents about their child's behavior.
After sharing your observations, let them know that other students have engaged in similar behavior in school. You may need to help them respond to their child in a measured way by discouraging them from punishing him or making him feel guilty or ashamed. You might tell them that you believe the issue is not what he did but rather where he did it. Suggest they convey to him in language that he is likely to understand that school is not the proper place for this behavior. Let them know how you plan to handle it in the future and what you intend to say to him when you meet with him privately. Ask the parents if they are in agreement with this plan and whether they want to participate in the meeting.

4. Have a private chat with the student.

In talking with the student, the last thing you want to do is scold him or say something that will intensify his embarrassment and shame from having been caught in the act. Instead, let him know in a calm, matter-of-fact manner that your concern is not with what he did but rather where he did it. Tell him that touching his private parts is not appropriate for school and is more suitable for the privacy of one's bedroom, making sure to use terms that he understands. You might tell him that just as you do not pick your nose in public or go to the bathroom in public, you do not touch your genitals in public. Also let him know that his classmates may be distressed by his behavior and start to avoid him.

5. Cue the student about his behavior.

Work out with him a private signal to let him know that he is touching himself and needs to stop. Make this signal as subtle as possible so that classmates do not become aware of the student's behavior, thus minimizing the chance of ridicule. The signal might be as simple as raising your eyebrows or scratching your head. You may have to get his attention before giving him the signal by saying his name or walking over to him and putting your hand on his shoulder. Tell the student that when he gets the signal he is to stop the behavior and place his hands on the desk.

6. Distract the student.

If one of your students appears to be masturbating, consider giving him an activity to do that requires him to use his hands or move around the class. This might be a puzzle, an art project, a handwriting assignment, or even an errand. You might also give him a ball that he can squeeze, which might provide him with an alternate way of releasing tension. In this way, you can inhibit his self-stimulation without either embarrassing him or disrupting the flow of your lesson. You can talk with him privately at a more convenient time.

7. Divert the other students' attention.

Classmates may become aware of the student's behavior. If so, divert their attention by getting them to focus on another activity without mentioning the student or his behavior.

8. Alleviate the student's stress.
Children sometimes masturbate to relieve tension. If this is the case with one of your students, identify the source of the stress and try to find ways to alleviate it. Possible sources of stress include academic difficulties, problems with peers, and conflicts at home. Young elementary children are especially prone to feeling upset about being apart from their parents. If you have a child who is experiencing this separation anxiety, it may be helpful to allow him to carry with him an item from home such as a picture of his family or a favorite toy.

See Also

School Phobia/Separation Anxiety

Teasing

Messiness

Identifying a messy student is not hard. Her desk is usually a sure giveaway. It may contain an assortment of items such as books, supplies, toys, crumpled papers, and food—all in a jumbled hodgepodge. Her desk may swallow up papers almost as quickly as you can hand them out. Her backpack may be just as much of a disaster zone. As a result, the student may spend much of her time in school searching for materials and redoing lost papers. And in the process, she may disrupt the class as she rummages through her desk or backpack.

What You Can Do

1. Build desk clean-up time into your class schedule.
Some students will not be able to keep their desk clean unless time is set aside for the task. Establish regular times when your students clean out their desks, perhaps on Friday afternoons. For students whose desks are already clean or who finish early, provide enjoyable activities for them to do while their classmates clean theirs. If a student's desk has gotten out of control and she is overwhelmed by the prospect of cleaning it, ask a classmate to give her some help. You might have the student put the items from her desk into a bag and take them to a table to sort through. Help her figure out what to do with the contents. Rarely used items might be taken home or placed on the classroom shelf or in her cubby.

2. Spot-check students' desks.
Praise those who have kept them neat. For a student who has not, give her a deadline for cleaning it out, and put her name and date on the board as a reminder to both her and you. Let her know that you will inspect her desk on that date, and make sure to follow through. If her desk is not cleaned up by the set date, have her stay in during recess until it is.

Elementary Teacher's Discipline Problem Solver

3. Give the student lessons in maintaining a neat desk.

Keeping a desk neat does not come naturally to many students. Some need to be taught how to reduce the chaos. As you help a student learn to organize her materials, keep in mind the goal is not to have her keep her desk meticulous but simply neat enough so she can find what she needs with little effort. Offer specific strategies for organizing her materials. Consider taping a list to her desk of items allowed inside, and let her know that toys are not to be among them. Allow her to keep no more than two or three books for silent reading in her desk. Also suggest she write the subjects on the spines of the covers of her textbooks so she can find them quickly.

4. Have the student remove unnecessary items from the top of her desk.

She may have difficulty focusing on her seatwork if there are extraneous materials atop her desk. Train her to clear her desk of materials except those needed for the seatwork before she begins the assignment.

5. Have the student clean out her backpack as a homework assignment.

Backpacks can also be black holes in which papers mysteriously disappear. Have the student clean it out at home rather than use valuable class time to do this. If necessary, ask for parents' help in the task.

6. Give the student a container for school supplies.

This might be a plastic zippered pouch kept in her binder or a resealable plastic bag or storage box kept in her desk. In this way, the student can find needed items quickly without having to take time to rummage through her desk or backpack.

7. Have students keep their papers in folders.

Help them solve the problem of lost papers by suggesting they buy folders to store them in. A student might have a different folder for each subject. Or she might have separate folders for completed work, work to be done, and papers for parents to see. With older elementary students, you might suggest they obtain a three-ring binder divided by subjects, with pocket folders that can go into the binder.

8. Send home completed work.   Designate a day each week when students will bring home work they have finished. Inform parents of the day so they can help their child sort through the papers.

See Also

Disorganization

Forgetfulness

Seatwork Problems

Motivation, Lack of

A motivational problem is not always easy to define, but teachers have no trouble recognizing it. This is the student whose attitude toward schoolwork screams, "I don't care." He is highly motivated when it comes to schoolwork—motivated to avoid it. He puts more work into avoiding academic challenges than tackling them. Although his test scores may convey high potential, his classroom performance may suggest something far different. When given an assignment, he may shrug his shoulders and complain, "Why do we have to do this?" and then give up at the first sign of trouble. He is often content with just getting by.

Motivational problems often emerge during late elementary school. The enthusiasm for school that students may have felt in kindergarten or first grade may take a back seat as the work becomes more demanding and their standing relative to classmates more apparent. They may come to believe that they are not able to succeed with academic tasks. As school becomes increasingly more difficult, they may begin to take academic detours. They may shy away from tackling difficult tasks, giving them little care or attention. Lacking confidence in their abilities, they may write off any successes as flukes, attributing them to luck, the ease of the task, or even teacher charity.

Your goal in working with a student who is unmotivated is to help him come to see school as a place where he can be successful and schoolwork as interesting, relevant, and meaningful. In particular, you face two challenges. The first is to change his thinking so that he comes to believe that he can be successful with academic tasks if he puts forth effort. The second is to figure out what motivates him, namely, to identify the settings, situations, and conditions that he responds to and can be used to foster his interest.

What You Can Do

1. Try to figure out why he is not putting forth effort.
Is he discouraged by a history of academic failures? Is he uncertain about what to do? Is he having

trouble concentrating in class? Is he showing signs of a learning disability? Does he find the work boring? To answer these and other questions, look for any patterns with the student by checking his school records, observing him in different school situations, and talking with his parents and previous teachers. And perhaps most important, talk with the student. He may be able to give you clues about his lack of interest in schoolwork, as well as suggestions about what you might do differently in the classroom to increase his effort.

2. Provide sincere appreciation for the student's performance.
Students who are unmotivated need more than the usual amount of encouragement. Provide generous recognition and praise for the student's efforts and performance, but keep in mind that he is probably skilled at discerning the difference between sincere feedback and empty praise. Selective praise that conveys genuine appreciation for his work will mean much more to him than vague or exaggerated compliments. Tell him specifically what you like about his performance, praising him for even small steps forward.

3. Help break the student's cycle of failure.
An unmotivated student is often a demoralized student. He may perceive school as a place of failure and frustration. Try to alter his perceptions by finding opportunities for him to excel and orchestrating some success experiences. Assign him work that he is capable of completing successfully but still gives him a feeling of accomplishment. Try to structure the assignment so that the beginning section is relatively easy, hopefully giving him the confidence to move on. If he struggles with a task, focus on what he has done well while gently correcting his mistakes without criticizing him. Help him understand that setbacks and mistakes are a normal part of the learning process. To enhance class participation, call on him when you are confident he knows the answer, perhaps even letting him know at the beginning of class that you will be asking him a particular question so he can think about a response. As he begins to enjoy more success, his confidence will grow, and he may become more willing to take risks.

4. Provide clear, concise, and explicit directions to the student.

Motivational problems can be compounded if the student is unsure what to do. After giving explicit directions, ask him if he has any questions. You might ask him to repeat the directions to you to ensure understanding. Have him do a sample problem, and then provide constructive and encouraging feedback. With complicated assignments, do an example for him.

5. Stay in close proximity to the student.

Help the student stay on task by seating him close to where you usually stand while teaching a lesson. Circulate among students while they are doing seatwork, making sure to spend time near the student who is prone to motivational problems.

6. Give the student work that is challenging yet achievable.

A student's motivational problem may reflect the difficulty level of the work. If he feels the work is too easy, he may race through it, giving it little thought or care; if he feels it is too hard, he may put forth minimal effort, perceiving he has little chance of success. If lack of time keeps you from individualizing instruction, consider using computer-based instruction, parent volunteers, peer tutors, and cooperative learning. If you sense the student is inattentive in class due to the slow pace of instruction and the teaching of topics he has already mastered, consider allowing him to skip topics that he can show he has mastered (perhaps through a unit test or end-of-year test) and give him more advanced work.

7. Give the student a choice of assignments.

He may be more likely to put forth effort if he has a say in the assignment. You might give him three assignments to choose from, each of which helps meet your objective. For example, in studying the American Revolution, you might allow him to do a book report, make an oral presentation, or do a related art project. Of course, you still reserve the right to require him to do certain critical assignments. Consider other ways to give the child some ownership over the learning process, for example, by having him select the book he will read or the topic for a paper or allowing him to choose the reward or classroom privilege he will receive if he reaches a goal.

8. Relate the lesson to the student's interests.

Find out about some of the student's interests (you might have him complete an interest inventory), and then try to integrate them into your lessons or classroom activities. If he has a paper route, for example, you might design math problems requiring him to calculate how much a child earns delivering papers under various conditions. If you are doing a transportation unit and you know the student builds model airplanes, have him bring in some models to show the class. If he is talented at art, have him help you design your bulletin boards. If he excels on the computer, have him become the class troubleshooter.

9. Give your lessons a real-world focus.

Students who are unmotivated often ask, "Why do I have to know this?" Try to give them some answers by helping them see how the lessons of the classroom can be applied to life outside the classroom. When teaching different shapes, have students point out examples of shapes in the classroom. Show how being able to count is essential when buying things at the store. In teaching about plant life, have your students make a leaf collection. Also plan field trips that show how the lessons they are learning work in real life. For example, if you are doing a unit on the environment, plan a trip to a recycling center.

10. Break the task into small parts.

Some students may put forth little effort because they perceive a task as too overwhelming. If so, present the task in manageable doses. Give the student one step at a time, and don't move on until he has mastered that step. As he gains skill and confidence, you can gradually expand the size of the task, give him more difficult problems, or move at a somewhat faster pace. Apply this same approach to homework. If the student struggles with math and rarely completes assignments, consider giving him half the problems of the other students, selecting problems you are confident he can do.

11. Vary your teaching style.

Consider altering your teaching style to spark the student's interest. This is especially important if your lessons include a steady diet of material to be memorized. You may find that a student who is in the dark when listening to classroom lectures may suddenly light up when given hands-on activities. For example, you might have students conduct a debate about a controversial historical issue, conduct an experiment to demonstrate a science principle, or do a cooking project to help them understand different types of measurement. These activities not only stimulate students' interests but help them retain concepts.

12. Focus on the student's progress rather than his performance relative to peers.

A student who is constantly compared to classmates who outperform him will eventually become so demoralized that he will shut down in school. You can avoid this by focusing on his improvement rather than his performance relative to his classmates. You might evaluate the student through a portfolio assessment in which you examine his work during the year and consider his progress as a measure of his performance. The student may receive a boost in confidence by seeing, through a review of his work samples, how much his work has improved over the course of the year.

13. Consider referring the child for a learning disability evaluation.

Your student's motivational problem may be masking a learning problem. If he has a learning disability, he may feel so frustrated and discouraged by his academic struggles that he may give up trying rather than risk trying and failing. If you suspect the student has a learning disability, talk with your principal about referring him for evaluation.

See Also

Dependent Behavior

Forgetfulness

Homework Problems

Participation, Lack of Class

Seatwork Problems

Participation, Lack of Class

Although teachers are often quick to point out to students that class participation is an important part of their grade, it is also an important part of their learning. By speaking up in class, they are learning to express their ideas in a way that others understand. And when they ask questions, they are learning how to obtain information to enhance their understanding of a topic. Class participation is also a valuable learning tool for teachers. Through your students' questions, you learn what your students do not understand and can adjust your instruction accordingly.

But just as speaking in front of a group does not come easily to many adults, speaking up in class is a struggle for many students. This may manifest itself in the classroom in a variety of ways, from not volunteering answers to questions to not asking for help to not speaking up in small-group activities to not talking at all.

Students may choose not to participate in class because they are unsure of the answers. Other students know the answers but are still reluctant to raise their hand. They may be afraid of giving the wrong answer and appearing foolish in the eyes of classmates. Or they may be intimidated by the teacher and fear what she might say if they answer incorrectly. Still others may shy away from participating because they are self-conscious about their language skills. They may have a speech defect, a problem putting their thoughts into words, or a lack of proficiency in English because it is not their first language.

You will have greater success in spurring a student to speak up if you can figure out why he is reluctant to participate. Whatever the reason for his reticence, however, your role is not to force him to speak; doing so will only make him more likely to clam up than open up. Rather, your role is to provide a supportive, encouraging climate that helps him feel more comfortable, more confident, and less fearful of speaking up.

What You Can Do

1. Create a supportive climate where students feel free to ask questions.

Make it clear to your students that you want them to ask questions. Tell them that their questions help you by indicating where you may not have been clear. Emphasize that there is no such thing as a dumb question, and make sure not to allow students to ridicule a classmate's questions. Even with your encouragement, however, some students will still feel uncomfortable posing questions in class, so make yourself available to them after class or at the end of the day.

2. Take the student's questions and comments seriously.

His reluctance to ask a question or volunteer an answer may be due to his lack of confidence. Help him gain the courage to participate by showing respect for his contributions and giving thoughtful answers to his questions. Listen attentively while he is talking, and do not interrupt him. Try to find something positive to say about his comments such as, "That's an interesting point. I never thought about it that way." or "That's a really creative idea." At the same time, avoid praising him excessively because this may draw attention to his reluctance to participate and make him feel uncomfortable. In response to one of his questions, you might come in the next day with a more complete answer, telling him you were curious about the question he asked so you decided to get more information.

3. Orchestrate his speaking experiences to ensure success.

Consider the following strategies:

- Ask him questions that you are confident he can answer.
- Let him know before class that you will be calling on him for a specific question so that he can prepare an answer. If you arrange to call on him, do it early to lessen his anxiety.
- When he does respond, reinforce his comments with positive statements and an encouraging smile.

- If you ask a question and he blanks out or says nothing, you might restate the question, perhaps in yes-or-no form, or lead him toward the right answer by providing a clue. Or you might let him off the hook by giving the answer while saying something like "That was a tough one" and then moving on.

- If he gives a one-word answer, ask him to tell you more or put it in a sentence, and praise him when he does.

- Avoid calling on students randomly or in alphabetical order.

4. Be patient in waiting for a response to a question.

The student may need more time to organize his ideas and formulate a response. As a result, he may be slow in answering a question. If so, give him extra time by waiting longer than you usually do for an answer. For example, if you normally wait a second or two before providing the answer or moving on to another student, consider waiting at least three seconds. If other students are clamoring to answer, ask for their patience as well.

5. Monitor class participation.

This will help you determine who is and is not participating and whether a particular student is improving. A simple way to keep track of student participation is to keep a seating chart on your desk and place checks next to the names of those who have contributed.

6. Give the student practice in communication skills by talking with him privately.

Find a few minutes every so often to talk with him about his favorite activities and interests. Or you might speak with him when he is doing an art project or writing assignment. Ask questions so he can explain what he is doing or writing about, but make sure they are not threatening. The idea is to help him feel more comfortable talking with one person so that in time he will feel more confident speaking up in class.

7. Encourage the student to ask for help.

He may be hesitant to seek out your help, even if it means not understanding a homework assignment or classroom activity. Tell him that you want him to tell you when he is confused about directions or assignments. Add that it not only helps him to ask questions but it helps you because you can learn where you have not been clear. Give him permission to come up to you at your desk or while you are working with a group.

8. Reduce the stress of giving oral reports. The following strategies may lessen the student's fears and increase his comfort level:

- Have him speak from his seat rather than in front of the class.

- Have him speak to the class about a topic he knows well and enjoys.

- Rehearse with him before he makes a presentation.

- Avoid bombarding him with questions.

- Allow him to make a presentation as part of a group. Once he feels comfortable doing this, encourage him to make an individual presentation.

- Do not criticize him for his oral report in the presence of classmates.

- Do not grade him for oral reports.

- If the idea of speaking in class throws him into a panic, do not push the issue.

- Provide the anxious student with alternatives to making an oral report such as a written report, an oral report to the teacher only, or an audiotape of the presentation made at home.

9. Give the student responsibilities that require communication. You may need to nudge him to do these activities, but don't hesitate if you are confident he can do them successfully. For example, you might encourage him to be a class messenger—a job valued by students that requires talking with school staff. Other possible jobs that demand communication skills: tutoring another student, being the leader of a small group if he is familiar with or skilled in the topic, or serving as a teacher assistant. Make sure to praise his performance, even if he struggles with the task.

10. Don't be concerned if a student with limited English proficiency is quiet.

The student may be reticent in class until he begins to feel confident speaking up. This does not mean, however, that he is not learning or that he is upset. In fact, he is probably observing very closely and absorbing new words and concepts. As his language facility increases, he will likely feel more comfortable speaking up.

11. Observe the student for any evidence of a speech or language problem.

It may be that the student is reluctant to speak up in class because he has a speech defect or difficulty putting his thoughts into words. Although articulation problems are usually evident to a teacher, difficulties in language usage may be more difficult to identify. If you have had few chances to hear the child speak because of his reticence, spend time observing him while he is talking with his peers or his parents to get a sense of his language skills. If your observations suggest a communication problem, bring this to the attention of your school's speech-language specialist, who may want to do an evaluation.

See Also

Dependent Behavior

Listening Skills, Poor

Self-Esteem, Low

Shyness

Passing Notes

Passing notes to other students in class is a time-honored communication system. For many students, exchanging secretive and often personal information can be an exciting way to pass the time in school, especially during a class they find boring. Although rarely a serious problem, note passing suggests that the students involved are not attending to the lesson. In addition, the contents of the notes, which may include gossip or rumors about other students, can sometimes trigger student conflicts.

A simple request to stop may be all that is necessary. After all, passing notes is just a matter of two students communicating with each other. If, however, it takes place during a test, disrupts your lesson, or gives rise to social difficulties, you may need to respond in a more serious manner.

What You Can Do

1. Explain your rule about note passing.
When discussing the dos and don'ts of your classroom, tell your students that passing notes is not allowed, and tell them why. You might explain that note passing can sometimes cause problems between students. It also suggests that the students passing notes are not paying attention in class. This should not be a major disciplinary concern, however, so do not spend a lot of time discussing it.

2. Address the problem in a low-key manner.
This is rarely an issue that warrants more than a quick reprimand, so do not make a big deal if you see a student passing a note. You might simply say, "Natasha, please put that away. Passing notes is not allowed during class," and then move on with your lesson.

3. Do not embarrass the student.
Although you may be annoyed at the student for not paying attention, resist any impulse you may have to take the note and read it. And certainly do not read it aloud or make the student read it. That will likely be humiliating to the student and engender a desire on her part to not cooperate with you in the future.

4. Move the student to the front of the class or near your desk.
Your concern should be less that she is passing notes and more that she is not paying attention. If you move the student closer to you so you can monitor her more closely, she will be less likely to pass notes and more likely to pay attention.

5. Separate note-passing students.
It is hard for students to pass notes back and forth if they are on opposite sides of the room.

6. If the note passing persists, treat it as a disciplinary matter.
If note passing occurs more than once, talk with the students after class and ask for their cooperation. Let them know that it interferes with your lesson and if it continues you will treat it as a disciplinary problem. If note passing occurs after that, consider giving the students an after-school detention or contacting their parents.

See Also

Attention Deficit

Disruptive/Uncooperative Behavior

Perfectionism

The perfectionistic student is not satisfied with merely doing well. She will labor endlessly over a composition as she tries to produce the perfect paper. She will redo assignments countless times and even then may feel that her final effort is not good enough. To say that she is tough on herself is putting it mildly. She considers anything less than perfection a failure.

Relentlessly self-critical, perfectionistic students set impossibly high standards for themselves and become frustrated when they fail to meet them. Extrinsic measures of success—grades, scores, records, awards, trophies—are of paramount concern to them. Even when they succeed, however, they find reason to be dissatisfied. The perfectionistic student who wins a spelling bee may get down on herself because she got one word wrong. The perfectionistic athlete who wins the race may fret about not breaking a record.

Students respond differently to their perfectionistic impulses. Some become compulsive workaholics, pouring every ounce of their energy into their work; others may fear failing and thus put forth minimal effort or opt for activities they know they can do successfully. They may conclude that it is safer not to try than to try and risk making a mistake. According to the perfectionist's code, failure is simply not an option.

Perfectionism is not the same as task commitment. There is nothing unhealthy about setting high standards or striving for lofty goals. But the healthy striving for excellence is far different from the unhealthy pursuit of perfection. The striver for excellence reaches for challenges; the perfectionist avoids them. The striver for excellence celebrates an accomplishment; the perfectionist experiences relief that she did not meet with failure.

The drive to excel can be a double-edged sword if the student becomes consumed with being the best at everything she does. When taken to an extreme, this passionate pursuit of perfection can lead to emotional difficulties. Unable to live up to her often unreachable standards, the perfectionistic student may experience intense disappointment and feelings of worthlessness. The challenge in teaching a perfectionistic student is to maintain a delicate balance between encouraging her pursuit of excellence and avoiding the perils of perfectionism.

What You Can Do

1. Provide a supportive, encouraging climate.
Adopt a sympathetic, patient approach with your students so they feel safe taking risks and are not afraid of your reactions if they make a mistake. At the beginning of the year, let them know that your goal for them is to improve rather than to perform perfectly. When a child does make a mistake, find a way to put a positive spin on it (for example, "You're very close" or "That's not quite right, but it's a very good guess").

2. Avoid putting down the student.
Although disparaging criticism should be avoided with all students, it can be especially disheartening for the perfectionistic student. Focusing on her flaws may only intensify her determination to perform perfectly and stifle her willingness to take risks. If you need to correct the student, do so in an emotionally neutral way that helps her understand the source of the problem without speaking negatively of her performance.

3. Accentuate the student's successes, and downplay her failures.
Help the student achieve success in school by giving her work that is somewhat challenging but not so difficult that she will lose confidence or become anxious. Demonstrate her successes to classmates by, for example, displaying her artwork on the wall or reading one of her essays to the class. (Get her okay before doing this.) Praise her for her efforts or accomplishments, but do not fall into the trap of only praising her for perfect performance. When she performs poorly on a task, do not sympathize with her or draw attention to her performance. If it was a tough assignment, let her know that you expected students to struggle with the task because of its difficulty.

4. Let the student know that mistakes are expected.
Give her license to make mistakes by explaining that they are a normal part of learning and typically reflect a specific weakness that can be corrected rather than a general lack of ability. In showing her that even accomplished people are far from perfect, you might point out that Babe Ruth struck out 1,330 times and that Thomas

Edison had over 1,500 failures before finding a filament that would work in a light bulb. You might even have your students share amusing mistakes they have made, making sure to chime in with your own. Also consider posting sayings in your class such as, "Making mistakes is part of being human, so if you don't make mistakes you are not human," or "We all make mistakes; that's why they put erasers on pencils."

5. Talk with the student about the downside of perfectionism.

Show how her very high standards can hamper her performance and productivity. Give her examples, perhaps citing her tendency to constantly redo papers or begin projects too late. Discuss how much time and energy it takes to try to produce perfect work and how she will miss out on important and enjoyable activities as a result. Also let her know that students do not produce their best work when they are worried and anxious and that her work may actually improve if she learns to relax.

6. Help the student set realistic goals.

Help set the student's sights on goals that she views as achievable and positive. Suggest that she develop concrete goals that represent realistic progress from her current level. You can show her the progress she has made by saving her earlier work and comparing it to her later work or by using tapes or charts to demonstrate improvement.

7. Challenge the student's faulty beliefs.

For some students, their need to be perfect is driven by the way they think. They may believe that others will perceive them as weak or flawed if their performance is anything less than perfect. They may think that when someone offers a suggestion or criticism, it means they are incompetent or a bad person. As the student talks about herself, listen for faulty beliefs that need to be challenged. For example, if she is fearful of making a mistake, ask her what she thinks will happen if she does.

8. Stress effort and learning in addition to evaluation.

Help the student appreciate that there is more to an educational task than the grade she earns or the recognition she receives. Comments such as, "I'm impressed with how much work you put into this project" or "It seems that you really learned a lot from working on that report," convey that schoolwork is not just about earning high marks. Reinforce this message by praising students who have put forth admirable effort, even if their final product is weak.

9. Keep a close eye on the student.
Help the student get off to a good start, which is often a problem for the perfectionistic student. Monitor her closely to see if she is becoming frustrated or distressed with her performance. If so, consider adjusting the difficulty level of the task or suggesting a change in strategy. Perfectionistic students often become bogged down with minor aspects of an assignment, so you may need to help her refocus on the more important parts of the task. Find a way to turn failures into successes; for example, if the student wants to throw away a composition or picture, try to salvage her effort by showing her what is good about it and building on it.

10. Spell out your expectations to the students.
When giving an assignment or project, describe precisely what you expect from the students in terms of content, format, and length. This will lessen the chance that the perfectionistic student will set unrealistic standards for herself. Also let the students know your primary purpose with the assignment so they do not get hung up with other concerns. For example, in asking students to submit notecards with research information for a report, you might tell them that your chief concern with the notecards is content rather than grammar and spelling.

11. De-emphasize the grading of the student's work.
Help the student see that her score or grade is not your sole concern. In reviewing her assignments, you might make comments rather than give her a grade or a number. Also highlight what she has done well, and indicate how she might improve, without making negative or discouraging remarks. In marking papers on which answers are either right or wrong, you might mark only the correct answers.

12. Encourage class participation.
The student may shy away from volunteering in class for fear of getting the wrong answer. In encouraging her to contribute,

make sure to spare her any embarrassment. Ask her questions that you are confident she can answer or that she has been prepared for in advance, or have her read correct responses from her paper. If you ask her a question and she blanks out or says nothing, try restating the question in a different form or leading her toward the right answer. Or you might let her off the hook by giving her the answer while saying something like "That was a tough one. I expected students to have trouble with that," and then moving on. Try to come back to her soon with a question you know she can answer.

13. Use a divide-and-conquer strategy with long assignments.

The perfectionistic student can feel overwhelmed by long or complicated assignments. Help lessen her anxiety and get her started by breaking the task into manageable steps. For example, if your students are doing a report, divide the assignment into the following parts: taking notes on notecards, making an outline, developing a rough draft, and writing the final draft. Set a deadline for completion of each step.

14. Encourage the student to finish assignments.

If the student is having difficulty completing tasks because she is rarely satisfied, use light pressure to get her to finish without punishing her. You might set a firm time limit for the task and insist that she submit the assignment, even if it is not finished or she is not completely satisfied. If she is constantly erasing, suggest she cross out instead; if the problem continues, consider removing the eraser from the pencil. If she is using paper after paper, consider setting a limit on the number of pieces she can use.

See Also

Participation, Lack of Class

Seatwork Problems

Playground Problems

For many students, recess is their favorite school activity. For many teachers who monitor recess, it is their least favorite. Recess is an activity that is fraught with problems, often of a disciplinary nature. This is not surprising. Because recess is highly unstructured, there is often limited supervision and children are engaging in physical activity.

The difficulties that you may encounter on the playground run the gamut of behavior problems. These may include two children arguing over the score of a game, a student ridiculing a classmate for his awkward physical skills, a student intentionally damaging playground equipment, a child crying because he has no one to play with, or a student upset about losing who is angrily accusing his classmates of cheating.

Because of the range of issues that arise on the playground, it presents you with opportunities to teach your students important lessons about such issues as displaying good sportsmanship, treating others kindly, resolving conflicts, and respecting property. Your students will learn these lessons most effectively if you deal with them immediately in the context of the problems that emerge during recess. It is important to tackle them head-on for another reason: if the problems that occur on the playground are not resolved, they may carry over into the classroom.

What You Can Do

1. Go over the playground rules.   If you are responsible for monitoring your students on the playground, explain your rules to them on the first day and periodically review them. If another school staff member has this responsibility, tell your students that another person is in charge of the playground but that you expect them to follow her rules without exception. In setting out playground rules, consider such issues as taking turns, sharing equipment, playing fair, treating playground equipment with care, and putting it away at the end of recess. Let them know that recess is a privilege and any student who cannot follow the rules will lose that privilege. If necessary, take your students to the playground and demonstrate the dos and don'ts of recess. Give special attention to the issue of teasing. Make it clear that ridicule or put-downs of any kind will not be tolerated and that no one is to be made fun of because of their athletic ability. Another topic you might put on your meeting agenda: being a good sport, namely, being both a gracious winner and loser.

2. Provide a range of activities.

Although most students opt for physical activities during recess, make sure to have items for students who prefer quieter activities. Have a box on the playground with such items as games, books, and art materials. In a similar vein, consider organizing cooperative activities for students who prefer to avoid the pressures of competition. As an example, you might have a group of students working together to assemble a puzzle or paint a mural.

3. Stay in contact with the playground monitor.

Ask the monitor to let you know if any of your students have had significant or continuing difficulties on the playground. Make sure your class knows the two of you will be in contact. Although consequences are most effective when implemented immediately on the playground, you might tell a misbehaving student you are disappointed in his behavior; then review the rules with him. Also ask the monitor to let you know if a student with a history of playground problems has been behaving appropriately during recess so you can acknowledge him.

4. Talk with the student about his behavior.

Help the student understand why his behavior is inappropriate and how it presents a problem. He may not understand, for example, that he created a safety concern or hurt another student's feelings. Give brief reminders to the student before recess about the importance of following the rules and the potential consequences if he does not.

5. Coach students with poor playground skills.

Some students need guidance about how to handle social situations. Give them help at the time the problem occurs, but treat it as a teaching situation rather than a disciplinary situation. If, for example, a student yelled at his teammate "How can you miss that ball? You really stink," you might take him aside and in a quiet way help him understand how he hurt the other student's feelings and what he might have said instead, for example, "Good try. You'll get it next time." When you see him handling a similar situation in a more appropriate or sensitive manner, let him know how proud you are of him.

6. Provide immediate consequences.

You will be more effective deterring future misbehavior on the playground if you respond immediately, especially with younger children. Similarly, if the playground is supervised by monitors, it is more effective for them to assign consequences at the time of the problem than tell you about it and have you give consequences later on. Of course, the monitor may still want to inform you, especially if the problem may carry over into the classroom, such as a fight between two classmates.

7. Have the student complete a playground report.

Keep a clipboard and pencil and paper handy. If a student has misbehaved on more than one occasion, remove him from the activity and have him fill out a form asking him to describe what happened, what he did, how his behavior might have affected other students, and what he can do differently next time. Keep these forms to help identify patterns and to review with the student at other times.

8. Have a problem-solving bench.

If students have a conflict on the playground, tell them that they either need to drop it and continue playing or talk it out while sitting on a bench set aside for that purpose. Help structure this talk by telling them they need to each tell their side of the story while the other is quiet and then together figure out a solution to the problem. Let them know that the point is not to figure out who is at fault or who started it but what each can do to solve the problem. Tell them that they must inform you as to how they solved the problem. Keep an eye on them as they try to resolve the conflict, and intervene if necessary.

9. Give the student a time-out on the playground.

If a student is not following the rules of the playground, you may want to have him sit down quietly for a short period, perhaps five or ten minutes. If he talks or gets up, then the time-out period starts from the beginning. The possibility of being benched, even for a short time, will be frustrating to many students and may be sufficient to get most to comply. If the misbehavior is serious or continuous, you may want to remove the student from recess for a longer period, perhaps a day or even a week.

10. Practice inclusion on the playground.

If a student is playing by himself and being ignored by his classmates, encourage other students to include him in their activity. Keep a watchful eye to make sure they are interacting with him in a kind manner. You might also give the isolated student a fun activity to do to lure other students to play with him.

11. Give the student a playground job.

You may be surprised to find that a student who can be a hellion on the playground can be a cooperative and reliable helper. If he is interested, you might have him be responsible for giving out or collecting playground equipment. Or you might have him serve as a safety monitor, although you may need to give him some coaching on how to do this in a fair and kind manner. Keep a close watch in the beginning to make sure he does not go too far in exercising control over classmates.

12. Avoid hurt feelings when choosing teams.

Here's a simple and effective way of avoiding the hurt of being the last student chosen. Appoint two captains, and have them alternate choosing players for their team. When about half the students have been chosen, have the remaining students alternate choosing which team they want to be on.

See Also

Aggressive Behavior

Bothering Classmates

Bullying

Friends, Lack of

Teasing

Pouting

The pouting student has a way of making her presence known. When told something she does not like, she may stamp her feet in frustration, fold her arms in defiance, and glare at you in anger. Pouting is her way of communicating her displeasure with your decision and giving you notice that she will put up a fight, even if nonverbal in form.

Her pouting may be triggered by a myriad of classroom situations—being corrected by the teacher, being chosen last on the playground, not getting called on during a lesson, not understanding the teacher's directions, or being called last to line up to go to lunch. It is hard for a teacher to predict what will give rise to sulky behavior.

Pouting is the student's way of protesting. Her resistance may take the form of clamming up and shutting down. She may refuse your overtures to join in with the other students and fail to comply with your instructions. Her silent demonstration may nonetheless have a large impact on your class. Her petulant behavior may distract you from your lesson and disturb the concentration of your other students. In addition, her pouting may give rise to peer conflicts, as classmates accuse her of acting in an immature way.

The student's pouting may convey different messages. She may not be used to things not going her way, and her pouting may be her way of telling you that she is frustrated. Or she may have had many experiences with failure, and her pouting may be her way of saying, "I'm not going to take it anymore." Or she may perceive your decisions as personal attacks on her, and her pouting may be her way of telling you that she is hurting. Or she may feel a sense of being ignored, and her pouting may be her way of gaining your attention and sympathy.

Whatever the reason for her behavior, helping the pouting child give up her hurt calls for a mild response or perhaps no response at all. Scolding the child who pouts will only make her more determined to continue her emotional display. A more effective approach is to help her learn more appropriate ways to express her feelings and get your attention. It also calls for showing the student, through your reactions to her, that she cannot get what she wants with immature or sulky behavior. In this way, she may come to see the futility of pouting.

What You Can Do

1. Look for a pattern in the student's pouting.
Observe when she is most likely to pout, what she is doing at the time, and what seems to trigger her sulky behavior. You may find, for example, that her pouting tends to take place on the playground or during tests or while waiting to get help from the teacher. This information may help you anticipate when the behavior will occur and take preventive measures. You might even write down brief descriptions of the pouting incidents and their context and inform the student you are doing this. Periodically review the information with her, letting her know the situations that seem to trigger the behavior and whether the behavior is increasing or decreasing. This will help raise her awareness of her pouting and may lead to a decrease in the behavior.

2. Have a private chat with the student.
If she pouts often when frustrated, validate her feelings by letting her know that we all feel disappointed when we do not get what we want. Let her know that it is okay to feel frustrated, but it is not okay to refuse to participate in class activities or follow your instructions. Suggest ways she can calm down when upset, including getting a drink of water, taking some deep breaths, or counting backwards from 10. Also help her understand the impact of her pouting, namely, that adults may perceive her as being disrespectful, and classmates may see her as acting like a younger child and start to avoid her.

3. Encourage the student to express her feelings in an appropriate manner.
While meeting with her privately, help her understand that there are more appropriate and effective ways of conveying her frustration and disappointment than pouting. Consider role-playing with her by giving her some situations that have previously elicited her pouting and having her try out other responses. You might suggest or model some responses of your own.

Elementary Teacher's Discipline Problem Solver

Encourage her to use "I messages" to convey how she is feeling without describing what others are doing to her. Let her know that it is not easy to convey feelings of disappointment in a calm and respectful manner but that you are confident she can learn to do it.

4. Redirect the pouting student.

You might put your arm around her and, without addressing her frustration, gently guide her to the next activity. Try to get her started in the activity as a way of distracting her from her distress. This may be especially effective with younger students.

5. Try to ignore pouting intended to get your attention.

If you conclude that the student is trying to get your attention or manipulate your reaction by pouting, try to avoid paying attention to her and certainly do not give in. Tell her that you do not respond to students who are pouting but you will be happy to talk with her when she stops. If she stops, give her immediate and positive attention. If she does not, walk away from her without giving her any further attention. Although you might talk with her later on about her pouting, you want to make sure she does not perceive a direct link between her pouting and your paying attention to her or giving her what she wants. If she does, her pouting will likely continue.

6. Praise nonpouting behavior.

Keep a watchful eye on the student's behavior, and if you see her handling frustration or disappointment appropriately and communicating in a respectful manner, acknowledge her with praise and attention.

7. Avoid confronting the student.

The challenge with the student who tends to pout is to get her to do what you want without provoking resistance. This calls for treading gently by avoiding harsh treatment such as punishing or scolding and using language that invites cooperation ("I would appreciate it if . . . ") rather than demands compliance ("You must . . . "). Teacher insistence often breeds student resistance. One way of eliciting cooperation is to give the student a choice of two options, both of which are acceptable to you. In this win-win scenario, the student feels a sense of control and you gain her cooperation. If you need her to stop a behavior and there is no choice in the matter, tell her you understand her disappointment and explain why she cannot continue. Suggest another activity that she enjoys and meets with your approval.

8. In disciplining the student, focus on her behavior rather than on her personally.

The student who pouts will often exhibit this behavior when reprimanded. This does not call for backing off from the way you discipline her. You want to use the same disciplinary measures for her that you do for other students, but make sure she understands that your concern is with her behavior and not with her as a person. As an example, if a student is constantly calling out, you might say, "Antonia, when you call out, other children do not get a chance to participate. Please raise your hand from now on," rather than "Antonia, you are being a rude and inconsiderate student. You know better than that."

9. If necessary, help ease the student's academic difficulties.

If your observations suggest that her pouting is related to academic frustration, help her understand that failure is a normal part of learning and that all students encounter academic difficulties at some point. You might tell her that Lincoln lost seven elections before being elected president. Let her know you understand her frustration, but then work with her to find ways to promote her academic success. As an example, if the student becomes readily frustrated with schoolwork, start out with problems or tasks that you know she can do and then, as her confidence grows, gradually increase the difficulty level.

10. Showcase the student's successes.

The pouting student is often a discouraged student. Look for opportunities to highlight her accomplishments to other students. You might, for example, have her tutor another student in a subject she does well in, display her artwork in the classroom, have her demonstrate how to do a math problem on the board that you know she can do, or read one of her essays to the class.

11. Find opportunities for the student to feel important in the classroom.

The child who pouts may be conveying through her behavior that she feels discouraged and inadequate. Try fostering a sense of importance by giving her classroom jobs or finding ways she can help others. Some possibilities: serving as line leader, being on the safety patrol, explaining to a classmate how to do an assignment, serving as the class computer expert, taking a new student on a tour of the school, or being a buddy to a student who speaks little English. Express your confidence that she can do this job well.

See Also

Crying, Frequent

Dependent Behavior

Disruptive/Uncooperative Behavior

Self-Esteem, Low

Whining

Racially Offensive Language

With the increasing diversity of America's schools, teachers are educating more and more students from different cultural backgrounds. Although this can be an enriching experience for students, it can present teachers with the challenge of dealing with racial prejudice.

Racially offensive comments can have a disruptive effect on your class. They can be very hurtful to the child who was the target of the comments. In addition, his academic achievement may suffer because he is unable to give his full attention to schoolwork. Racial prejudice may also have an impact on the rest of your class by creating a tense classroom climate that diverts students from learning and you from teaching.

Teachers play a vital role in combating racial bias. In responding to racially offensive language, keep in mind that your primary goal is to challenge and change the perceptions of the students who have made the derogatory remarks. You will be more likely to accomplish this goal by helping them see the inaccuracy, unfairness, and hurtfulness of their comments rather than by punishing or yelling at them.

In addition to dealing with individual incidents of racial bias, you need to look at the larger picture and find ways to promote racial tolerance and understanding in your class. Toward this end, you need to encourage children of different backgrounds to interact in school so they learn to feel comfortable with each other and realize they have more similarities than differences. It is hard for prejudice to flourish in an environment of understanding and companionship.

What You Can Do

1. Make it clear to your students that racial comments are prohibited.

As part of your discussion with your class about ridicule, let your students know that they are not permitted to make offensive comments of any kind to their classmates. Using terms that are appropriate to your students' age, explain that offensive comments include not only teasing, name calling, and put-downs but negative comments about race, religion, or ethnic background. Let them know that you will take comments of this nature very seriously. Ask your class for a show of hands to demonstrate that they agree with and will follow this rule.

2. Be aware of any biases you have.

Although we all like to think of ourselves as unprejudiced and fair-minded, it is the rare person who does not have some stereotypical views of people from backgrounds different from ours. There is also a tendency to view differences as deficits. Examine your own cultural perceptions, and be careful that they do not limit your understanding of a child from that culture or send biased messages to your other students. Rather, be a positive role model; show them how to reach out to and show respect for those from different racial or ethnic groups.

3. Have a discussion with your class about diversity.

Ask your students to name some ways that children are alike. You may need to prompt them by asking, for example, "What do you think makes all kids your age happy? Sad? Frustrated?" Then ask them for some ways that children are different. To reinforce the point that all children are different in some way, have them raise their hands or go to a corner of the room, depending on the color of their eyes, or their place of birth, or their favorite foods, or the color of their hair. Emphasize that it is okay to be different. Go one step further by telling them they should take pride in their background, even if different from most of their classmates.

4. Conduct a lesson about dealing with racial bias.

Help your students understand at a level appropriate to their age what discrimination is, citing specific examples. Talk with them about how children sometimes make fun of others who are different in some way, perhaps because they wear glasses or have an unusual hairstyle or have a different skin color. Tell your class that these comments can be very hurtful to the student being talked about. Ask them if they have ever been made fun of for some aspect of their appearance or background and how it felt. You might share an experience of your own.

Racially Offensive Language

Also help them learn how to respond assertively but not antagonistically if a student makes a comment about their skin color, ethnic background, or religion. You might suggest that they say something like "That's a really mean thing to say. And besides it's not true," and then walk away.

5. Challenge racial comments publicly.

If a student makes a racially biased comment in class, respond to it then and there and do it so your other students can hear you. Let the offending student know that these comments are hurtful to others and unacceptable in your class. If the comment reflects a lack of knowledge, provide information to refute what he said. In this way, you are providing support to the student who was the target of the comments and giving a message to all your students that such comments will be taken seriously and challenged. You may also want to speak with both the offending and offended student privately.

6. Speak to the offending student.

Your purpose here is not to punish or yell at him but rather to challenge and change his perceptions. Reinforce what you said in class, namely, that such comments are unacceptable and can be hurtful, but tell him that you don't think he is a mean person. Find out if he understands what the words he used mean and why they might hurt another's feelings. Ask him if the other student did anything to anger him or if he was upset or feeling hurt for another reason. Find out if he was ever made fun of for any reason and how it felt. Ask him if he has any suggestions for how he can make it up to the student. You might suggest that he write a letter of apology. If the offensive comments persist after this discussion, contact the parents and ask for their support in solving this problem.

7. Speak to the offended student.

Talk to her privately, and let her know that you are sorry she had to hear those comments. Let her know that what was said was untrue as well as unkind. Tell her that you have spoken to the student who made the comments and you believe it is unlikely to happen again. Encourage her to come to you if anyone makes offensive comments to her, and let her know that you will respond immediately.

8. Put students in heterogeneous cooperative learning groups.

There is no better way of helping children of different backgrounds learn about and feel comfortable with each other than by bringing them together for a common purpose. An effective way of doing this is to arrange for children to work together in cooperative learning groups. Similarly, you may want to arrange for students to get to know each other by arranging for them to sit together at lunch or be partners during learning activities. These experiences may help to reduce bias by helping children from different backgrounds appreciate that they share much in common. It is no surprise that studies show that prejudice is reduced when students have a chance to get to know each other through such activities as an athletic team or the school band.

9. Help your students understand their own cultural backgrounds.

By learning about their own heritage, students may be more respectful of children from backgrounds different from theirs. Probably the best way to help a child learn about his cultural heritage is to go right to the source—his family. Have your students interview their parents and grandparents to find out where they came from and what some of their family traditions were. Teach them how to construct a family tree, and have them do one for their own family, noting when and where family members were born and what their occupations were.

10. Use multicultural teaching materials.

Look critically at the materials you use to make sure they are sensitive to different racial and ethnic groups and present them in a favorable light. You might, for example, make sure that your read-aloud books are relatively free of stereotypes and have characters from various cultural backgrounds, that you have dolls of different racial groups, and that you use paints and markers that include a variety of skin tones.

11. Make sure your bulletin boards reflect a multicultural society.

It is important that all your students see themselves reflected in the images of people displayed in your classroom, so make sure the pictures include people from different racial and ethnic groups. Do this all year round, not just during Black History Week. You may want to establish a picture file of people of diverse backgrounds and then change the pictures on display every so often.

Racially Offensive Language

12. Foster respect for children from different cultural backgrounds. One way of doing this is to have international days when students bring in foods that are characteristic of their culture. Be a participant in this event by bringing in a dish from your own cultural heritage. You might also have music of different cultures playing in the background.

See Also

Angry Outbursts

Bullying

Rude/Disrespectful Behavior

Sexually Offensive Behavior

Teasing

Rude/Disrespectful Behavior

Although the basic mission of school is to teach children the three R's, a fourth R merits teachers' attention: respect. Just as students need to master reading, writing, and arithmetic, they also need to learn the importance of acting respectfully toward their teacher as well as their classmates. Helping children learn to relate in a kinder and gentler manner to others has taken on added significance in recent years, as individuals in our society have arguably grown more contentious and less civil toward each other.

Children, it is said, can be cruel. We only need witness the unkind things they may do to their classmates, such as calling them names, pulling their chair from under them, making a snide comment, or excluding them from games to appreciate their capacity for cruelty. But it is also true that they are not innately so. If students are acting in a rude or unkind manner toward a fellow student, there is an underlying reason for their behavior. They may be upset with or angry at the student or someone else; they may be frustrated by their academic difficulties; they may be looking to gain status with their peers. Whatever the reason, you certainly do not want to ignore or excuse their behavior, but you want to try to understand its source and then try to address those concerns. If you fail to confront one student's rude behavior, you may be facing a chorus of disrespectful voices.

Just as children have a capacity for cruelty, they also have a capacity for caring. An important part of helping students learn to act in a respectful manner is to try to stimulate and nurture this innate potential for kindness. As with an academic subject, students may need specific lessons in respectful behavior, including help in learning how to be kind to one another as well as opportunities to practice this behavior.

What You Can Do

1. Model respectful behavior.
Probably the best way to encourage your students to act respectfully toward you and classmates is to act in a respectful manner

toward them. As the saying goes, example is the best teacher. You can provide a positive example by fostering a climate of acceptance and support and by treating students in a kind and patient manner without talking down to them. Look for opportunities to show them they are important and be attentive to their concerns. Avoid sarcasm or put-downs of any kind. If you are taking a child to task for misbehaving, you can talk to her in a firm manner and get your point across without being rude or impolite.

2. Talk with your class about the importance of acting respectfully.

When you describe your rules to the class in the beginning of the year, make sure that a rule about acting respectfully is on the list. Give some examples of kind and unkind behavior, asking students to offer some ideas of their own. Help them understand how acts or words of unkindness can cause a child real pain. You might invite students to talk about times when they were victims of unkindness or volunteer an experience of your own.

3. Have a private talk with the student.

If you observe a student acting in a rude or impolite manner, take her aside and talk with her. If you confront her publicly, she may feel compelled to continue to act disrespectfully to show her peers that she can stand up to you. Tell her that you are disappointed in her behavior. Let her know that her comments might have hurt the other child's feelings, but add that you are sure she did not mean to hurt the other child. Inquire if she is upset about something that somebody said or did. Ask her what she could have said instead, perhaps offering some examples of your own. Ask her to apologize to the child.

4. Teach the vocabulary of kindness.

Make it easy for your students to talk kindly to each other by giving them the words and phrases they need. On the bulletin board, put up a list of "Terms of Respect" that includes phrases that can be used to convey kindness, courtesy, and caring. This list might include such phrases as "please," "thank you," "excuse me," "I like the way you . . .," "Do you want to play with us?" "You did a great job," and others. Have students suggest some of their own.

5. Role-play social situations with your students.
Consider posing some common school scenarios and asking your students how they might handle them in a respectful manner. In this way, they can hear what their classmates might say and do and also have a chance to try out their own responses. Give them feedback by having them consider whether their response is likely to get their point across without resulting in a conflict with the student. If you find that younger students are unable to talk about these situations, you might act them out using puppets. The following are some examples of situations that you might present:

- A student cuts in front of you in line.
- A student calls you a name.
- A student takes the ball away from you on the playground.
- You accidentally bump into a student in the hallway.
- A student calls you out in a kickball game, and you are sure you were safe.

6. Encourage students to use "I messages" to express their feelings.
Although ignoring a rude comment can be an effective way for a student to respond, she may also get the point across by conveying her feelings directly to the offending student. Teach her to express her feelings without eliciting an angry or hurtful response by talking about its impact on her. For example, a student who has been made fun of might say to the teaser: "It hurts my feelings when you talk about me that way. I really don't appreciate it, and I'd like you to stop."

7. Establish a class signal to alert students to disrespectful behavior.
Develop a nonverbal signal such as a thumbs-down sign to let students know that they are saying or doing something that is rude or disrespectful. You may need to say their name first to get their attention. In this way, you can nip disrespectful behavior in the bud with minimal disruption to your class. You may even start seeing your students give the signal to their classmates.

8. Catch the student being kind.

Acknowledge her when you see her acting in a kind or helpful manner to either you or her classmates. Describe the specific behavior that you observed. Do this publicly (unless you think it would embarrass her) to spur other children to engage in acts of kindness. As an example, you might say to a student, "Jesse, it was so nice of you to sit with Julio after he hurt himself on the playground. That was a very caring thing to do." Make a special effort to find something positive to say about students who are prone to unkind behavior, even if it is a small gesture.

9. Have a courtesy display on the bulletin board.

When you observe an act of kindness by one of your students, describe the act with the student's name on a 3" × 5" card or a heart-shaped piece of paper and tack it to the display. Encourage students to tell you about actions of classmates for posting on the display, or have them write out the cards and submit them to you. This may give rise to a chain reaction of compliments that has a contagious effect on your class.

10. Encourage students to show appreciation to each other.

Here are some ways to do this:

- Establish a box that students can place notes in complimenting their classmates for something they said or did. At the end of the week, read these notes to the class.

- Name a "student of the week," and then develop a poster about her that includes positive comments from classmates.

- Have a class meeting periodically in which students gather in a circle and compliment or express appreciation to a classmate. Only allow positive comments, and make sure that all students are acknowledged at least every other meeting. You may need to get the ball rolling by being the first to talk about a student's act of kindness.

11. Reward the entire class for kind behavior.

Keep a jar on your desk, and every time you observe an act of kindness by one of your students, put a marble in the jar. Once the jar is full, give the class a special prize or privilege that it has previously selected.

12. Have a raffle to encourage kind behavior.
Every time you observe a student engaging in an act of kindness toward you or another student, give her a ticket that she can deposit in a box in the classroom after writing her name on it. At the end of the week, draw a ticket from the box and give the student with the winning ticket a special prize or privilege. Obviously, the more tickets a student earns, the greater her chance of winning the raffle.

13. Pass around a kindness necklace.
If you see a student acting in a kind or courteous manner, give her a necklace to wear. Tell your students that if they are given the necklace, they are to pass it on to another student whom they have observed to be acting kindly. You might do this one day a week or month, but let your students know that you expect them to act kindly all year round.

14. Do class projects that involve helping others.
These projects may help your students experience the satisfaction of giving to others and stimulate their kinder and gentler impulses. The activities are only limited by your imagination. Some examples: tutoring younger children, writing letters to soldiers who are stationed abroad, singing a holiday song for senior citizens in a nursing home, and raising money for a cause endorsed by your students.

See Also

Argumentative Behavior

Back Talk

Racially Offensive Language

Sexually Offensive Behavior

Teasing

School Phobia/Separation Anxiety

A student who is absent frequently from school demands the teacher's attention. Although it may be that he is genuinely sick, it may also be that he is absent for reasons other than illness. If so, this could reflect some anxiety related to school and be the precursor to a more significant problem.

In most cases, a child's anxiety about attending school can be resolved and the child returned to school quickly with teamwork by parents and the teacher. In some cases, however, this anxiety can take the form of resistance to attending school. At its most extreme, this school resistance may become school phobia, also called school refusal. This is an intense anxiety reaction, often related to difficulty separating from parents, that results in a determined refusal to attend school.

This problem requires your immediate attention. Prolonged absence from school can give rise to significant academic and social difficulties. In addition, the longer the student is absent from school, the greater his anxiety about returning and the harder it is to get him back in school.

The school-resistant child may appear sad and withdrawn in school, often seeming on the verge of tears. He may shy away from interacting with classmates and seem tentative about doing schoolwork. He may make regular visits to the school nurse, complaining of stomachaches or headaches. Anxiety about being in school may turn into frequent resistance and in some cases full-fledged refusal. Persuasion, parental threats of punishment, even pressure from the principal may be futile in getting him back in school.

Kindergartners and first graders are especially prone to anxiety about school, although most students with beginning-of-school jitters eventually adjust as they begin to feel secure in the setting, trusting of the teacher, and comfortable with their classmates. Children may also experience school-related anxiety at the beginning of the week, after a school vacation, and after an absence due to an illness or an operation.

For some students, their resistance to school may be related to issues within the family. For others, it may stem from events in school. Some anxiety-provoking situations that may give rise to school resistance include difficulties with schoolwork, ridicule or bullying by classmates, an embarrassing incident, lack of acceptance by peers, loss of a close friend, and fear of a strict teacher. In identifying what may be causing a child's anxiety about school, think about what may have changed for him and observe carefully his interactions with peers.

What You Can Do

1. Make a call home.   If one of your students has been absent for even a short time, contact the parents to find out the reason. This call will convey your concern to the parents and the student. If you find that he will be out for a lengthy period, you might arrange for his classmates to write him some letters telling him they hope he comes back to school soon. When he returns, instruct your students to say simply that they are glad that he is back and not to bombard him with questions about why he was absent.

2. Make the student's immediate return to school a high priority.   Urge the parents of a school-resistant child to send him to school, even if he is upset. Reassure them that the school has dealt with this problem many times and most children adjust and calm down after a short period of discomfort. Let them know that the school will try to make their child as comfortable as possible and will cope with his distress as well as his tantrums. Be empathetic and understanding in talking with them, inasmuch as they will have their own anxieties about their child's problem. Advise them not to argue with or yell at their child before school but to tell him in a calm, matter-of-fact way that all children must go to school and that it is not possible for him to stay home. Urge them to stay the course by resisting their probable impulse to give in to the child and keep him home.

3. Consider adjusting the student's schedule.

Although ideally you want the student to return to school with the same schedule as his classmates, you may find that the only way you can get him to come to school is to make some adjustments in his school day. These adjustments might include these:

- Have the student go home for lunch.
- Have the parent come to school to eat lunch with him.
- Allow the student to call home during the day.
- Arrange for the parent to stay in school for part of the day (for example, by volunteering in the library).
- Arrange for the student to attend for part of the day.

With time, you will want to gradually phase out these adjustments, as the child begins to feel more settled in school. What you want to avoid is placing the student on home instruction; this will only make it harder to get him to return to school in the future.

4. Try to get to the root of the problem.

If the child's physician has ruled out a medical basis for his absences and you suspect they are due to anxiety about school, schedule a meeting with the parents to try to understand the reasons for the absences. You might involve the child in part or all of this discussion. If he has difficulty putting his concerns into words, mention some potential sources of anxiety in school. His reactions may tell you that you have hit a nerve: he may look away, pause, or become teary-eyed when you mention a sensitive area. If you are able to pinpoint the source of his distress, take his concern seriously and work together to develop some solutions. As an example, a teacher of a school-resistant student found from talking to his parents that he did not think he could wait until his class went to the bathroom, and he feared having an accident. This was easily resolved by changing the bathroom time.

5. If the student becomes upset in school, weather the storm.

Brace yourself for a crying episode after the parent drops him off, although you may be surprised at how quickly he calms down. These behaviors may be his way of testing your resolve. Although you may need some support from a classroom aide or the principal if his behavior is disrupting the class, strenuously avoid the impulse to call the parents to have them pick up their child. That will only make the next day that much harder. If he complains of a stomachache or headache and you conclude it is anxiety-related, send him to the nurse but make sure she is aware of the importance of keeping him in school.

6. Distract the student if he exhibits distress.

Try distracting him by involving him in an activity that he enjoys. Most likely, he will calm down relatively quickly.

7. Make the school setting inviting for the student.

Find out from his parents what kinds of activities are comforting to him, and try to incorporate them into the class routine. Also try to find a few minutes each day to talk with him about his interests or the activities he enjoys so that he comes to see you and, by association, school in a positive light. In addition, help him develop friendships with classmates so that he comes to feel a sense of belonging and acceptance in school.

8. Encourage the student to carry a security item.

You might ease his anxiety and help him cope with the separation by suggesting he carry an item during the day that connects him with home, such as a picture of his family or a favorite doll, book, or toy.

9. Reassure the student while acknowledging his fears.

Using a calm, supportive voice, tell him that you understand that he is nervous about being in school and away from home. If he is experiencing beginning-of-school jitters, let him know that many children find the first days of school hard because it is an unfamiliar place, with people in it they may not know. Listen intently to his concerns and fears while reassuring him that school will feel a little bit better each day. If you find that his anxiety about school is fueled by horror stories he has heard from other students, make sure he understands that his fears are unfounded.

10. Reassure the parents as well.
As the student shows signs of becoming more comfortable in school, give his parents a call to let them know. This will help give them some peace of mind and reinforce the message that sending him to school is the right approach, even in the face of his protests.

11. Reward the student for school attendance.
Work out a plan with the parents to provide incentives to the child for attending and participating in school. For example, he might receive points for participating in class, not crying in school, staying in school all day, and completing assignments. These points could be exchanged for special privileges or tangible rewards in school or at home. As his attendance stabilizes, you can gradually phase out the rewards.

12. If the attendance problem persists, suggest the parents obtain professional help.
Your school's guidance counselor, social worker, or school psychologist should be able to recommend a mental health counselor to the parents. Keep in mind that the initial focus of this counseling should be to help the parents take firm steps to get their child back in school at the earliest possible time.

See Also

Bullying

Crying, Frequent

Lateness

Self-Esteem, Low

Teasing

Seatwork Problems

Students may experience the same problems with seatwork that they do with homework. They may not attempt it. Or they may attempt it but not complete it. Or they may complete it but do it inaccurately or sloppily.

Seatwork problems may result from various factors, including difficulty understanding the directions, an inability to do the work, distractibility, poor time management, or lack of motivation. Although the causes vary, the results are often the same. The student may have mastered the art of procrastination and have trouble getting down to work. He may take the path of least resistance by doing as little as he can. And the work that he does do may be done haphazardly. Although he may come to believe that his failure to complete seatwork will not catch up to him, it almost always does.

How to respond to a student with seatwork problems depends on its cause, and thus you need to figure out the reason he is not completing the in-school assignments. This requires that you adopt a problem-solving mode in which you identify the source of the difficulty and then, if warranted, adapt your expectations and tailor your instruction to his needs.

What You Can Do

1. Set out clear expectations about seatwork.
Spell out precisely what your students need to do and how much time they have. Also describe your standards for written work. You might, for example, tell them that sloppy, crumpled, or torn papers are not acceptable, explaining that you cannot help them if their papers are not readable. Make sure they have the time and materials to complete the task. Encourage them to ask questions if they are confused about some aspect of the assignment.

2. Devise a system for students to get your attention.
You can have students alert you in a nonintrusive way that they need help by placing a visual cue on their desk. This might be a small flag stuck in a piece of clay, a 6" × 8" card

folded in half like a tent, or a Styrofoam cup placed upside down on the desk. Using these signals enables students to alert you that they need help while continuing to work until you can get to them.

3. Provide incentives to students who finish their seatwork.

You might, for example, allow students who have completed their seatwork to engage in pleasurable activities of their choosing. Or you might schedule a recreational activity at the end of the week for those who are up-to-date with their seatwork and homework. Students who have work that is outstanding must spend that time completing the work in class or in another supervised setting. These incentives may spur students to finish their work, but be on the lookout for students who rush through their work carelessly in order to participate.

4. Hold the student accountable for the seatwork.

If you are confident that the level and amount of the work are within the student's ability, require him to complete it. You might give him the seatwork he did not complete as homework (in addition to his regular assignments) or have him stay in during recess or after school to finish it.

5. Problem-solve with the student.

Talk with him in a nonjudgmental way to try to determine why he is having problems with seatwork: Does he understand the directions? Is the work too difficult? Is it too easy so that it holds little interest for him? Is he having problems concentrating? Are the assignments too long? If you can zero in on what may be impeding his seatwork, try to modify the task in accordance with his need. If the work is too difficult, you might give him an easier assignment. If he has difficulty reading and the task is to answer chapter-end questions, you might let him know the page where each answer can be found. Other accommodations are discussed later in this chapter.

6. Seat the student away from distractions.

Try to find a spot where you can monitor him closely and help him stay on task but where there are few distractions. If possible, avoid seating him near the pencil sharpener, window, or hallway—locations that are sure to divert his attention. You might want to seat him near your desk unless there is a lot of student traffic there. Also consider placing him next to an attentive student who is diligent about completing seatwork. A study carrel might enable the student to focus on his seatwork, but avoid this if the student feels singled out.

7. Help the student unclutter his desk.
Part of his difficulty in finishing seatwork may be due to the clutter on his desk, which causes him to have trouble focusing. Instruct him to eliminate these visual distractions by putting away all materials on his desk except those needed for the seatwork assignment.

8. Monitor the student's understanding of directions.
His failure to complete seatwork may be due to his confusion about what to do. If so, you might clarify his understanding of directions by having him repeat them to you. Also encourage him to check with you or another student if he does not understand the directions. Many students will choose to sit at their seat doing nothing rather than ask the teacher for help.

9. Signal the student that he is off task.
Arrange a private signal with him to encourage him to focus on the seatwork assignment. This signal might be a nod of the head, a wink of the eye, or a tug of the ear. If necessary, call his name quietly to get his attention.

10. Use a timer to keep the student on task.
Set the timer to go off at varying intervals. If the student is working when the timer goes off, give him a token or sticker while praising him for his attention to task. After he attains a set number of tokens or stickers, allow him to exchange them for classroom privileges or material items.

11. Arrange a seatwork buddy for the student.
Ask a responsible classmate to help the student complete seatwork. Tell the student to see his buddy for help before coming to you. Another source of peer support is to place him at a table with other students and make it clear that group members are expected to assist others in their group.

12. Allow the student to use a computer.

The student may be more motivated to complete seatwork if he can do it on a classroom computer. This option may be particularly appealing to students with handwriting difficulties.

13. Focus on quality rather than quantity.

If the student is having trouble completing seatwork but you are confident it is at the right level for him, consider reducing its length. He may be able to master the concepts with a shorter assignment. As an example, rather than give him twenty math problems, you might give him ten by having him do the even problems only. If your priority is that he complete the entire assignment, you may find that in his eagerness to finish, he may race through the task, producing careless or inaccurate work.

14. Provide the seatwork in chunks.

By giving him the seatwork in parts, it will seem more manageable to him and he will be more likely to tackle it. Allowing him to get up after each set also gives him a short break. As an example, if the assignment is to do ten problems, you might initially give him five problems. After he completes them, check them over to make sure he is on the right track. If so, give him five additional problems. As he does well with this pattern, you can increase the size of the chunks you give him.

15. Give the student some control over the seatwork assignment.

He may be more inclined to do the work if he has some say in the assignment or the way it is done. This might be as simple as allowing him to write with a colored pen or pencil of his choice or having him choose where he does the work (for example, at a table rather than at his desk).

16. Have the student begin his seatwork with you.

This way, you can assess if he understands what to do and how to do it. Once he completes a problem or two successfully with your assistance, let him continue on his own.

17. Prod the perfectionistic student to finish the task.
If you have a student with perfectionistic tendencies who wants to do a task perfectly or not at all, let him know there is nothing wrong with making a mistake (you might tell him that's why pencils have erasers). Try setting a firm time limit for the task, and ask him to hand in the assignment, even if he is not completely satisfied. If he is using paper after paper, consider limiting the number of pieces he can use. If he is constantly erasing, tell him to cross out instead or remove the eraser from the pencil.

18. Consider whether the student has a learning problem.
His problems completing seatwork may suggest the presence of a learning disability. Find some time to work with the student one-on-one to determine whether he understands the work and is able to do it successfully. Also review other work samples and his standardized test scores. If these point to the presence of a learning problem, talk with the principal about arranging an evaluation to determine whether he has a disability.

See Also

Attention Deficit

Disorganization

Forgetfulness

Hyperactivity

Listening Skills, Poor

Motivation, Lack of

Talking, Excessive

Self-Esteem, Low

Self-esteem, namely how a student views and values herself, can have a marked effect on almost everything she does—the way she engages in activities, the way she deals with challenges, the way she interacts with others. It can also have a significant impact on her academic performance, notably her desire to learn, her ability to focus, and her willingness to take risks. Positive self-esteem is one of the building blocks of school success and thus provides a firm foundation for learning.

Just as self-esteem can affect school performance, so too school performance can affect self-esteem. Children's experiences in school help to shape their perceptions of themselves as competent and capable learners. This process of self-assessment can begin early. Research shows that as early as kindergarten or first grade, students are already making judgments about their competence relative to classmates. The child who has difficulty keeping pace with her peers academically is likely to experience low self-esteem.

The student with high self-esteem is comfortable with who she is and what she can do. In contrast, the student with low self-esteem may feel that she cannot do anything right. These self-perceptions may affect how she responds in the classroom. She may become discouraged by experiences with failure, give up easily when frustrated, and shy away from academic challenges. The student with low self-esteem may also experience social and emotional problems. Fearful of rejection, she may withdraw from peers and spend most of her time engaged in solitary activities. She is also at increased risk for disciplinary problems in school.

Your challenge in working with children with low self-esteem is to restore their belief in themselves so they persevere in the face of academic challenges. You do not need a formal program to promote self-esteem, however. You shape self-esteem every day in the course of interacting with your students. Although you cannot teach your students to feel good about themselves, you can nurture their self-esteem through a continual process of encouragement and support. At its most basic, this means showing appreciation for the things your students do well, expressing confidence that they will improve in the areas where they don't do well, and adapting instruction so they can experience success.

What You Can Do

1. Provide an accepting atmosphere in which students feel valued.

Although you cannot give your students self-esteem, you can help nurture it by conveying a warm, supportive tone in your classroom. Treat your students with respect, especially those who are different, and do not allow them to make fun of or put down classmates. Help ease their anxieties about schoolwork by telling them that mistakes are expected and a normal part of learning.

2. Avoid acting in ways that your students perceive as belittling.

What you say or do can have a marked impact on your students' self-esteem. Even small actions or casual comments can boost their morale or send their spirits nose-diving. Bear in mind that they may construe ambiguous comments in unintended and often negative ways, so be clear in your communication.

3. Provide praise but make it specific and genuine.

Students are expert at distinguishing genuine feedback from empty compliments. Although they may dismiss vague words of praise as insincere and perhaps even phony, praise that suggests thoughtful appreciation of their work or effort will be meaningful to them. Toward this end, let a student know in specific terms what you like about her work or behavior and, if she is progressing slowly, praise her for small steps forward. If you sense that she is uncomfortable being praised in front of her classmates, tell her in private or send her a note. You might call her parents in her presence with news of a particular accomplishment.

4. Support the student academically.

Success is the best antidote to low self-esteem, and academic mastery is a surefire remedy for lack of academic self-confidence. Help chart a path toward success by carefully analyzing her weaknesses and finding ways to provide support, which might include extra help after school, remedial instruction, special education, outside tutoring, or peer tutoring. You might also adjust her classwork by giving her tasks that are within her ability and likely to lead to success. Also make sure she understands the directions—a problem for many students.

5. Help the student develop a realistic appraisal of her strengths and weaknesses.

Students with low self-esteem tend to dwell on their failures and dismiss their successes. They may discount as unimportant what they do well and give undue weight to what they do poorly. Help the student modify her perceptions by making a list with her of her strengths. At the same time, if she struggles in school, talk about a couple of areas where she has difficulty but express your confidence that with hard work she will improve. Make sure to let her know that every student has weaknesses, perhaps using the analogy of a student who has a vision problem and wears glasses but is healthy.

6. Show the student visible evidence of her progress.

Although expressing confidence in a student's ability is important, pep talks may not be enough. Help her appreciate her improvement by pointing to concrete signs of her growth, perhaps by taping her oral reading at the beginning of the year and comparing it to her later performance, showing her papers from earlier in the year and contrasting them with later papers, or demonstrating how the math problems she struggled with during the first marking period now come so easily to her. You might also have her place index cards with spelling or reading words she has mastered in a box to document her growth.

7. Highlight the student's accomplishments.

Look for opportunities to showcase the student's successes to her classmates. You might, for example, read one of her compositions to the class, display her artwork on the bulletin board, have her demonstrate how to do a math problem that you are confident she knows, or, if she is an ESL student, have her talk to the class in her first language. If she has a particular hobby or interest, suggest that she talk to the class about it. If necessary, have her rehearse in advance.

8. Help the student feel important through her classroom contributions.

You might give her classroom jobs or find ways that she can help others. Tell her that you are giving her this responsibility because you are confident she can carry it out well. You might, for example, have her take care of the rabbit in the class, take lunch money to the office, collect homework, help another student with a computer problem, read the school's morning announcements, answer the school phone while the secretary is at lunch, or tutor a student in a lower grade.

9. Talk with the student about her interests.

A student can gain self-esteem from involvement in activities that she cares about. Find a few minutes every day to talk with her about her favorite hobbies, sports, television programs, or musical groups. If necessary, ask her parents for this information to give you a basis for talking with her. Suggest ways she can pursue her interests in greater depth. You might even bring in a book or item from home related to one of her interests.

10. Help the student deal with adversity.

If she meets with academic difficulties, help her appreciate that failure is a normal part of learning and that everyone experiences disappointment or frustration at some point. You might tell her that Thomas Edison had over 1,500 failures before finding a filament that worked in a light bulb. Acknowledge her frustration, but then move on to helping her develop strategies for improving. Express your confidence that with hard work and your support she is likely to succeed.

11. Encourage a sense of belonging.

Students with low self-esteem are often isolated from their classmates. You can promote a student's peer involvement by finding ways to integrate her into activities either in or out of school. You might organize an activity for a group of students that includes her. Or you might ask a couple of friendly and accepting students to play with her during recess or invite her to eat lunch with them. If you have students pair up in class, assign her a kind and easygoing partner. You may also want to encourage her parents to arrange social contacts with classmates, perhaps suggesting potential playmates, or sign her up for community activities.

12. Let parents know of their child's successes. Although teachers are quick to let parents know when their child has a problem, they are not nearly as diligent about notifying them when she has a success. Consider sending a note home or calling parents when their child does something noteworthy, and tell the student you are doing this. This gesture may take you only a couple of minutes, but it can brighten the student's day and engender positive responses from the parents to their child.

13. Focus on the student's behavior rather than on her as a person when disciplining her. If a student with low self-esteem misbehaves in class, treat her as you would any other student, but make sure she understands that your concern is with her behavior and not with her as a person. For example, if a student is constantly calling out, you might say, "Rebecca, when you call out, other children do not get a chance to participate. Please raise your hand from now on," rather than "Rebecca, you are being a rude and inconsiderate student."

See Also

Crying, Frequent

Friends, Lack of

Shyness

Special-Needs Students

Suicide Threats

Teasing

Sexually Offensive Behavior

Students may exhibit sexually offensive behavior as early as elementary school. These behaviors may take the form of a student calling a child a name with sexual overtones, spreading sexual rumors about another student, making sexual comments to a classmate, and even touching another student inappropriately. Gender bias may also surface in the early years. Boys may tell girls they are not allowed to play in a game, or they may speak in a derogatory manner to female staff members.

The students who are the targets of this offensive behavior may experience embarrassment, distress, anxiety, and even fear. It can also make other children feel uncomfortable and insecure. Yet this behavior often continues unchecked because students are reluctant to report it or take on their harasser. They may be too embarrassed to tell you; they may fear retaliation; they may not want to be perceived as a tattletale, or they may believe that telling you would accomplish nothing or even make the problem worse.

As a result of this reluctance to report it, you need to keep a watchful eye for this type of behavior. And if you find out it is occurring, you need to take it seriously and respond immediately. Although it can be difficult to distinguish playful teasing from sexually offensive behavior, err on the side of not dismissing complaints. It is important that you give these incidents serious attention for another reason: parents have been successful in some cases in suing school districts for failing to protect their children from sexual harassment by another student.

If one of your students is engaging in sexually offensive behavior, find out if your school district has a sexual harassment policy and, if so, what types of behavior are included and to whom it is reported. Because of the sensitivity of this issue, make sure to discuss the student's behavior with his parents as well as the principal. You may also want to request to have the principal present if you are meeting with the student or his parents to provide support and verify what was said.

What You Can Do

1. Take reports of sexual comments seriously.
If a student tells you that another student is making sexual comments to her, follow up in every case. Do not dismiss a student complaint out of hand. Talk to the two students individually, and take notes on what they say. Suggestions for handling these meetings are discussed later in the chapter. Consider informing the parents and the principal, who may also want to speak with the students.

2. Respond immediately if you hear a student making sexual comments.
Tell him in a serious tone that his comments are inappropriate and you don't want to hear that kind of language again. Say this so your other students can hear you to give them the message that you take this behavior seriously. After this reprimand, proceed with your lesson or activity without giving the student any additional attention. Depending on the nature of his comments and whether this has occurred before, you may want to meet with the student privately and contact the parents.

3. Assess if the student understands the meaning of his words.
Although he no doubt appreciates the power of the words he used to get people's attention, he may not grasp their meaning. If you conclude he does not, make a judgment based on his age and your comfort level as to whether to explain what they mean. As an alternative, you might ask parents to do this.

4. Write down the student's comments.
Make sure he sees you doing this. He may ask what you are writing, but even if he doesn't, let him know you are making a record of his comments because you are considering showing them to the principal as well as his parents. You might have the student sign the paper, indicating that he made those comments.

5. Meet with the student privately.
Take him aside and, using a stern but not humiliating manner, let him know that his comments are unacceptable in your class and will not be tolerated. You may need to tell him the words he used that were objectionable. If this is the first time he has used this kind of

language, consider telling him that you will not be taking disciplinary action this time but you will if it happens again. If his language was insulting toward girls, you might inform him as to how offended you are when he treats females disrespectfully. Also let him know that other children may not want to be friends with him if he continues to use that kind of language.

6. If he continues to make sexual comments, provide disciplinary measures.
You may find that your public reprimand or private talk does not curtail the student's inappropriate comments. If so, consider providing some consequences, which might include after-school detention, loss of recess, or loss of a classroom privilege. Try to tie the consequence in with the setting where the behavior occurs. For example, if he is making these comments on the playground, you may want to make him stay in during recess for a period of time. Given the sensitive nature of the problem, you will also want to contact the parents if you haven't already.

7. Minimize contact between the students.
If the student is directing his offensive comments to a particular child, find ways to lessen their contact. If this means that a student needs to be moved or inconvenienced, make sure it is the student who is making the comments. For example, if a student is harassing another student on the school bus, ask the bus driver to assign the harassing student a specific seat, perhaps right behind the driver.

8. Meet with his parents.
Although it is often helpful to talk with parents when their child is exhibiting behavior problems, it is especially important to do this if he is making sexual comments. This can be a sensitive issue that calls for keeping parents informed of what their child is saying, what you are doing in response, and how classmates are reacting. Also obtain the parents' perspective on their child's behavior, including why they think he is making these comments and whether he is using this language at home. Ask for their support in trying to discourage this behavior. Consider involving the child in the meeting with his parents so he can see that both you and his parents are of one mind about the inappropriateness of his comments and the need for it to stop.

9. Contact other school staff about the student.   A student who is making sexual comments to other children is likely to make them in areas with minimal supervision, including the lunchroom, the playground, the hallway, and the bus. Talk with the adults who supervise these locations to let them know about the student's behavior, to get their observations, and to ask them to monitor his behavior carefully. Check in with them periodically regarding his behavior, and let the student know you will be doing this.

10. Talk with the student who was harassed.   Let her know that the comments made to her were very inappropriate and that she did nothing wrong. Tell her that she did not deserve to be treated in this manner and that you will talk with the offending student and take steps to get him to stop. Ask her to tell you if it happens again. You might want to give her suggestions about how to react if it does. Suggest a response such as the following: "What you said is really mean, and I don't like it, so stop it." Then tell her to walk away and ignore him.

11. Talk with your other students.   A student who is making sexual comments is often trying to impress or gain the attention of his classmates. Find a time to talk with your class when the student is not there, and ask them to not giggle, laugh, or join in if a student makes inappropriate comments. Suggest they respond in one of three ways: (1) ignore the comments, and go on with what they were doing; (2) tell him in a direct but not mean way that they do not like what he said, and then continue what they were doing without getting in an argument with him; or (3) let you know. You might give them an example of what they could say to the student.

12. Promote positive images of females.   In choosing books to read to your students, include stories of strong women who are accomplished in some respect or successful in facing challenges. With older elementary children, you may want to help them understand how the media may sometimes depict females in an unflattering manner. Introduce the concept of stereotypes, and point out examples of how girls and women can be portrayed on television, in magazine articles, and even in song lyrics in a restrictive and often negative manner.

See Also

Aggressive Behavior

Bullying

Masturbation

Racially Offensive Language

Rude/Disrespectful Behavior

Teasing

Shyness

The shy child is anything but a discipline problem. In fact, she is just the opposite. While many of her classmates work hard to get attention, sometimes in disruptive ways, she works equally hard to avoid it. Fearful of drawing attention to herself, she prefers to blend into the background. More spectator than participant, she tends to hang back rather than dive in. The shy child is anything but a risk taker.

She may only speak with the teacher and even then in a low-key voice. When asked a question, she may gaze downward and give monosyllabic responses, sometimes nodding or gesturing instead of speaking. Easily embarrassed, the shy child may hesitate to speak up in class. Reading aloud, giving oral reports, even doing show-and-tell may cause her considerable anxiety. And if she has a bad experience, she may be even more reluctant the next time. During recess, she may keep to herself; you may see her sitting against the wall or wandering the playground alone.

Her shyness may be misinterpreted by peers. They may see her as unfriendly and conclude that she doesn't want to play with them. As a result, they may begin to avoid her, thus reinforcing her shyness and denying her opportunities to learn how to socialize. In reality, the shy child usually wants to be involved with her classmates but may lack the social skills to do this effectively. She may not know how to begin or sustain a conversation so that making and keeping friends can be a major issue for her.

Teachers may also misread the shy child. They may mistake her reluctance to participate for lack of understanding. They may conclude she is academically slow and avoid calling on her in class on the assumption that she does not know the answer. Low teacher expectations may give rise to a self-fulfilling prophesy as her confidence lags and her effort declines, causing her to withdraw further. In other cases, the teacher may conclude that the shy child is simply a serious, well-behaved student who warrants little attention. Although it is true that a shy child is often a diligent student, she often needs the teacher's attention to give her the confidence to take risks in school and draw her out.

What You Can Do

1. Determine if the student's shyness is a problem for her.
It may be that despite her quiet, low-key style she is adapting well in the classroom and with her peers. If so, there may be little need for intervention. However, you may find that her shyness is interfering with her ability to make friends, her academic performance, her confidence speaking up in class, and her willingness to take advantage of school opportunities. If this is the case, help bolster her confidence in interacting with others, but make sure not to add to her anxiety by placing her in very uncomfortable situations. Also be careful about leading her to believe that there is anything wrong with her being shy.

2. Build rapport with the student.
The more successful you are in developing a trusting relationship with her, the more likely she is to develop the confidence to reach out to peers. Find time to do some activities with her that she enjoys, perhaps letting her teach you a game or skill that she does well. A shy child is often lacking in confidence and self-esteem, so be especially warm and nurturing with her, and make sure to praise her accomplishments. Encourage her to ask you for help when she does not understand something.

3. Make time to talk with the student privately.
Shy children may need practice speaking with individuals on a one-to-one basis. Even a few conversations with her every week can help improve her comfort and skill in interacting with others. Ask her about her interests or her activities, and use these as the basis for your conversations.

4. Place a shy student near the front of the room.
In this way, the child may be more willing to speak up in class because she will be less aware of the rest of the students. And by being closer to you, you can talk with her more easily. Also place students next to her who are likely to befriend her.

5. Help the student feel more comfortable speaking in front of the class.

You might ease her anxieties about public speaking by the following:

- Pose questions to her that you are confident she can answer successfully.

- Lead her to the correct answer with a hint if necessary.

- Have her speak to the class about a topic she knows well.

- Have her speak from her seat.

- Allow her to make a presentation as part of a group.

- Do not grade her for oral reports or penalize her for lack of class participation.

- Permit her to satisfy the requirement to make an oral report in a less threatening way (for example, a written report, an oral report to the teacher only, or an audio- or videotape of the presentation made at home).

6. Give the student a little push.

You may need to nudge her to do activities that require verbal interaction, even if they are mildly anxiety-provoking for her, as long as you are confident she can do them successfully. As one example, you might have her serve as the class messenger, which requires talking with school staff. Find something about her performance to praise. Give help if necessary, but you can gradually lessen your assistance as she appears more confident.

7. Put on your social director's hat.

The shy child may keep to herself, but this is probably due more to fear than desire. She most likely wants to be involved with her classmates, but staying to herself is often the less painful option. If she is socially isolated, orchestrate some interactions with her peers. You might organize an activity for a group of students, including the shy child. Or you might ask a couple of friendly and mature students to ask her to play during recess or join them at their lunch table. If you have students pair up in class, assign her a kind and easygoing partner. You may also want to encourage the student's parents to arrange social contacts with classmates, perhaps suggesting potential playmates. Also recommend that they involve their child in community activities she is interested in and where she is likely to do well.

8. Teach the student some basic social skills.

She may fail to understand some of the rules of social interaction that come so easily to her peers. Entering social situations may be especially difficult if she does not know the right words to use. If she does not, take her aside and teach her some "door openers" (for example, "Do you want to be my partner?"). If she is receptive, try role-playing with her. Impress upon her the importance of smiling and maintaining eye contact. In addition, give her some ideas of what she can talk about with peers during recess or after school.

9. Help the student adapt to new situations.

New activities often throw the shy child for a loop and may cause her to withdraw. If so, help prepare her for the new activity by giving her some advance notice and letting her know what she will likely encounter. Help bolster her confidence by having her rehearse or role-play a new situation (for example, have her practice an oral report with you or her parents).

10. Arrange for the student to work with younger children.

You may find that a child who is uncomfortable interacting with children her own age is surprisingly at ease with younger children. These kinds of activities may bolster her confidence when interacting with students in her own grade. You might, for example, send her into a kindergarten class to read a story or lead a game on the playground.

See Also

Crying, Frequent

Dependent Behavior

Friends, Lack of

Participation, Lack of Class

Self-Esteem, Low

Sleeping in Class

It is not very often that elementary students fall asleep in class, but when they do it can be a distraction to you and your students. It can also signify a problem that warrants your attention. If you have a student who is nodding off frequently, do some digging to find out why.

A student may fall asleep in class for a variety of reasons, including the following:

- He is going to bed too late.
- He is having trouble getting to sleep.
- He is bored in school and finds the work tedious.
- He has a learning problem and is trying to avoid having it exposed.
- He is depressed.
- He is not feeling well.
- He is not eating properly and as a result has little energy.
- He has a medical problem such as an allergy, diabetes, or hypoglycemia.
- He is experiencing a side effect of medication.
- He is using drugs or alcohol.

Knowing why the student is falling asleep will help guide you in figuring out how to respond and whether to deal with this as a medical concern, an emotional difficulty, a motivational problem, or a disciplinary issue.

What You Can Do

1. Wake up the student. Ask him if he feels all right and if not send him to the nurse. If he claims to be feeling okay, suggest he get a drink of water and go to the bathroom to wash his face to help overcome his fatigue.

2. Figure out why the student is sleepy.

Begin by talking with the student in private. Ask him why he gets so tired in school. He may not be able to give you a specific answer, so you will probably need to probe further. Ask what time he goes to bed, whether he is having trouble sleeping, whether he is on medication, and whether he is having any medical problems such as allergies. You might also talk with last year's teacher. Ask her if he tended to fall asleep last year, what the pattern was, and what strategies she found effective. Also look for a pattern by examining when and where he falls asleep in school. Toward this end, you may want to keep a diary. And of course you will want to talk with his parents.

3. Schedule a conference with the parents.

Ask the parents to come in to school so you can talk with them face to face. Be candid with them about their child's behaviors. They may be surprised to hear that he is falling asleep in school. Brainstorm together to try to figure out the reason for his sleepiness, and then come up with an action plan that you all support for how to deal with his falling asleep. You might want to suggest to the parents that they obtain a medical examination of their child.

4. Allow the student to take a nap—sometimes.

Some kindergartners or first graders may still need a nap during the day. Indeed, if you are teaching kindergarten, you may want to build a rest period into your class schedule, although you might phase it out during the school year to help prepare your students for first grade. You might allow an older student to go to the nurse to nap if your efforts to rouse him are unsuccessful. If he continues to fall asleep in class, contact his parents.

5. Seat the student at the front of the class or near your desk.

He will be less likely to fall asleep when seated near you, and if he does you will be sure to notice him. If he is seated elsewhere in the class, move toward him if you see him nodding off. Your close proximity may serve as a wake-up call. You might also consider seating him near the window; the light and fresh air may help to heighten his alertness.

6. Call on the student unexpectedly.
If he senses that you may call on him at any time, he may work harder at staying awake. If you notice that he is starting to nod off, ask him a question or give him a task to do in the classroom. The point here is to heighten his alertness, not to humiliate him, so give him a question that you are confident he can answer.

7. Present lessons that tap the student's interests.
You can make your lessons more stimulating for the student by learning about his interests, perhaps through an interest inventory, and then integrating them into your classroom activities. For example, if you are teaching a lesson on fractions and you know the student is a baseball fan, you might demonstrate how to work with fractions by figuring out baseball averages.

8. Have the student work with a small group or a partner.
In this way, he will not be able to fade into the background. He will be expected to contribute to the group, and his group members are not likely to be understanding if he dozes off.

9. Keep the student active.
Give him activities to do during those times of the day when he is most prone to falling asleep. In fact, incorporating physical activity into your class schedule is a good practice to follow with all of your students. These activities might include doing stretching exercises, playing Simon Says, having them take a bathroom break, or assigning students classroom errands such as taking a message to the office. Tailor these activities to the student. If, for example, he tends to fall asleep while watching movies in class, you might ask him to help operate the audiovisual equipment.

10. Make it hard for the student to sleep.
If a student falls asleep often and you are confident it is not related to illness or a side effect of medication, you might consider removing his desk the next time he falls asleep so he has no place to rest his head. Give him a clipboard or a hard surface to write on. Let him have his desk back when he tells you he is confident he can work without falling asleep.

Elementary Teacher's Discipline Problem Solver

11. Get help from your other students. Encourage students to help a classmate who is nodding off or has fallen asleep by touching his arm and saying his name.

12. Hold the student accountable for missed work. If he falls asleep in your class and as a result misses work, let him know that he is responsible for making it up. This may mean getting information from classmates or finishing the work during recess or taking it home for homework.

13. If the student is on medication, inform his parents about his sleepiness. It may be that fatigue is a side effect of the medication. If so, the prescribing physician needs to know this so he or she can consider adjusting the dosage. Because physicians cannot always predict a child's reactions to a medication, it is important that they have specific information from teachers and parents about the child's behavior.

See Also

Motivation, Lack of

Participation, Lack of Class

Special-Needs Students

With the current trend toward inclusion, namely, placing special education students in regular classes, teachers are being asked to deal with a wide range of academic and behavioral problems. Disciplining students with disabilities or special needs can present challenging issues for teachers.

It is important with all students presenting behavioral problems to try to understand what underlies their behavior. This is no less true for children with special needs. The behavioral difficulties these students present often result from feelings of discouragement, frustration, and inadequacy. The student with a learning disability may misbehave because she feels discouraged by her academic difficulties and wants to deflect attention from her deficiencies. The student who is ridiculed by classmates because of a physical disability may act out in a misguided effort to gain their approval. The student with a reading problem may lash out in anger due to her mounting frustration with her inability to decode words. If you can identify what lies beneath the student's overt behavior, you can provide her with the appropriate support and guidance.

In disciplining students with disabilities, teachers must bear in mind an important principle. Students with disabilities cannot be disciplined for behavior that is a direct result of their disability. To do so is to discriminate against them for their disability, which is contrary to law. At the same time, if a student's behavior is not directly related to her disability, then she can be disciplined the same way as students who do not have disabilities.

In practical terms, this means that a student with a reading disability can be disciplined if she continually yells out in class. The rationale is that her behavior is not the result of her disability. In contrast, a student with Tourette's syndrome who vocalizes often in class cannot be disciplined for this behavior because it is directly related to his disability. This is not only the law but it is good educational practice. Students should not be disciplined for behavior they cannot control. Because behavior often has multiple causes, however, whether they can control it or not can be a difficult judgment to make.

What You Can Do

1. Model respectful behavior toward the student. Your class will look to you for cues about how to interact with the student. Foster a climate of acceptance and support by treating her in a kind, sensitive, and patient manner, but do not talk down to her. Speak with her in a friendly way, and do not hesitate to joke with her. Also use language that is suitable for her age and places her on an equal level with her peers. As an example, in asking a classmate to go with her to the library, it is more respectful and sensitive to say, "I'd like the two of you to go" than "Take her with you."

2. Find opportunities to stroke the student. She may be frustrated by her limitations and in need of emotional support and acknowledgment. Her accomplishments, however, may not take the same form as those of other students. Small steps may represent giant leaps for the child with special needs. In an honest and sincere manner, praise her for these gains in the presence of classmates (or privately if you sense she will be embarrassed by public recognition).

3. If the student is in special education, become familiar with her IEP. The IEP, a document required for all special education students, should include a comprehensive description of her educational strengths and weaknesses. In addition, if she is presenting behavioral problems, it may contain management strategies in the Behavior Improvement Plan section, as well as modifications of the school disciplinary code for this student. If so, this is important information for you to know. If the IEP does not have these elements and you think they should be included, talk with the special education staff about convening a meeting of the IEP team (of which you are a member) to revise the IEP.

4. Discipline the student when she knowingly misbehaves. Although you may feel sympathetic to the student, she should not be automatically exempt from discipline because of her disability. If you are confident her misbehavior is not a result of her particular problem, do not hesitate to set limits in the same way you would with other students. She needs to know when her behavior is inappropriate (she may not always know) and understand that her behavior has consequences. Bear in mind, however, that the ultimate purpose of discipline is to teach, not to punish or humiliate. And the child with a disability is clearly able to learn from consequences. As part of your discipline, tell her clearly and concretely what she did wrong and what she needs to do differently next time. Also consider imposing some reasonable consequences such as loss of recess, after-school detention, or loss of classroom privileges.

5. Determine whether the student understood the inappropriateness of her behavior.
Your response to her behavior may differ, depending on whether or not she understood that she was behaving improperly. Talk with her and ask her to tell you what she was doing that was unacceptable. If she violated a class or school rule, ask her to tell you what the rule is. If she is fuzzy on these issues, help her understand why her behavior was inappropriate and what the rule is that she violated. To confirm her understanding, have her repeat the rule back to you. Also ask her how she might have handled the particular situation differently, making sure to offer your own ideas.

6. Make accommodations for the student.
Her behavioral difficulties, which can run the gamut from withdrawal to crying to lashing out at classmates, may result from her frustrations in school related to her special needs. Be creative in finding ways to make accommodations in class to lessen this frustration or distress. Here are some examples:

- Reduce background noise for the student with a hearing impairment.

- Give the student with an auditory processing problem extra time to process information presented orally.

- Ease up on the amount of writing required of a student with a hand-writing problem.

- Allow the student with Tourette's syndrome to leave the class at any time.

- Provide short, simple, and clear directions to the student who is a slow learner or is cognitively impaired.

- Provide alternatives to reading aloud for the student with a reading disability.

- Prepare the autistic child for changes in school routine.

- Describe to the visually impaired student events she cannot see.

7. Consider whether peers are negatively influencing the student's behavior.
She may be acting out in reaction to her treatment by classmates. She may be feeling left out or may be the target of ridicule. Or classmates may blame her for behavior she did not do. Feeling upset or angry, she may express herself by misbehaving or trying to get even. If you suspect this may be going on, observe the student carefully in different school situations, including the playground, to find out if peers are including her and treating her appropriately. If you find this to be a problem, find ways to help her connect with her peers.

8. Talk with your class about the student.
If you find that her classmates are mistreating her, find a time when she is out of class to talk with them. Without singling out particular students, let them know what you have observed and express your disappointment in their behavior. Tell them you expect them to be kind to the student and include her in their activities. If her behavior is unusual, help them understand why she may behave that way, but emphasize her similarities with them more than her differences. Also avoid using labels or disability language that sets her apart from other students. Help them understand that she has the same feelings and sensitivities as other students. Ask for their ideas as to how they might react to her differently and include her in school activities.

9. Stop teasing immediately.
The student with special needs may be ridiculed by her classmates and made the butt of jokes. If so, take the students aside who are doing the teasing and help them understand how upsetting and hurtful ridicule can be. Tell them in strong terms that this behavior is unacceptable and is not allowed in your class. If they persist, contact their parents or take disciplinary action. Although it is important that the student learn to stand up for herself, she may not have the skills to cope adequately with peer

ridicule. You may need to teach her steps she can take and things she can say when someone teases her.

10. Help the student blend in with other students.

Because the student with special needs may stand out in a regular class, it is important to help her fit in with her peers and give her a sense of belonging by treating her as much like her classmates as possible. Give her the same privileges or items that you give to other students (for example, a book for keeping a journal), make sure to involve her in your class routines (for example, leading the class in the Pledge of Allegiance), and expect her to comply with the same rules as other students as long as they are within her ability (for example, expect her to cover her textbooks).

11. Obtain the help of special education professionals.

If the student is receiving special education, she should have a team of people that you can call on to support you. If she is mainstreamed in your class for part of the day, work closely with the student's special education teacher, who will likely have suggestions on how to manage her behavior. Indeed, the teacher may already be using a behavior-management system with her that you can implement as well. Also consider talking with the school psychologist, who might offer you ideas for managing the student's behavior and may be available to provide counseling to her.

12. Assign the student a classroom buddy.

This buddy may ease the student's frustrations by helping her understand directions, complete assignments, and follow classroom routines. Select a student to provide this help who is responsible and sensitive. Check in with her periodically to make sure she is not feeling overwhelmed and is getting her own work done. You might alternate buddies so that no one student feels burdened by the job.

13. If the child's behavior is severely disruptive, request an aide.

It is not uncommon for a special education student who is mainstreamed in a regular class and presenting significant behavioral problems to be assigned an aide.

A classroom aide may assist other students as well. If an aide is assigned to your class, clarify your expectations with her, including her response to the student's misbehavior and her involvement with other students. The decision to assign an aide can be made by the IEP team, so talk with the special education staff and ask to convene an IEP meeting. Also inform your principal of this request.

See Also

Attention Deficit

Disorganization

Homework Problems

Listening Skills, Poor

Seatwork Problems

Self-Esteem, Low

Teasing

Special Subjects

It is not just regular classroom teachers who face the challenge of dealing with discipline problems. Teachers of special subjects such as art, music, and physical education also confront behavioral difficulties. Indeed, students may be more inclined to act up in these classes because they see them as a break from having to work and an opportunity for having a good time. It is no surprise then that students who are angels in their regular class may be transformed into hellions when they go to "specials."

Specials teachers have the additional burden of instructing many more students than the regular classroom teacher. As a result, they have fewer opportunities to convey their expectations to students and shape their behavior. Moreover, their classroom activities are often highly stimulating, which may increase the likelihood of acting-out behaviors.

If you are a specials teacher, you need to give careful consideration to behavior management in your classroom. Lay the groundwork for good discipline by engaging in such practices as communicating your behavioral expectations, establishing and posting clear rules, consistently applying those rules, setting firm limits, and providing discipline when necessary. If you fear that structure stifles creativity, reconsider this notion. Structure and limits are key educational tools that can help bring about a climate in which creativity can emerge.

What You Can Do

1. Let your students know that your class is not playtime.
Students may come into your class with the attitude that it is a time to have fun but not a time to work. If so, you are likely to see behavior problems, perhaps even from generally cooperative students. Quickly disabuse them of this notion. Tell them that you hope they have a good time in your class but that you expect them to work hard, pay attention, and behave appropriately. If you find that a staff member is conveying the message to them that special subjects are a

time to have fun, you might talk with that person and ask her not to describe your class in that way.

2. Establish and post your classroom rules.
State the rules simply, clearly, and in positive terms (for example, "Walk in classroom" rather than "Do not run"), and do not have more than five. Post them where your students can easily see them. Go over the rules the first week, and reinforce them during the school year as necessary. You might consider using the same rules the regular teacher uses.

3. Post the rules the regular teacher uses.
Obtain a copy of the rules employed by the students' regular teachers, and post them in your classroom. Although this will involve extra work on your part, gathering the various teachers' rules and posting a new list every class, it may be worth the additional time if it results in an increase in student cooperation. Using the same rules posted in their regular class will provide continuity for the students and emphasize to them that you expect the same behavior in your class that they exhibit in their regular class.

4. Set the tone at the beginning of class.
If the students are allowed to talk with their classmates at the start of class while you are getting organized, it will be hard to settle them down. Let them know that you expect them to enter class quietly and be ready to follow your instructions or begin the task outlined on the board. Follow through on this by starting your lesson as soon as students are seated and before they have a chance to misbehave.

5. Enlist the help of the student's regular teacher.
If you have a student who is misbehaving in your class, talk with her regular teacher. Find out if the child is presenting similar problems in his class and how he handles her. More specifically, ask which strategies are effective with her, which should be avoided, what incentives are motivating for her, which students she should or should not sit next to, and whether there is anything about her background that is important for you to know.

6. Remind troublesome students of your rules as they enter class.

If you have a student who has presented behavioral problems in your class, have a brief talk with her as she walks in the door. Greet her in a positive manner, and then remind her of your rules, especially those she has violated in the past. If she is cooperative during the period, let her know how pleased you were with her behavior. If you think it will spur her to continue to behave well, you might even call her parents to let them know how well she performed in your class.

7. Record in writing the student's misbehaviors.

Make sure she sees you doing this. If she asks what you are writing down (and even if she does not), tell her that you are taking notes on what she is saying and doing so you have an accurate record of her misbehavior to show both her teacher and parents.

8. If a student misbehaves, consider removing her from the activity.

If you have taken steps to quiet a disruptive student and she continues to misbehave, making it difficult for you to teach, you might exclude the student from the class activity. If she enjoys the activity, giving her a time-out may be sufficient to gain her cooperation in the future. Have her sit out for a set period (the younger the student, the shorter the period), and allow her to return to the activity if she has been quiet and complied with your instructions while in time-out. If she disrupts the class while in time-out or resumes her misbehavior after returning to the activity, consider sending her to the office.

9. Contact the student's parents.

Even though you are not her regular teacher, you have every reason to contact her parents if she misbehaves in your class. If feasible, invite them in for a meeting; otherwise, speak with them on the phone. Describe her behavior in your class, and then ask for their suggestions for dealing with her in school. After agreeing with them on a plan for managing her behavior, bring the student into the conference (if she is not already attending). Encourage the parents to say in their child's presence that they disapprove of her behavior and expect her to follow your rules. Another option for contacting the parents: have the student phone them in your presence and have her describe to them her classroom behavior. Her discomfort at doing this may be sufficient to deter future misbehavior. And don't forget to contact her parents when she behaves appropriately.

10. Post a notice from the regular class teacher.

This strategy requires cooperation between the regular and the special teachers. If the regular teacher informs you that her students have been particularly difficult on the day you see them, you might put up a sign in your class from the regular teacher that says something like the following: "This class has been behaving poorly today. Please let me know of any students who misbehave during this class so I can take appropriate action. I can also give you students' telephone numbers in case you need to contact their parents." Work with the regular teacher to come up with wording that suits your situation. Do not post this notice every time you have this class. Reserve its use for those days when the students have been misbehaving and the regular teacher anticipates a problem in your class.

11. Sign on to the regular teacher's behavior-modification plan.

If a student who is prone to problems in your class is already receiving points or tokens for good behavior from her regular teacher, ask her teacher if you can participate in this plan to help manage her behavior in your class. Make sure to keep it simple. If, for example, the student has a point card that she uses in her regular class, you might have her bring it to your class and then assign her points based on her behavior with you. She can then use these points to earn rewards or privileges from her regular teacher.

12. Figure out a system for cleaning up.

This is a particularly important issue for art teachers. Having an efficient system will lessen your stress and decrease the chance of discipline problems. Try out various approaches, and see which works best for you. You may find that it is too chaotic to have your students cleaning up simultaneously as they scurry around the class in a hurried manner. If you have tables in your classroom, consider assigning one student to be in charge of cleaning up for each table and then alternate that job each week. Another approach is to identify the various clean-up jobs and assign one or two students to each job, again alternating these jobs so each child participates in the clean-up. You might also spur students to clean up efficiently by offering a reward to the table or class that cleans up the best. Whatever system you use, make sure you have students begin cleaning up early enough to finish before the period ends. If there is extra time after the students have finished cleaning up, use this time to review concepts or vocabulary you have taught the students or highlight student projects to the rest of the class.

13. Do activities with the students as they line up to leave. If the classroom teacher is delayed picking up the students, they may exhibit problems while waiting in line. Try to prevent this by preparing in advance some activities to do with them that are both fun and educational. As an example, you might play "Art Jeopardy" or "Music Jeopardy" with them, in which you provide the answers and the students provide the questions.

See Also

Disruptive/Uncooperative Behavior

Hallway/Lining-up Problems

Spitting

Few behaviors are more disconcerting to a teacher than spitting. A student may spit on school property as a way of appearing cool or gaining the attention of peers or the teacher. The challenge for the teacher is to try to stop the student from spitting without giving him excessive attention for this behavior.

Spitting *on somebody* is a different matter. This is often a hostile or angry act that can be highly upsetting to the target of the spitting. Consider responding as you would if a student had hit another; take firm and prompt steps to ensure this behavior does not happen again.

What You Can Do

1. Find out if the student's spitting has a physical cause.

Frequent spitting may result from a medical problem, perhaps of a bronchial nature. Talk with the student's parents to find out if this is the case. If so, work with them and the student to come up with ideas about what he can do when he needs to spit. For example, you might suggest that the student carry a package of tissues with him or keep some in his desk. He might keep a bag in his desk for disposing of used tissues. If he needs to use the bathroom to spit, you might suggest to the student a signal he can use in class to alert you that he is going to the bathroom.

2. Take the student aside and talk with him.

Ask him why he spits, and solicit his cooperation in trying to stop. Let him know that spitting in school is inappropriate unless done in the toilet. Tell him that if he needs to spit, he can get a tissue from you or obtain a pass to go to the bathroom but that he is not allowed to spit on school property, either inside or outside. Help him understand that spitting shows a lack of respect for school property and that his classmates may find this behavior offensive and avoid him as a result. Ask him how he might feel if he were to step on the spit of another student.

3. Have the student clean up the area where he spit.

If he spit on the playground, have him get a pail of water and pour it on the area. If he spit on the floor of the school, have him get some paper towels and wipe the area well. You might even have him spray disinfectant on the floor. Direct him in a calm, matter-of-fact manner without engaging in a verbal confrontation, but insist that he obtain the supplies and clean up the area himself. If the student continues to spit on school property, you might expand his clean-up responsibilities. You might also encourage other students to tell him that they find his spitting disgusting and ask him to stop.

4. If a student spits on another student, take immediate action.

Let the student know in a very firm manner that this behavior is unacceptable and will not be tolerated in your classroom. Insist that he apologize appropriately to the other student. Consider notifying the student's parents, perhaps by having him call to inform them of his behavior. You might also provide a consequence in school, such as having him stay in during recess or miss a desirable school activity. Give thought to alerting the nurse to determine if there are any health concerns for the student who was spat on.

5. Help the student learn to express his anger more appropriately.

If the student's spitting on another student was his way of hurting a peer with whom he was angry, suggest to the student other, more appropriate ways of expressing his anger, for example, by simply telling him in a direct way why he was angry with him. You might even suggest what the student could have said. This incident may also indicate the need for you to get the two students together to resolve their dispute.

6. Talk with your class about spitting.

If a number of your students have engaged in this behavior, have a brief discussion with the whole class. Let your students know that you find spitting repulsive, but give them an opportunity to voice their own opinions, trying to draw out students who are disgusted by spitting.

See Also

Aggressive Behavior

Bullying

Rude/Disrespectful Behavior

Stealing

Students may steal for a variety of reasons. Some, especially younger students, may steal an item simply because they want it and haven't developed the necessary impulse control to curb this behavior. Others may steal out of a feeling of hurt and anger; their actions may be their way of expressing their distress or getting back at someone who they believe has wronged them. Still others may steal in an effort to gain status with their peers or attention from their teacher.

Whatever the motivation, in responding to an incident of stealing, you want to try to arrange for the item's return to its owner, identify the guilty student, and respond to him with a mix of firmness and understanding. If there have been a number of incidents of stealing in your class, you will want to consider how to prevent their recurrence. Because these incidents can create conflict and distrust among your students, you need to deal with these situations promptly and sensitively.

Although your first priority is to have the stolen item returned to its owner, you also want to take advantage of this incident to teach the student responsible behavior. At the same time, you want to be measured in your response. If you blow the incident out of proportion, you may frighten your class and the guilty student may not return the item or come forward. Similarly, avoid dwelling on the issue to the extent that it creates tension among your students and cuts into your teaching time.

What You Can Do

1. Ask for the item to be returned without assuming it was stolen. Tell your class that an item is missing, and ask if anyone knows where it is. Although you do not want to refer to the item as "stolen," let your students know that, if someone took it, this is stealing and it is important that the item be returned immediately.

2. If you believe it was stolen, provide a way for the student to return it anonymously.
Let your students know that you are more interested in having the item returned to its owner than finding out who was responsible. Tell them that you would like it returned by the end of the school day and no questions will be asked. Designate an unmonitored area in the school where the item can be left.

3. Do not threaten or punish the entire class in an effort to find the culprit.
This will only incur the anger of your students and is unlikely to bring forth the guilty student. Moreover, punishing the whole class may create an unhealthy climate in which students begin to accuse or suspect each other in an effort to avoid punishment. Similarly, avoid putting pressure on students to inform on each another. It is more important that you have a classroom in which students support and trust one another than that you identify the student. At the same time, students should know that they can come to you in confidence if they are certain who took the missing item.

4. Ask students to do the "write" thing.
If you are intent on finding the culprit because the missing item is valuable, you might have your students note, in writing, whether they were involved. Tell them that your primary interest is in having the item returned to its owner. Have each student write on a piece of paper either "I did not take the (name of item)" or "I took the (name of item) and am sorry I did it," and have them sign the paper, fold it in half, and hand it to you. You may be surprised at students' willingness to admit their responsibility. If a student owns up to having taken the missing item, keep this information confidential and thank him privately for acknowledging his mistake. In deciding how to respond to him, place the focus on helping him understand the consequences of his behavior and factor in his willingness to take responsibility for his behavior.

5. If you know who stole the item, arrange for its return.
Make sure not to accuse a student or impose consequences unless you are certain he is guilty. If, however, you are certain that he stole the item, confront the situation

directly. Do not ask him if he stole the item because this will only invite him to lie or put up a vigorous defense. Rather, let him know that you are aware that he took the item and that you expect him to return it to its owner and apologize. If he does not have the stolen item, let him know that you expect him to replace it or pay for it. If you decide to provide the student with additional consequences, remember that your goal is to deter future incidents, so be measured in your actions. Whatever action you take, do not let other students have any input into your response to the student. This is your call.

6. Educate the student about stealing and its consequences.

What you say to the student will of course depend on his age and whether he has done this before. If he is a kindergartner or first grader, he may have a limited notion of property rights and may need some help in understanding that stealing is wrong. An older elementary student will likely understand that his actions were wrong but may need some assistance in grasping the consequences of stealing, both for him and the person he stole from. Help him understand that if classmates become aware of his involvement, they may come to suspect him when other items are missing. If appropriate, you might also mention that stealing is against the law and that if he were to do this when he were older, the consequences would be much more serious.

7. Consider informing the principal and the parents.

If one of your students has taken an item of value or stolen on more than one occasion, inform the principal and talk with the student's parents, preferably in a conference. (You might even have the student make the call to his parents to let them know what he did.) At the meeting, let them know the steps you are taking in school and emphasize that your interest is more in preventing its recurrence than in punishing their child. Encourage them to do the same. If the student no longer has the item and has to replace it or pay for it, suggest to the parents that they have their child do some extra chores as a way of earning the money.

8. Figure out what motivated the student and try to meet his needs in a socially appropriate way.

In trying to understand what prompted his actions, consider the circumstances: what he stole, how often he stole, from whom and in what setting he stole, and what happened before the incident. If, for example, you conclude that the student stole from a classmate as an expression of anger toward him, consider addressing the conflict between the students, perhaps through a conflict-resolution procedure. If you believe that the act of stealing was a reaction to feeling hurt, try to identify the source of the student's distress and take steps to ease his pain. If you conclude that his behavior was his way of trying to impress his classmates, find opportunities for him to gain recognition from his peers in socially appropriate ways.

9. Conduct a class meeting.
If stealing has happened in your class on more than one occasion, it is time to have a discussion with your students. Let them know how you might feel if someone had stolen something from you. Ask your students if they have ever had something taken from them and how they felt. With younger students, you might talk about the concept of ownership in a way they understand; with older students, you might focus on the consequences of stealing.

10. Make sure the student is not shunned by his classmates.
If you know who stole the item, keep this information to yourself and certainly do not reprimand him publicly. But if your students find out through other sources, take steps to avoid the student being condemned or rejected by peers. The class will likely take its cue from you in terms of how to treat the student. Although you want to avoid a lengthy discussion of the incident, you might describe the student as having made a mistake rather than having done some terrible act or having a serious problem. And of course do not refer to him as a thief. Remind your students that many of them have made mistakes. In the days after the incident, be on the lookout for any signs that the student is being shunned.

11. Encourage responsible behavior.
Look for opportunities to compliment the student when he behaves in a responsible or trustworthy manner. You might also create opportunities for him to help others (for example, by having him read to some kindergarten students) or demonstrate his honesty (for example, by having him take the lunch money to the office).

Stealing

12. Discourage your students from bringing valuable or desired items to school.
This will help prevent future incidents of stealing. Inform parents of this rule during Back-to-School Night or in a letter you send home regarding class rules and procedures. If children do bring items in from home, ask their parents to put their name on them.

13. Consider ways to discourage stealing in your classroom.
Limit the times that students have access to your classroom without adult supervision. Make sure to place your purse in a secure spot, and consider locking the door when you leave the classroom. If the stealing of items such as pencils or erasers has become a problem, keep some extras on hand that students can use to lessen the temptation to take these items from classmates. Another way to discourage stealing is to lend students desirable items in the classroom for short periods (for example, the weekend), but keep track of the borrowed items and insist on their return. Brainstorm with your students to see if they can come up with other ideas to prevent stealing.

See Also

Aggressive Behavior

Bullying

Vandalism

Substitute Teacher

A substitute teacher has one of the more challenging jobs in education. She is an outsider with no knowledge of or personal connection with the students she is being asked to teach, yet she is expected to pick right up where the regular teacher left off. She has all the responsibilities of a teacher but little of her authority.

Some students may be thrilled at having a substitute, viewing this as a "day off." Others who have a strong bond with the regular teacher may be distressed by her absence and feel a need to display their loyalty to her. As a result, a substitute may face a class filled with students looking to take advantage of her position and test her limits.

You can help make the job of the substitute easier if you do some advance planning for the days that you are absent. As part of your beginning-of-the-year planning process, consider developing a "substitute survival kit." The more information you can provide to the substitute, the more likely she is to have a productive and problem-free experience and the easier it will be for you when you return.

What You Can Do

1. Convey your expectations to your students.
Let them know that your classroom rules are in full effect when there is a substitute and that you expect them to be on their best behavior. Tell them that she will be giving you a report of their behavior and collecting their classwork. Help them understand that being a substitute is a difficult job. Ask them for suggestions about what they might do to assist the substitute and make her feel welcome. Inform them that teachers have different ways of teaching and that they should follow the instructions of the substitute, even if they differ from your approach.

2. Refer to the substitute as a "guest teacher."

If your students think of the substitute in this way, they are more likely to be respectful and cooperative. This will also reinforce the message that she is there to teach rather than baby-sit.

3. Create a handbook for the substitute.

This is perhaps the most useful step you can take to help her. This guide should contain a class roster, a seating chart (consider using self-stick notes in case you change the seating arrangement), school and classroom procedures, a school map, the bell schedule, your daily schedule, lesson plans for the day, and the location of materials and supplies. In addition, it might include the following information to help the substitute deal with any behavior problems or special situations:

- A copy of the school's code of conduct

- A list of your classroom rules

- Some practical management strategies that you have found effective with the class or a description of your management system (but keep it simple)

- A brief and easy-to-understand description of any reward or incentive system that you use

- Your technique for gaining your students' attention (for example, by turning the lights on and off)

- A beginning-of-the-day activity or brain teaser to give to the students as soon as they enter class in the morning

- The names of responsible students she can call on for assistance

- Students with medical concerns, including restrictions (for example, a student who is excused from physical activity)

- Students with academic, emotional, or behavioral problems and helpful strategies for dealing with them

- The name and room number of one or two teachers who can provide help or answer questions

- A request for the substitute to leave you a note describing how the day went and listing the names of students who misbehaved or were especially helpful

4. Indicate the phonetic pronunciation of your students' names on the class roster.
As the student population has grown increasingly diverse, the first challenge a substitute typically faces is pronouncing the students' names correctly. Providing her with a pronunciation guide may help avoid embarrassing situations for the students as well as the substitute. You might also note the names students prefer to be called by.

5. Request a specific substitute.
If you have had experience with a substitute who has good management skills and knows your students, request that the school use her when you are absent.

6. Provide activities for students to do when they have completed their work.
Behavior problems tend to arise when students have free time and no structured activities. You can sidestep this problem by giving the substitute some appealing activities students can do when they are finished with their work or at the end of the day. Some examples: videos, crossword puzzles, games, word searches, brain teasers, trivia questions, arts and crafts projects, books on tape, books to read aloud to the class, riddles, fun math problems, a book of poems (especially one by Shel Silverstein), and jokes. Make sure to let the substitute know where you keep this activities folder.

7. Talk with your class about their response to the substitute.
If she indicated the class was cooperative and well behaved, express your appreciation to your students. You might even find some way to reward them. However, if she reported some behavior problems, address those directly, either with the whole class or the individual students. This will let students know that they are accountable for their behavior on days they have substitutes. You might also ask them to tell you about the topics they covered with the substitute.

8. Have students evaluate their own behavior.
If the substitute reported that the class was uncooperative, you might have students report on their own behavior as a way of holding them accountable. They may surprise you with

their honesty. For example, you might have each student complete the following:

My behavior for the substitute was

a. poor

b. fair

c. good

Complete the following questions if you answered "poor":

In what way did you misbehave?

How will you behave differently with another substitute?

The act of filling out this form may be sufficient to motivate students to cooperate next time. Keep the forms of the misbehaving students on file to help identify patterns and give you a behavior record if you decide to contact the parents or give the student a consequence.

See Also

Disruptive/Uncooperative Behavior

Suicide Threats

Teen suicide is a problem of alarming proportions. An estimated 500,000 teenagers attempt suicide every year in this country, and about 5,000 succeed. Younger children may also threaten or commit suicide, although their rate of suicide is significantly lower than it is with adolescents.

The low rate of suicide among young children does not mean they are immune to experiencing profound distress or sadness. Indeed, young children can become depressed and even suffer the despair and desperation that underlie suicidal threats, but they usually lack either the cognitive skills to plan such a complex task or the means to carry it out.

Elementary school children may sometimes make comments or behave in a way that suggests they feel like killing themselves. Even if you conclude that a student is not serious about this threat or is unable to follow through on it, the fact that he is making these comments is cause for concern and reason for your follow-up. Young children who talk about wanting to kill themselves are no doubt feeling pain. But for most of these children, their talk of suicide is more an effort to end their pain than it is to end their life. For many, it is also an effort to gain attention, sympathy, and support from people who are important to them.

Children's thoughts may drift to suicide in part because of their immature thought process. They may feel desperate about their situation and conclude that there is no way out from their pain and hurt. They may feel a sense of hopelessness because they do not see any alternative to their present situation. In short, they feel powerless to change their situation. Believing there is no solution to their pain, they entertain thoughts of suicide.

Although suicide threats by children of elementary school age are rare, feelings of depression are not. You need to be aware of students who may be exhibiting signs of depression or suicidal thoughts. If you have a student who is exhibiting these signs, you need to take action, including alerting your principal, informing his parents, and trying to obtain professional help for the student. A child who is feeling depressed or suicidal can be helped. If he does not receive help, in some cases his feelings of sadness and despair will fade with time. In other cases, however, they may build to the point that he thinks about suicide as a way of easing his pain.

What You Can Do

1. Recognize the warning signs of suicide.
Just as teens who are contemplating suicide may communicate their intentions in subtle ways, so too younger children may signal their distress indirectly. These warning signs are often their cry for help—their way of letting us know they are hurting. The following is a list of behaviors that, when considered collectively, may suggest a child is feeling distress and possibly has a desire to kill himself. Keep in mind that a child who displays one or even a number of these behaviors is not necessarily suicidal. They do suggest, however, that the child may be depressed and in need of emotional support.

- An oral comment or written note indicating a desire to die
- A previous suicidal attempt
- Statements of hopelessness (for example, "I wish I was never born")
- Compositions or artwork involving death
- Increased absenteeism from school
- Unexplained decline in academic performance
- Dramatic personality changes (for example, angry or agitated behavior)
- Risky or reckless behavior (for example, walking across a busy street carelessly or jumping from a high point)
- Withdrawal from family and friends
- Loss of interest in activities that he previously enjoyed
- Giving away his favorite possessions to friends or family
- Unusual neglect of his physical appearance
- Frequent physical complaints such as stomachaches or headaches
- Self-inflicted injuries such as cuts, scratches, or burns
- Significant change in sleeping or eating habits

2. Monitor at-risk children closely.

Children who experience significant family changes or disturbances, whether it be abuse, abandonment or rejection by a family member, separation, divorce, death, or financial stress, may learn the hard way about the fragility of life. These children are particularly vulnerable to depression and perhaps even to suicidal thoughts. If you have a student who has gone through difficult family circumstances, you should be particularly attuned to any signs of emotional distress.

3. Take every threat seriously.

The fact that a threat is made by a young child should not diminish your concern. And the fact that a young child may be unable to follow through on the act, even if he has suicidal intentions, should not lessen your response. Nor should you ignore a threat because it was made casually or in jest. A threat of suicide, even when made by a young child, even when said in jest, can be a desperate cry for help. We cannot take the risk of not responding to this threat. Although a comment relating to a desire to die may not be indicative of suicidal intentions or even distress, you or another professional need to talk with the student to find out if this is the case. Ignoring or trivializing a child's threat when he is feeling distressed will only intensify his desperation.

4. Respond in a caring, compassionate manner.

If one of your students has communicated orally or in writing his desire to die, take him aside as soon as possible and talk with him. (If necessary, find someone to take over your class.) Ask him what he meant when he said or wrote that. Encourage him to speak about what is upsetting him by listening attentively without criticizing him or even offering advice. Respond in a sympathetic, soothing manner, and help him feel that he has been understood. Acknowledge his feelings and perceptions, even if they seem trivial to you. If he perceives a problem as serious, then it is serious—to him. Reassure him, however, that other children have experienced similar pain and distress and with time and help from adults have eventually felt better. Let him know that it is important that you let his parents know of his distress so they can help him and that you also need to inform the principal. He may be upset with you or plead with you not to tell his parents, but you have an obligation to inform them.

5. Make use of the school's resources.

Do not feel that you have to shoulder this problem alone. Notify the principal of your concern. In addition, other school staff members, including the school psychologist, guidance counselor, and social worker, can talk with the student and meet with his parents. Your school might even have a suicide prevention team that can be called upon when a student is in distress. If you choose to obtain the help of another staff member, try to select a person who has a relationship with the student. Then talk with the student, letting him know that there is a person in school you want him to talk with who can help him. Rather than send him to see this person, arrange to walk with him to her office. Make sure to follow up with the counselor that day and discuss the arrangements for informing the parents. Also talk with her about whether she will be able to provide continuing support to the student in the future.

6. Contact the parents.

If one of your students is very distressed and has expressed feelings of wanting to harm himself, it is essential that you notify his parents the same day you become aware of this information. Try to have the parents come in for a meeting, and consider involving the principal and any other staff members who talked with the student about his concerns. Encourage the parents to obtain professional help, and be ready to offer them some recommendations. Informing the parents is not just the professional thing to do; it is the legally prudent thing to do. Some schools have been held legally liable for not notifying parents in a timely manner of their child's suicidal comments or providing him with adequate supervision. You may want to document, in writing, that the parents were notified and that they were encouraged to get professional help.

7. Follow up with the parents.

Talk with the parents within a week of your conference to offer your observations of how their child is doing, to elicit their perspective, and to find out if they have been able to find professional help. If so, encourage them to have the counselor or therapist call you so you can obtain her insights and suggestions.

8. Be discreet in informing other school staff about the student.

It is important that other staff involved with the student, such as the specials teachers, be informed of his emotional distress. This will encourage them to find ways to lessen his stress and bolster his confidence and sense of belonging. Be selective in giving out this information, and only give as much information as is necessary for others to provide the necessary emotional support.

9. Reach out to a student in distress.

Try to connect with him by greeting him at the door every morning in a warm, friendly manner and finding something positive to say to him. Listen attentively when he speaks with you, and show respect for his concerns. Find a few minutes every day to talk with him about his interests, perhaps sharing one of your hobbies with him or bringing an item from home related to one of his interests. You might call his parents to find out about his favorite hobbies, collections, sports teams, television programs, or musical groups. Or you might have all your students fill out a form at the beginning of the year asking for this information. Consider these other ways of reaching out to the student: be his partner on a field trip; have lunch with him on occasion; make a home visit; call him at home after he has had a difficult day, and contact his parents after he has had a good day.

10. Help the student gain a sense of importance.

His distress may stem in part from feelings of worthlessness. You can help enhance his self-worth by finding opportunities in school for him to help others or perform a useful task. Some possible tasks are these:

- Serving as class messenger
- Taking care of the class pet
- Reading the morning announcements
- Being on the safety patrol
- Tutoring a classmate
- Taking a new student on a tour of the school

- Being a buddy to a classmate who speaks little English

- Assisting classmates with computer problems

- Answering the school phone while the secretary is at lunch

- Participating in a school project such as a canned food drive

11. Help the student cope with failure.

If part of his distress is related to academic problems, find ways to give him confidence and boost his morale. Allow him to express his frustration and acknowledge his feelings, but then move on to helping him understand the source of his difficulties and giving him strategies for improving. Help him appreciate that struggle is a normal part of learning and that accomplishment rarely comes without setbacks. Suggest to him that with your help and his perseverance you are confident he will succeed.

12. Notify parents of their child's successes.

Teachers are usually very diligent about informing parents when their child has a problem but less so when he has a success. It only takes a few minutes for you to call his parents or send a note home when their child does something especially well. Tell the student you are doing this. A gesture like this can brighten his day and elicit praise and encouragement from his parents.

See Also

Crying, Frequent

Self-Esteem, Low

Swearing

Profanity has become an increasingly common part of children's everyday language. This no doubt reflects the frequency with which they hear foul language in the media, as well as in the casual conversation of adults. Its commonplace use in society, however, does not mean that you need to be accepting of its use by your students.

In responding to a student who has used profanity, try to identify the reason for his swearing. Students may use profanity for a variety of reasons. Some may swear to gain the attention and notice of their teacher or classmates. Some may swear to impress their peers and gain acceptance. Some may swear as a way of expressing strong emotions such as anger, distress, or frustration. Some may swear to distract the teacher from focusing on their misbehavior. And some may swear to get back at somebody who has hurt them or is trying to control them. If you can identify the reason for the student's use of profanity, you can respond to him more effectively.

Although the use of profanity is typically confined to one or two students, occasionally this can become a classwide problem. This may happen if your students come to see swearing as a way of appearing cool. If this happens, you will need to devise strategies to use with your entire class.

What You Can Do

1. Do not ignore profanity from your students.
It is important that you respond in some way to foul language. Failing to respond may convey to your students that this language is acceptable. Confronting swearing is also important because some students may use profanity so habitually that they do not realize that they swore or their language was inappropriate. Address the issue of swearing, even if you are not sure who made the comments. If this happens, do not spend a lot of time on this problem, and do not ask for help from your students in trying to identify the offending student. Rather, let your class

know that this kind of language is unacceptable, perhaps using an "I message" such as "I expect that students in this class will talk respectfully to each other." And then return to your lesson.

2. Keep in mind that a young student may not realize the inappropriateness of his language.
The student may tell you that he thought these words were okay to say because he heard his parents or friends or people on television use them. If so, you might say to him, "I understand that you may have heard other people use those words, but they are not okay to use in school." Help him understand that these words can hurt others' feelings and cause peers to avoid him. Be specific with him about which words are objectionable, and suggest other words or phrases he can use instead.

3. React calmly to foul language.
If you perceive that a student is swearing to get your attention or make you upset, react in a low-key, restrained manner, avoiding expressions of emotion. Paying considerable attention to the student or getting upset by his swearing may give him precisely what he is seeking and reinforce his impulse to swear. Instead, inform him in a calm, brief manner that his language is unacceptable and that there are more appropriate ways to gain your attention. If you opt to give him consequences, do so matter-of-factly. Avoid lecturing him, justifying your decision, or engaging in a debate. Then return to what you were doing.

4. Consider giving a mild consequence.
You may conclude that the student's inappropriate language calls for some disciplinary measure. If so, you might have the student stay for detention or miss part of recess. You might establish a rule with your class that students who swear will lose 5 minutes of recess for every incident. With younger students who need an immediate consequence, consider giving them a time-out of short duration, explaining that students cannot remain with other children if they use offensive or inappropriate language.

5. Inform the parents by mail if he swears again.
Have the student complete a form that asks him to write down exactly what he said and what prompted

him to use that language. Then add comments of your own. Put the form in an envelope, and have the student address it to his parents. Place the envelope in your desk, and tell the student that you will send the envelope to his parents if he uses profanity again.

6. If the student swore out of anger or frustration, address this concern.

Try to find out the source of the student's distress, although you may want to give him a chance to cool down before talking with him. You might say the following: "I know you said those words because you were upset, but let's try to figure out some other way of dealing with this. Help me understand what you were so upset about." After identifying the source of his distress, suggest ways to deal with the situation. For example, if his swearing reflected his frustration in understanding or completing schoolwork, find ways to give him some extra help. In addition, help him find ways he can express his emotion without using profanity or offending others.

7. Teach the student substitute terms for swear words.
Using profanity may help students blow off some steam or express frustration. Help the student find inoffensive words or phrases they can use when they make a mistake or are frustrated or upset. The student may have some ideas of his own, or you might suggest some, such as "darn" or "shoot." He may even be open to using nonsense words for this purpose. If appropriate, you might suggest that he express his distress or frustration by putting his thoughts in a journal or writing you a letter.

8. Use a signal to cue the student about his language.
Arrange to give the student a silent signal (for example, putting your finger to your lips) when he uses profane or inappropriate language. Let him know that you expect him to stop using offensive language immediately upon receiving this signal. In this way, you can deal with the problem of swearing with minimal disruption to your class.

9. Encourage the student to emulate a peer model.
If the student is swearing as a way of gaining status with peers, help him learn how to interact with his

peers by observing and emulating a student with good social skills who does not use profanity.

10. Recognize the student when he uses language responsibly.
If you find yourself frequently reminding a student about his use of profanity, it may be that he is swearing to elicit your attention. If so, look for opportunities to give him praise and attention in class when he speaks or acts responsibly. You may even want to create these opportunities by, for example, assigning him class chores or talking with him after class about his interests. Be sure to praise him when he speaks in a kind or appropriate manner to another student, especially in situations that might have previously given rise to his swearing. Make this a practice with your other students as well. In this way, all of your students will learn that they are likely to be recognized when they speak or act appropriately.

11. Practice what you teach.
Students often take their cues about how to behave and speak from their teacher, so it is important that you pay attention to the language you use with your students. This means making sure to never use offensive language of any kind with your class, including sarcasm and name calling. When you are upset or frustrated, model for your students how to speak to them in a way that communicates your feelings without using inappropriate language.

12. Hold a class meeting.
You may experience an outbreak of profanity in your class if it comes to be perceived as a way to appear cool. If this happens, you need to have a discussion with the entire class. Your students may be more sensitive to the reactions of their classmates than your own, so make sure this is more of a dialogue than a lecture. Begin by asking why they think students swear. Hearing classmates suggest that students swear because they want attention or want to appear tough may be enough to deter students from swearing. You might also ask some of the following questions:

- Why is profanity not allowed in school?
- How might other students feel if you swear at them?

- Has anybody ever sworn at you? If so, how did you feel?

- What might others think of you if you swear?

- Would you use profanity in front of your friend's parents? If not, why not?

- If you're feeling upset or angry about something, what can you do to express your feelings other than swear?

After eliciting these reactions from students, have them offer some ideas for eliminating foul language from school.

13. Develop a classwide incentive system to encourage appropriate language.

If foul language has become a problem with a number of your students, you might deal with this problem through behavior modification. As one example, you might draw five smiling faces on the board at the beginning of the week. Every time a student uses inappropriate language, erase one face. If there is at least one face left at the end of the week, then give the class a reward. As an alternative, print the word LANGUAGE on the board and erase one letter for every incident of swearing. Reward the class if one or more letters remain at the end of a week. You can of course adjust the standards to suit the needs of your class.

See Also

Angry Outbursts

Back Talk

Racially Offensive Language

Rude/Disrespectful Behavior

Sexually Offensive Behavior

Tourette's Syndrome

Talking, Excessive

Some students just love to talk. They seem to have opinions about everything and are not shy about expressing them. They may stop talking in response to a teacher request but 5 minutes later may be at it again. Their talking may become contagious. If students see that their classmates are allowed to get away with it, they may start as well. The resulting chatter can significantly disrupt your classroom activities.

Excessive talking can impede your ability to teach a lesson and your students' ability to concentrate on that lesson. In extreme cases, the noise may reach the point that you are unable to teach at all, undermining your authority and engendering considerable frustration. Once you have lost control of your class, it is difficult to get it back.

Excessive talking can thus result from a failure to exercise your authority in class. It may also stem from other causes, including boredom with the lesson or confusion about what to do, causing their attention to shift to other concerns. In addition, students may start to chat with each other if the lesson or seatwork period goes on too long.

In your effort to gain quiet, you need to pay attention to the nature of your instruction, as well as the structure in your classroom. This structure needs to include a clear rule regarding talking and a willingness to enforce that rule consistently without antagonizing your students. Also bear in mind that you do not want to discourage all talking by your students. Indeed, students talking among themselves can be a real source of learning, as exemplified by cooperative learning groups.

What You Can Do

1. Communicate your rules regarding talking.
In conveying these rules to your students, make it crystal clear when students are allowed to talk and when they are not. You might, for example, tell them it is okay to talk when

Elementary Teacher's Discipline Problem Solver

they raise their hand and are called on, when they need information to finish an assignment, or when they have completed their seatwork, as long as they talk in a whisper. You might also tell them they are not allowed to talk when you are teaching, when a classmate is asking or answering a question, or when they are taking a test. Let them know the consequences of not following these rules. Teach them the signal you will use to cue them to stop talking.

2. Remind students of your rules prior to an activity.

Because students have difficulty resisting the temptation to talk, you may need to remind them of your rules periodically. Do this right before entering a new activity so your students know whether they must be quiet or can talk softly. You might even appeal to their sense of fairness by explaining your rule ("Please remember there is no talking in the hall because it will disturb students in other classes"). Another way of reminding them is to praise students who are doing what you asked ("I like the way that Sarah is walking quietly").

3. Change the seating arrangement.

After you have gotten to know your students and their talking patterns, take a look at how they are seated. If they are seated in groups, consider placing your chattier students in groups with quiet children. If they are seated in rows, consider separating talkative students and seating them next to quiet students or near where you typically stand in class. You might find that placing your students' chairs in a U shape (if you have room to do this) discourages talking because students are more visible to you.

4. Talk with the student.

Help the student understand the impact of her talking on your ability to teach, her ability to keep up with the work, and her classmates' ability to focus. Rather than simply telling her, however, it may make more of an impression if you elicit this information by asking questions. If many of your students talk excessively, speak with the entire class. You might role-play by having one of the more talkative students talk about a topic to the class. As she does, ask a few students to talk nonstop with each other. After the exercise, ask the student how she felt and what ideas she has for quieting noisy students.

Talking, Excessive

5. Cue the student to stop talking with a prearranged signal.

Talk with her privately, and agree on a signal you will give her when she is talking and you need her to stop. Get her agreement to this plan, and ask for her suggestions about a signal. Some possibilities: pausing while you are speaking, raising your eyebrows, tugging on your ear, or winking. You may need to say her name to get her attention before signaling, but do not stop class to reprimand her. The idea is to give her a reminder without interrupting the flow of your lesson.

6. Stand by your students.

If a student is talking while you're teaching, move in her direction while continuing to present your lesson. Stand there for a minute or two, perhaps making eye contact with her. Your presence will likely be sufficient to quiet her down. It is a good practice generally to move around the room in an unpredictable manner and vary where you stand when you present your lessons.

7. Stop and wait.

Tell your students that if anyone is talking while you are speaking to the class, you will stop talking and wait for her to stop. Make eye contact with the guilty student. If she continues talking, you might say, "Alexandra, I'm waiting." Or you might ask talkative students questions during the lesson (for example, "Christine, can you explain in your own words what I was just saying?"). This technique may encourage them to stop talking and pay attention and may help keep all your students on their toes.

8. Gain quiet by signaling your students.

The following are some ways to quiet a noisy class. You may want to vary the signals you use, or they may lose their effectiveness over time.

- Hold up two fingers in a V shape to signal students to stop talking, raise their hands, and look at you. This works equally well in an auditorium and a classroom.

- Flip the lights off and on a couple of times. As students look at you, put your finger on your lips to alert them to be quiet.

- Say, "Stop what you are doing and look at me" while raising your hand. When students see you doing this, they are expected to stop talking and raise their hands. Wait until all hands are raised before speaking.

- Say, "Give me 5–4–3–2–1," and expect students to be quiet and looking at you by the time you get to 1.

- Clap out a beat, with students expected to imitate your beat and then look at you quietly when they are finished. Students will find this fun.

- Play a note or two on a piano or toy horn.

- Ring a bell or chime and then say, "1–2–3, all eyes on me."

9. Do not bail out a student who has been talking.

A student who is gabbing with her neighbor may miss out on directions or part of the lesson. If she asks you to repeat them, tell her she will need to figure out another way of getting the information. Let her know that she would have heard the directions if she had not been talking. You might avoid this problem by saying to your students before giving directions, "I'm only saying this once."

10. Consider whether your instructional decisions are giving rise to talking.

Take note of the occasions when your students are most likely to talk. You may find that they are talking because they are bored with the work and have finished it quickly, or find it too difficult and have given up, or are losing focus due to the length of the seatwork periods. You may need to modify your instruction or the assignments to increase their attention to task and decrease their talking. You will find that talking is lessened if you can avoid lengthy lectures and long periods of seatwork, provide work that is challenging but not frustrating, and encourage student participation in your lessons.

11. Give students activities to do if they finish their seatwork early.

These activities might include reading at their desk, doing an art activity, working on the computer, listening to an audiotape (using headphones), assisting another student, or going to the library. You might put a list of allowed activities on the board. Make it clear to students whether they must be quiet or are allowed to talk with classmates after finishing their work. If the latter, let them know they must use a quiet voice or speak in a whisper.

12. Find productive outlets for students' talking.

Look for ways to channel their expressive impulses into useful activities. One way of doing this is to set up cooperative learning groups in which students must interact with each other to complete an academic task. Other activities that can take advantage of students' proclivity for conversation are leading the Pledge of Allegiance, reading the morning announcements, serving in student government, reading to younger students, and giving a new student a tour of the school.

13. Use a noise meter.

Try this simple strategy for quieting a noisy class. In the morning, draw a noise gauge on the board and divide it into five or ten parts. Each time the noise reaches an unacceptable level in your class, fill in the gauge up to the next point. If the noise is really loud, you might go up an additional increment. If the gauge becomes filled to the top, consider imposing a consequence that you have previously discussed with the class. You can also use this in a positive manner by rewarding the class at the end of the day if the gauge has not risen above a certain point. Start with an empty gauge every day. The advantage of this technique is that it helps you quiet the class without speaking to your students. Just your walking toward the gauge may be sufficient to lessen the talking.

14. Set a timer to go off at random times.

Use a dial timer that can be set for different time periods and will ring at the end of the period. Vary the length of the time periods, and do not let your students know when it will go off. When it rings, assess whether the class is quiet and on task. If it is, place a marble in a jar and then reward the class when the jar is completely filled. You can modify this behavior-incentive plan by changing the length of the time period, the size of the jar, and the nature of the reward. You might use stickers, tokens, or points rather than marbles. Whatever system you use, if there is a reward to be earned, students will discourage their classmates from talking to ensure they make progress toward getting the reward.

Elementary Teacher's Discipline Problem Solver

15. Keep track of their noisiness using a stopwatch.

Start the stopwatch as soon as the class becomes noisy, and stop it when the class quiets down. Make sure your students see you doing this. Let them know that the amount of time they have been talking may be taken away from their recess or made up after school. You might also reward them if they can keep the time they were noisy under a standard you have set.

16. Use a device to monitor classroom noise.

One such device is called a Yacker Tracker. It works like a stoplight but is sensitive to sound. The green light remains lit until the noise goes above a certain level, at which point the yellow light comes on. If the noise rises above a second level, the red light comes on or you can arrange for a siren to go off. You can select the noise levels that trigger the lights (or siren) coming on. This device frees you from having to monitor the noise level in your class. You may want to establish a class consequence if the device turns red. Doing this may help keep noise to a minimum and make it less likely that students will intentionally cause the device to change colors. The Yacker Tracker can be purchased for $39.95 on the Web at www.schoolaids.com and may also be available at your local teachers' supply store.

17. Play music in the background.

You may find that you can discourage students from talking and even enhance their concentration if you play soft music (for example, classical music) while they are working. Even though they may protest your choice of music, you may be surprised to find it has a calming effect.

See Also

Assembly Problems

Back Talk

Calling Out

Disruptive/Uncooperative Behavior

Making Noises

Tattling

Elementary students, especially those in kindergarten through second grade, are quick to tattle. They may tell the teacher about their classmates' misdeeds for a variety of reasons. They may want to get the teacher's attention. They may want to curry favor with her. They may want to get another student in trouble. They may obtain a sense of power and importance from tattling. They may tattle as a way of figuring out what is allowed and what is not. Or they may believe that rules are sacred and feel compelled to inform the teacher if a rule is being violated.

Whatever the reason, tattling can disrupt classroom lessons and sap your energy as you try to resolve student conflicts. Tattling can cause you to feel more like a referee than an instructor, with more time spent resolving disputes than teaching lessons. And if you don't find a way to contain this problem, you may find that you have a tattling epidemic on your hands, with a constant stream of students eager to report on their classmates.

The dilemma for the teacher is whether to respond to tattletales. Although your teaching obligations preclude your dealing with every dispute that arises, you want to make sure that no student is being hurt physically or emotionally by a classmate. The following strategies will help you walk this line in a way that allows you to spend most of your time teaching while ensuring that students are safeguarded.

What You Can Do

1. Teach your students the difference between tattling and telling.
Discuss the issue of tattling with your class. With younger elementary students, you may have to describe what tattling is. Ask students how they feel when someone tattles on them, making sure to elicit the point that students are likely to be upset with classmates who tattle. Tell your class that the only time they are allowed to report a student's behavior to you is when a classmate is doing something that is hurtful, destructive, or dangerous. Explain what you

mean by hurtful ("when a student does something to hurt another student or make him feel very upset"), destructive ("when a student damages school property or property belonging to another person"), and dangerous ("when a student does something that can cause him or others to be hurt"). Inform your students that when they report these incidents to you they are not tattling but rather telling important information. Give your students some situations, and ask them to identify whether they are examples of tattling (and thus not allowed) or telling (which is not only allowed but encouraged). For example, you might ask them to categorize the following:

- "Sarah just hit Jessica."

- "Tamika is picking her nose."

- "Billy didn't do his homework."

- "Eric said he was going to beat up Ryan after school."

2. Help students learn to ignore behaviors that do not affect them.

When a student complains to you about a classmate's behavior that does not affect him (for example, "Patrick is not staying in single file"), let him know this is not his concern. You might say, "I'm happy to see that you know how to behave, but I would prefer that you not tell me about behavior that does not concern you." Another response might be to ask, "Are you trying to get a student in trouble or out of trouble? I'm only interested in what you have to say if you're trying to get a classmate out of trouble." Some teachers use the phrase "M.Y.O.B." to give the message to students to "mind your own business."

3. Encourage students to settle problems on their own.

If a student complains about something a classmate has done to him, encourage him to solve the problem without your help. You might give him some ideas about how to respond (for example, "Did you tell him to stop?"). If appropriate, you might suggest an area of the class where the students can go to talk about the problem. If you find that a number of your students have difficulty asserting themselves with their classmates, consider doing some role-playing with them so they can gain the confidence and skills to stop classmates from doing things they do not like.

4. Don't automatically dismiss a student's concern.
Keep in mind that a complaining student may be alerting you to a problem that warrants your involvement, so screen his concern before dismissing it. Be especially attentive to reports suggesting that a student is being bullied, especially if you are getting similar reports from various students. Studies of bullying indicate that teachers sometimes fail to respond to reports of students being taunted, threatened, or harassed. If you are not sure whether it is an issue requiring your attention, tell the student you will get back to him, and then keep a watchful eye on the students to observe their interactions. If you conclude that bullying is taking place, you may want to intervene rather than encourage the victim to stand up to the bully. In bullying situations, there is often an imbalance of power that makes it difficult for a weaker, smaller student to confront a stronger, bigger classmate.

5. Stop a student before he even gets a chance to tattle.
If you sense a student is about to tattle on a classmate, stop the student before he completes his thought and say to him, "Are you about to tattle on another student, or are you going to tell me important information that a student is doing something that is hurtful or destructive?" If he tells you the latter, let him finish his thought.

6. Set up a situation box.
This strategy is appropriate for students who are able to communicate in writing. Put a covered shoe box on your desk with a slit in the top. Place a note pad next to the box. Let your students know that if they have a concern about a classmate and need your help in dealing with it, they can write a note and leave it in the box. Tell them that you will read the notes before the end of the day and that you will follow up with the student who wrote the note if you think help is needed. Reassure them that they can still see you without leaving a note to report a student doing something hurtful, dangerous, or destructive. If you decide to follow up on a concern, ask the student if the problem is still going on. You may find that his concern has faded. You may also want to talk with him at the beginning of recess. His eagerness to go to recess may help you gauge his level of worry.

7. Recognize students for non-tattling behavior.
Praise students for handling peer issues on their own, especially if they have a history of tattling. Similarly, reinforce students when they come to you with important concerns relating to the physical or emotional welfare of students. Students may feel as if they have "ratted" on somebody. Reassure them that what they did was far different from tattling. You may say something like, "Melissa, thank you for telling me this. You did the absolutely right thing in coming to me."

8. Do not put students in charge of their classmates.
Putting a student in a position of authority over his classmates will often give rise to the student telling you about students who have been noncompliant, which will engender student conflict. You can give students responsibilities in the classroom; just make it clear that being in charge of their classmates is not one of them.

9. Pay attention to the frequent tattler.
A student who tattles often may be looking for attention from you. Try to identify if there is an underlying concern—perhaps low self-esteem or peer ridicule—and respond in a supportive manner without reinforcing the tattling.

See Also

Complaining, Frequent

Dependent Behavior

Friends, Lack of

Whining

Teasing

Teasing is a pervasive problem in our schools and can be a painful experience for the students who are on the receiving end. It can give rise to anxiety and low self-esteem and, if frequent and ongoing, can leave psychological scars that last longer than those from physical blows. School performance may also be affected. A student upset about teasing may have problems concentrating in class and may be reluctant to attend. Teasing is not just a problem for the targets of ridicule. It makes all students feel uncomfortable. In addition, teasing may beget more teasing, which can give rise to physical conflicts.

Although teasing often engenders hurt feelings, that is not always the intent of the teaser. A child who teases may be trying to build herself up by tearing others down. It may also be her way of trying to boost her status, influence, and popularity with her classmates. Maligning others may be her misguided way of trying to fit in.

Whatever the teaser's intent, students should not have to put up with being put down. They need to know that you will take this problem seriously and that they will be protected. Toward this end, you need to send a strong message that ridicule will not be tolerated in your classroom. If teasing is allowed to continue unchecked, you may find other children engaging in similar behavior.

Because your students may be reluctant to tell you they are being teased, you need to be alert for signs that they are being ridiculed. Possible signs include avoidance of school areas such as the playground, withdrawal from peers, unusual fearfulness or anxiety, difficulty focusing in class, and a reluctance to come to school.

What You Can Do

1. Establish a clear anti-teasing policy in your class. Tell your students very early in the year that in your class all children are to be treated with respect and kindness. This means that teasing, name calling, using put-downs, and

Elementary Teacher's Discipline Problem Solver

other cruel behaviors are not allowed under any circumstances. Teach them what the words "zero tolerance" mean, and inform them that this concept applies to teasing. Tell them that you need their help in creating a classroom where students can express their ideas without fear of being ridiculed. Explain the possible consequences for students who violate this policy. Remind them of the class policy periodically.

2. Promote a climate of cooperation and caring.

You can help discourage teasing by reinforcing acts of kindness and communicating values of cooperation and tolerance in your classroom. Show your students that everyone is deserving of respect by relating in a caring manner to all of your students. Be careful that your playful comments are not misinterpreted. For example, saying "I missed you, freckle-face" to a girl who is returning from an absence may be embarrassing to her. Help your students understand the behaviors you expect by putting a list of "caring behaviors" on the bulletin board.

3. Discuss teasing at a class meeting.

Because teasing is such a common problem in elementary school and can consume so much of your time, it is important to have a serious talk with your class about this issue. Help them understand how hurtful teasing can be. Ask them to talk about times they were teased (without mentioning anybody's name) and how it felt. Tell them that if they see a student being teased, they should try to come to his aid or let you know, but they should not join in. Let them know that children who tease are often unhappy and are trying to make themselves feel better by putting down others. Saying this may deter the teasers in your class, who may not want to be viewed in this way by classmates.

4. Help your students gain insights into teasing through class activities.

Consider doing the following with your class:

- Read stories to your class about teasing. Stimulate discussion by asking the following questions:

    How do you think the child felt about being teased?

    How did he deal with it?

Did it help?

What else could he have done?

Do you have any ideas about why children tease others?

- Present realistic scenarios to students that may give rise to ridicule (for example, a student's zipper is open), and ask for suggestions about what they could say.

- Give students the assignment of making a list of hurtful comments they hear classmates make during the course of a week. Tell them to write down what was said and how the child being teased responded without recording any person's names or profane language. At the end of the week, hold a class meeting, and have students discuss what they observed and what conclusions they reached about why children engage in teasing, how it affects children, and what are effective ways to respond.

5. Demonstrate the power of words.
One teacher uses a simple exercise to help her students think before they tease a classmate. She takes out toothpaste and construction paper and tells the class that the toothpaste represents hurtful words and the construction paper the student being teased. She has a student come to the front of the class and squeeze the toothpaste onto the paper. Then she asks her to put the toothpaste back in the tube. When she is unable to do this, the teacher makes the point that just as toothpaste, once out of the tube, cannot be put back, hurtful words, once out of your mouth, cannot be taken back.

6. Figure out why the student is being teased.
Ask yourself if the student's behavior is drawing the attention of other students and eliciting the teasing. The following are some examples of these behaviors: crying in class, wearing dirty clothes, nose picking, and having an unfashionable haircut. If you identify behaviors that are giving rise to peer ridicule, help the child change the behaviors but do it so that he does not feel accused of doing something wrong.

7. Have a one-on-one talk with the offending student.

If you sense she did not mean to upset her classmate, help the teaser understand how hurtful ridicule can be. If you sense, however, she was trying to be hurtful, let her know in a serious but not humiliating manner that this behavior is unacceptable and must stop immediately. Let her know that you will monitor her closely. Talk with her about how her behavior will cause classmates to avoid her. Ask how else she might have responded, while offering suggestions of your own. For example, if she was frustrated by a student missing a ball during a kickball game, suggest she opt for a put-up rather than a put-down ("Good try, Sarah. You'll get it next time"). And finally, ask if she is upset about something, as children who tease often are.

8. If a student persists in teasing others, take disciplinary action.

The purpose should be to deter her hurtful behavior rather than to humiliate or embarrass her. Assign a consequence that is proportional to the severity of her actions. This might be serving an after-school detention, missing recess, or not being allowed to attend a school activity. You might also contact her parents to inform them of her actions and to ask that they convey to her that teasing is unacceptable.

9. Role-play with the student being teased.

Assume the role of the student being teased so you can model what to say, perhaps using some of the responses listed next. Then reverse roles and have the child practice what to say in response to ridicule, as you give feedback. Also model the use of positive self-talk. For example, if a child is called stupid by a classmate, suggest that he say the following to himself: "When Rowena says I'm dumb, it's because she's trying to get others to pay attention to her. But she's got the problem, not me. I get better grades than she does anyway."

10. Help the student prepare some ready responses.

Show him how to deflect the teasing or defuse the situation without provoking his tormentor or appearing upset. Suggest he respond simply and firmly to the offending student or else say nothing. If he is open to responding, advise him to speak confidently while looking the student in the eye, and then walk away without engaging her in conversation. The following examples may show the teaser that the student is not as passive as she thought:

- "Please don't say those things. You really hurt my feelings." This is the straightforward approach.

- "Teasing kids is a pretty nerdy thing to do." This appeal to the student's desire for peer approval may encourage her to back off.

- "Could you say that again?" Asking the student to repeat herself may take the wind out of her sails.

- "Thanks for telling me. I didn't know that." An unpredictable comment such as this may throw the student off stride.

- "That's the nicest thing anybody's ever said to me." A humorous response may be effective in disarming the name caller.

- "That's your opinion." A short, simple response such as this, followed by the student walking away, will get the point across.

- "I don't want to argue with you. Do you want to play a game with me?" A conciliatory approach might soften the student.

11. Tell other school staff about a student who is being teased.
Children who tease others are likely to make their comments outside your presence. Alert other adults who supervise the student, including the bus driver, lunch and playground monitors, and specials teachers, so they can keep a watchful eye and intervene if necessary. You may want to suggest that they separate the two students as much as possible.

12. Help the student being teased to connect with his peers.
The more involved a child is with other children, the less he will be a target for teasing. If he is isolated from his peers, help him establish friendships by encouraging involvement in activities where he feels confident and is with peers who are kind and accepting. Pay particular attention to lunch and recess, when teasing is likely to occur. Also encourage his parents to set up play dates with classmates.

13. Help the student who is being teased frequently to gain recognition from peers.

Find a way to highlight the student's strengths and talents in the presence of his peers so they learn to see him in a new light. If he is skilled at doing cartoons, have him show some of his drawings to the class. If he is interested in magic, have him demonstrate some tricks. If he is a whiz on the computer, have him become the class troubleshooter. If he has special needs, help classmates learn something about him that lets them see that he has many of the same interests they do.

14. Use peers to help vulnerable students.

Students who are teased may have little status with their peers. If so, help them gain a sense of belonging in the classroom by finding some respected classmates to befriend them. You might even ask older students to spend time with children who have been rejected by peers.

See Also

Bothering Classmates

Bullying

Playground Problems

Rude/Disrespectful Behavior

Toileting Problems

Teachers are sometimes called upon to deal with issues that fall well outside the scope of education. Toileting is one such issue. You may have a student who wets or soils herself in school. This behavior can be a source of embarrassment and distress to the student, as well as a disruption to your class, if other students become aware of it. This is not an issue that you can ignore, especially if it gives rise to ridicule and rejection from peers.

A child's toileting problem may stem from a variety of causes. She may have a physical problem such as a urinary tract infection that causes her to urinate involuntarily, or constipation that leads to leakage and soiling. The problem may also stem from her reluctance to use the toilet in school because of discomfort in going to the hall bathroom or intense involvement in an activity. Her failure to use the bathroom in a timely manner may result in a toileting accident.

In some cases, the behavior may be purposeful. She may wet or soil herself to avoid an activity that is uncomfortable for her. For example, in an effort to avoid going out on the playground where she is the target of teasing, a child may have an "accident" right before recess and be sent to the nurse's office.

Toileting problems command your attention because of the social and emotional implications for the student. A child who wets or soils herself in school is frequently the target of ridicule and often shunned by classmates. Fearful that other children may learn of her problem, she may shy away from peer interaction. Self-esteem may plummet as she comes to feel ashamed of her behavior and begins to believe there is something wrong with her. In responding to a child with a bladder or bowel control problem, it is critical that you be sensitive to her emotional well-being and guided by the principle of preserving her dignity and self-esteem.

What You Can Do

1. Involve the parents.
If a child has wet or soiled herself in school on more than one occasion, it is imperative that you talk with her parents to gain information about the problem at home and work together to solve the problem in school. You may want to involve the nurse in this meeting. In talking with them, keep in mind that this is a sensitive issue to discuss with them because they may feel embarrassed by their child's behavior. Although you want to be tactful in your presentation, you also want to be direct and honest. This conversation may touch upon the following points:

- Find out if the child wets or soils herself at home and what, if anything, seems to trigger it. Ask if she has the necessary toileting skills and what practices they follow to avoid accidents.

- Ask the parents if there are any stresses in the child's life that may help explain the problem.

- Suggest that they talk with their child's doctor if they have not already done so to find out if there is a physical basis for the problem. For example, it may be that she has a urinary tract infection that causes her to lose control.

- If the child is coming to school smelling of urine because of having wet herself during the night, suggest she take a shower in the morning.

- If the parents are following a treatment plan to deal with the problem, find out how you can support that plan at school. For example, if they are rewarding her every time she goes to the bathroom at home, discuss whether you should follow the same procedure in school.

2. Have a private conversation with the student.
This is no doubt an awkward and sensitive subject for her, so tread gingerly, adopting a matter-of-fact and nonjudgmental tone. Let her know that you want to help her solve the problem, especially because other children may tease her or avoid her if it continues. Although you do not want to ask why she had an accident, you

Toileting Problems

do want to ask if she knows when she has to go to the bathroom. If so, tell her to let you know any time she feels the urge and you will let her go right away. Also talk with her about the procedure to follow if she has an accident.

3. Remind the student to use the bathroom.
She may have a toileting accident because she forgets to go or avoids going to the bathroom. With this student, the key is to make certain she goes to the bathroom regularly. Make sure she goes during the regularly scheduled bathroom breaks, but let her go at other times if she needs to. Work out with her a subtle, nonverbal signal (for example, a wink of the eye) to alert her when you think she should go to the bathroom. You might get her attention before signaling her by calling her name. If you have a watch with an alarm, you might set it to go off at the time you want her to go or on an hourly basis as a reminder to you to signal her to go. With an older student, you may want to suggest to her parents that they get her such a watch and set it to go off on an hourly basis to remind her to use the bathroom.

4. Keep a change of clothes handy.
Ask the parents of a child who is prone to toileting problems to send in an extra set of clothes, but in case they don't, have a set available. You might want to keep the clothes in the nurse's office.

5. Handle toileting incidents in a discreet and private manner.
In this way, you minimize the possibility of other children becoming aware of the incidents and lessen the chance of teasing. Take the child aside, and suggest she go to the nurse's office to clean herself or change her clothes. Give her as much responsibility for caring for herself as is consistent with her age. A kindergartener or first grader may need help in cleaning herself up, but an older student should be able to care for herself. Talk to the child in a matter-of-fact manner without any hint of annoyance or distress. You might say something like the following: "Sometimes students have accidents because they are so involved in what they are doing they forget to go to the bathroom. In the future, if you feel an urge to go, tell me and I'll let you go right away."

6. Allow the student to use a private bathroom.
It may be that she is resisting going to the bathroom because she is uncomfortable using a stall in the hall rest room. If so, allow her to use a private bathroom such as the one in the nurse's office, especially if she is cleaning herself or changing her clothes after an accident.

7. Look for patterns with the incidents.
This information can help you figure out if the toileting incidents are accidental or intentional. Keep a log of when they happen and what occurs before and after. Do they occur at the same time of the day? For example, do they happen right before lunch or during a stressful activity such as a test? What typically happens after the incidents? Is she sent home or to the nurse? Answering these and other questions will help you figure out if she is trying to avoid an activity and what steps you can take to help her feel more comfortable in that activity. For example, if the response to a toileting incident is always to send her home, it is a safe bet that her behavior is her way of getting to go home.

8. Encourage the student.
She is likely embarrassed and upset about her toileting difficulty and would probably like nothing more than to have it go away. When you talk with her, do not add to her stress by yelling at her or suggesting that she is to blame for her behavior. And certainly do not punish or humiliate her in an effort to get her to change. Rather, talk with her in a supportive manner, and give her confidence that with help from you and her parents the problem will improve. Make sure to find positive aspects of her class performance to praise so she does not think your relationship with her is dominated by her toileting problems.

9. Talk with the rest of your class.
If the child is being ridiculed or shunned by classmates, talk with them when the child is out of the class. Help them understand that she has a genuine problem and that nobody wants to make it go away more than she does. Tell them that most children run into difficulties of some kind and that they would not like it if other children made fun of them when they did. Ask for their cooperation in not teasing or rejecting her.

Tell them that the best thing they can do if the problem occurs is to continue what they are doing without talking about it, but reassure them that you will deal with it promptly. This does not need to be a long conversation. Indeed, it is better if it is short and to the point.

10. Stop the teasing immediately.
If you become aware that the student is being ridiculed for her toileting problem, put an end to the teasing right away, but do so in a calm manner without dwelling on the issue. If you respond in a harsh manner, you may incur the students' anger and may make them more inclined to continue ridiculing her. If you belabor the issue publicly, you will embarrass the student.

11. Check on the student if she is in the bathroom a long time.
If a child has a history of toileting problems, you may want to send an adult (if available) to check on her. She may have wet or soiled her pants and need some assistance in cleaning herself.

12. Monitor the student's fluid intake.
If the child is wetting herself in school, keep her drinks from the water fountain to a minimum. Of course, you do not want to deny her water completely. If you have questions about appropriate drinking restrictions, talk with the school nurse. Also let the child's parents know you are doing this, and get their okay.

13. Address toileting in the student's IEP.
If the student is a special education student and is wetting or soiling herself, suggest that this issue be addressed in the IEP. This will spur the members of the IEP team to develop a plan to deal with this problem that everyone is committed to following.

See Also

Bathroom Problems

Hygiene, Poor

Teasing

Tourette's Syndrome

Tourette's syndrome (TS) is a neurological disorder that is characterized by tics, which can take the form of repeated, involuntary, and rapid body movements (motor tics) or uncontrollable verbalizations (vocal tics). A child with TS typically exhibits both types of tics. This disorder can present issues of classroom management for the teacher, as well as self-esteem and peer acceptance problems for the student.

Although the symptoms of TS vary from person to person, the majority of individuals with this disorder have mild cases. Most students with TS are able to attend regular classes and lead productive and independent lives as adults. The behaviors associated with TS generally lessen with age. In fact, studies indicate that 20 to 30 percent of children with TS outgrow this problem in their teens or early twenties.

The behaviors that you see with TS vary with each child and may include rapid blinking of the eyes, twitching of the mouth, or jerking of the head. In some cases, the behaviors are more disruptive, such as kicking, touching other people, or jumping. Involuntary vocalizations might include repeated throat clearing, grunting, yelping, or saying words or phrases repeatedly. On very rare occasions, the person with TS will use offensive language (for example, obscenities) involuntarily. The symptoms of TS may wax and wane in intensity and may even disappear for weeks or months at a time.

TS may have an impact on a child's school performance. Although children with TS typically have the same cognitive ability as other children, many have learning and attentional difficulties. Staying in their seats, sticking with tasks for a sustained period, and organizing their work can be problematic for them. In fact, about half of children with TS have attention deficit disorder, according to some estimates.

Students with TS may also have problems controlling their impulses, so they may be easily frustrated and quick to lose their temper. They may also act in an aggressive or socially inappropriate manner. As a result, peers may perceive them as different or even disturbed, which may give rise to ridicule or rejection. The social and emotional problems that often accompany TS can be more upsetting for the student than the physical symptoms or the academic difficulties. The challenge in teaching a child with TS is thus not just dealing with behaviors he can't control but helping him feel more comfortable in the classroom and accepted by his classmates.

What You Can Do

1. Recognize that you play a key role in detecting TS.

Because the diagnosis of TS relies largely on behavioral observations, you may be the first to spot the problem. If you observe a student in your class displaying tics, begin to observe him systematically, jotting down the form and frequency of the tics and the situations and times they occur. You might also ask the school psychologist to observe the child. Contact the parents to inform them of your observations.

2. Provide support and understanding to the parents.

Parents of children with TS may have almost as tough a time dealing with the disorder as their child does. In addition to possibly feeling guilty that he may have inherited the disorder from one of them, they may be distressed and confused by his unusual behaviors. Help ease their distress by reacting in a supportive and understanding way and reassuring them that their child will be treated with care and concern. You will want to talk with them in the beginning of the year to learn about the particular behaviors their child may exhibit, strategies for responding to him, and potential side effects to any medication he may be taking.

3. Have a one-on-one talk with the student.

Tell the student that you are aware of his medical problem and that you know he lacks control over his tics and is not misbehaving. He will appreciate hearing this, as he is likely sensitive to being perceived by others as strange or uncooperative because of his behavior. Ask him for suggestions about what you can do or not do to make him feel comfortable in class.

4. Help your class understand TS.

Obtain permission from the student and his parents before talking with the class, and ask if they would like to be present for and participate in the discussion. Make a brief presentation to the class, explaining that their classmate has a medical problem that causes him to behave the way he does. Students will be more sympathetic to him if they learn that his behaviors have a medical basis and thus are not under his control. The Tourette's Syndrome Association (telephone 1-718-224-2999) offers a brochure titled "Matthew and the Tics" for teachers to read to their students or for students to read on their own.

5. Encourage positive peer interaction with the student.

Your students are likely to look to you for guidance about how to respond to the child with TS, so try to model an understanding, accepting approach. If you observe classmates who are teasing the student with TS, take them aside and try to elicit their understanding and cooperation. If another student is making noises in class, ask him to stop because the child with TS may think the student is making fun of him.

6. Permit the student to leave class at any time.

The student with TS may be able to hold off expressing his tics for a short time, but he still may need a place where he can go to release his symptoms and thus avoid the embarrassment of doing it in public. This might be the nurse's office, the bathroom, or a corner of the library. A study carrel in your classroom might provide him with the privacy he needs. Give the student a signal to use to alert you that he needs to leave the room.

7. If the tics are not disruptive, try to ignore them.

The best response to the student's tics is no response at all. Drawing attention to them will only make him more self-conscious about his disorder and create a social barrier between him and other students. If the tics are disruptive and hard to ignore, look for ways to lessen their disruptiveness. As an example, if the student compulsively taps his pencil, you might place a piece of foam rubber on his desk.

8. Allow the student to release excess energy.
The student with TS, similar to a student with an attention deficit disorder, may have difficulty sitting still for a long period. Moreover, the buildup of tension resulting from having to sit quietly may worsen the TS symptoms. Allow the child to move around during the day by, for example, letting him go to the water fountain or bathroom or serving as classroom messenger.

9. Be on the lookout for medication side effects.
Although there is at present no cure for TS, medication can be helpful in lessening its more extreme symptoms. But the medications for TS can have significant side effects, including drowsiness, sluggish thinking, memory problems, and social withdrawal. Some children even become school phobic during the initial stage of the medication. Ask the parents to let you know when their child is beginning or changing medication so you can inform them of any side effects.

10. Don't be afraid to discipline the student.
Teachers must walk a fine line with a student with TS, trying to be understanding without being overprotective. As a general rule, treat him as you do other students. If he is misbehaving and you believe his behavior is under his control, don't hesitate to use the same disciplinary measures you would use with other students while suggesting alternative ways of behaving.

11. Orchestrate opportunities for the student to shine.
The child with TS is often lacking in confidence and may not feel accepted by his classmates. Take advantage of his strengths and interests to find areas where he can excel in the classroom. For example, if he is good at math, have him demonstrate how to do some challenging math problems on the board. If he has a special skill, encourage him to show the class.

12. Make accommodations if the student has handwriting problems.
A student with TS may have poor or illegible handwriting because of difficulties controlling his hand movements. If so, limit the amount of material he must write by hand or give him extra time. Design worksheets that require limited

writing, and avoid making him recopy assignments that are done sloppily. Allow him to decide whether he wants to write in manuscript or cursive. You may find that he can use a computer more effectively than he can write by hand.

13. Provide test-taking alternatives.

The student's tics and handwriting difficulties may place him at a significant disadvantage when taking timed tests so that the test results fail to reflect what he knows. In addition, his vocal tics may disrupt other students taking a test. To deal with this problem, you might give him extra time to do the test, provide an alternate test setting such as the library, or give him an oral rather than written exam.

14. Consider recommending the student for a special education evaluation.

Although most students with TS can learn effectively in regular classes, some may need special education. Recommend an evaluation for the student if his TS behaviors are significantly impeding his learning. If determined eligible for special education, he may receive individualized instruction in a regular or special education classroom. As an alternative, the student may qualify to receive special accommodations in school through Section 504—a federal law that mandates that public schools provide accommodations for students with disabilities.

See Also

Attention Deficit

Hyperactivity

Seatwork Problems

Self-Esteem, Low

Special-Needs Students

Teasing

Vandalism

Vandalism by students is a major problem for schools. Although it is more common in secondary schools, elementary students also engage in this behavior. Vandalism in schools may take various forms, from writing in books to writing on desks, from marring walls to smashing windows, from cutting up school bus seats to taking apart school furniture. Even though the principal is typically responsible for dealing with students who have engaged in vandalism, you play an important role in its prevention by attending to the reasons underlying this behavior.

Students may engage in vandalism for a variety of reasons. For some, it is their way of venting anger or frustration toward the school, perhaps stemming from social difficulties or academic failure. For others, it is an effort to curry favor with peers by impressing them with their daring. And for still others, it is an innocent act reflecting their lack of understanding about appropriate behavior.

Whatever the motivation, vandalism can have a marked impact on a school district. It can drain resources that are needed for important student programs and thus requires a strong, effective response from schools. Failure to provide firm consequences for vandalism will only encourage other students to engage in similar behavior.

What You Can Do

1. Model concern for school property.
Demonstrate to your students through your own actions how you value school property. You can do this by treating items in your room with care, whether by the way you have arranged books on the shelves or the attention you have paid to decorating the room.

2. Talk with your students about caring for others' property.
Students may need some guidance about the importance of caring for property that belongs to another person or the school. Talk with them about what to do if they lose

or damage property that is not theirs, including replacing it or compensating the person. You might ask them what they would expect to happen if another student damaged their property. Work in the issue of school property, and discuss how it needs to be treated with respect so other students can enjoy it.

3. Praise students who treat property with care.

Recognize students when you observe them handling materials carefully ("Jeffrey, I really like the way you have taken care of your books by covering them"). This not only conveys the message that care of school property is an important value but suggests to students that handling classroom materials with care will gain attention from you.

4. Try to understand the student's motivation.

As discussed earlier, students may destroy property for a variety of reasons. It may be their way of venting frustration with their academic difficulties. Or they may be frustrated with you, perhaps feeling you treated them unfairly. Try to identify the student's motivation by observing him carefully, taking note of what triggers the behavior. Although it is important to address these underlying concerns, this does not lessen the importance of holding the student accountable for the vandalism.

5. Have the student write down what he did.

With an older student who is able to write relatively well, have him describe on paper what he did. Also instruct him to discuss the possible consequences of school vandalism. Inform him that you will put this paper in his school file and will remove it at the end of the year if there are no further incidents of vandalism. You might also send his written statement to his parents, with the student's knowledge.

6. Make sure you are certain of a student's guilt before accusing him.

Do not accuse a student of vandalism unless you have convincing evidence of his culpability. If you suspect him of having done it but have no proof, tell him in private of the problem and ask if he has any knowledge of what happened. If he denies it, don't pursue it any further with him. If you falsely accuse him of having engaged in vandalism, you risk alienating him and perhaps incurring his wrath for the remainder of the year.

Vandalism

7. Inform your principal. Make sure to let your principal know of all but minor incidents of vandalism. Your school may have a specific policy for how it handles vandalism. It is also important to let the principal know if the student or parent needs to compensate the school in some way for the damage.

8. Inform the parents. You will be more effective in preventing future acts of vandalism if you have the parents' support. Whether you contact parents for a particular incident should depend on the extent of the damage. If the student has put gum under his desk or written in a book, you can handle this matter without informing the parents. If the incident is more serious, especially if it requires that the school be compensated in some way, parents must be notified. Check with your principal to see who should notify them.

9. Avoid lecturing the student. Certainly you can talk with him about the consequences of vandalism, but long lectures about how wrong vandalism is will have minimal effect. And trying to persuade the student to express remorse for his acts will accomplish little. Instead, focus on working out a plan for him to make restitution for what he did. Let the student offer his ideas for doing this.

10. Have the student make amends. Having the student remedy the problem he created is the best way of holding him accountable for his behavior. In devising a suitable plan, consider the nature of the damage and the age of the student, and make the punishment fit the crime. If the student has torn a page from a book, you might have him carefully tape it back in the book. If he has put gum under his desk, you might have him stay after school and remove gum from under all the desks, using a paint scraper. If he has written on the desk, have him clean all the desks in your classroom. If the damage is such that the parents must pay for it, suggest that they find some way for their child to do chores at home to work off the cost in a way that is compatible with his age.

11. Eliminate evidence of school vandalism immediately.
By showing the students that defacing school property will not only be punished but will be removed within a week of its occurrence, you will discourage others from engaging in this behavior.

12. Help the student feel a sense of belonging in school.
A student will be less likely to damage school property if he feels a sense of ownership and pride in the school. Try to involve him in activities that give him a good feeling about school so he is more likely to defend it than vandalize it. This is of course a good practice to follow with all students. Here are some possible activities: planting a garden, decorating one of the school's walls, and painting walls that have been defaced. You might also get ideas from students on how to improve the school building and then try to implement some of them.

13. Use math to help the student understand the consequences of vandalism.
Find out from the principal the cost of repairs for the previous year for vandalism. Have students figure out how many pizza parties the school could have had if there had been no vandalism.

14. Make the student responsible for specific school property.
Surprise the student who has engaged in vandalism by showing trust in his ability to care for school property. For example, you might allow him to help out with audiovisual or athletic equipment. Tell him that you are confident he can handle this task in a responsible manner. He will not want to disappoint you.

See Also

Angry Outbursts

Bathroom Problems

Playground Problems

Weapon, Possession of

The tragic school shootings of recent years loom large in our memories and remind us that the violence that we see all too often in the world has invaded our schools. As abhorrent as these events are, the reality is that gun violence in schools is rare and especially so in elementary schools. Yet when an incident involving a gun does occur, even if it involves just the act of a student bringing a gun to school, it can send shock waves through the student body, creating widespread fear and anxiety.

Schools must be safe havens. Students must not only *be* safe in school, they must *feel* safe in school. And parents too must have the peace of mind that comes with knowing their children are safe. Under conditions of fear and vulnerability, teachers have difficulty teaching and students have difficulty learning. When students fear they will be targets of violence, anxiety about going to school increases and concentration while in school decreases.

Although it is highly unlikely that one of your students will use a weapon on a classmate, you may have to deal with a student who comes to school with a weapon. In responding to such a student, your first priority is to ensure the safety of your students. You need to alert your principal as soon as possible and let her assume responsibility for handling the problem. Your involvement does not end here, however. You may need to deal with the student if he returns to the classroom and consider the impact of the incident on your other students.

In determining whether an item constitutes a weapon, you and the principal need to exercise careful judgment, especially in light of the potentially severe consequences of being found to be in possession. For example, you might reasonably conclude, after talking with the student, that a penknife brought to school by a well-behaved, mild-mannered student is not a weapon. You might tell him not to bring it to school anymore and pursue it no further. Schools have sometimes gone overboard in making this judgment. As just one example, in one school district a second-grade student was suspended for bringing in a key chain that had a little toy gun attached to it.

What You Can Do

1. Find out your school district's policy on weapons.
Your school board most likely has a policy for dealing with students who bring weapons to school. Many school districts have implemented a "zero tolerance" policy for weapons, requiring that the school take serious disciplinary action (for example, a ten-day suspension or expulsion) if a student is found to be in possession of a weapon on school property. This policy may be dictated by the state.

2. Take seriously all threats to bring a weapon to school.
Let your principal know what the student said, even if he is young and you believe this is not a credible threat. The principal will want to assess the seriousness of this threat. Even if she concludes it is not serious, she or another school staff member (for example, the school psychologist) will want to talk with the student about what motivated him to make this threat and what he could have done differently.

3. Encourage students to tell you if they observe something dangerous.
Students sometimes have their fingers on the pulse of potentially dangerous situations in school. Find a time to let your students know that they should inform you of any dangerous situations that could cause harm to students. Do not mention weapons, as this may unnecessarily alarm some students.

4. If you become aware a student may have a weapon, take action immediately to ensure student safety.
If a child tells you that a classmate has a weapon, ask to see that student in the hall. Using a calm but serious voice, ask him if he has a weapon, making sure to use specific and clear language such as, "Do you have a knife, gun, or anything that could be used to hurt somebody anywhere in school?" If he says he does, insist that he tell you where it is. Whether he acknowledges or denies possession of a weapon, arrange to escort him to the office immediately. Tell the principal what you know, and allow her to take over from there. If a weapon is found, she will want to contact the student's parents and follow school policy, which may require that the police be contacted. The principal will also need to make

decisions regarding the disciplining of the student and his appropriateness for remaining in the classroom.

5. Confer with the parents.
The principal may ask you to be present at her meeting with the parents. She may ask a police officer to participate as well. This meeting has several purposes: to inform the parents of their child's behavior, to assess the seriousness of the threat, to apprise the parents of the actions to be taken, and to gain their support for the school's actions. The discussion with the parents will of course vary, depending on the child's behavior, but it should include some or all of the following issues:

- The parents' ideas on the underlying reasons for their child's behavior
- The child's history of aggressive or violent behavior
- The child's access to weapons
- Steps the parents have taken to prevent this access (for example, making sure the gun is unloaded, storing the gun in a locked cabinet, placing the bullets in a separate locked location, putting a safety locking device on the gun, or removing the gun from the home entirely)
- The child's exposure to violence in the media, namely in the television shows he watches and the computer and video games he plays

It is important that the child be brought in to this meeting so he can hear both the principal and his parents say that bringing a weapon to school is a very serious and dangerous act and is never to happen again. If a police officer is present, have him talk with the student about the potential consequences of bringing a gun to school.

6. Let parents know of services available to help their child.
A student who has brought a weapon to school will likely need some help to deal with his underlying motivation, as well as his possession of and access to weapons. Ask the guidance counselor or school psychologist to recommend to the parents a private counselor to work with the child and family. You might also contact community agencies or the police department to find out if they have or know of a videotape or educational program for children about the consequences of gun violence.

7. After the incident, talk with the student.

You may want to have a school counselor join you in this discussion. Ask the student why he brought the weapon. You may find that he was only trying to impress his peers and exercised poor judgment. Also consider a more aggressive motivation, however. Find out if he was feeling angry with a student or staff member and if so why. Inquire if another student has been threatening, hurting, or bullying him so that bringing the weapon was his way of fighting back. If it becomes clear that the student was seeking to get revenge for something that was done to him, take steps to deal with this situation and monitor the situation closely in subsequent weeks, perhaps by having the counselor meet with him weekly. Also encourage the student to let you know whenever he is upset or angry about something.

8. Find a way to bond with the student.

A student who brings a weapon to school may feel he has no one there he can talk with or trust with a problem. You can make it more likely that he will seek you out when he is upset or angry by making a special effort to reach out to him. Try to gain his trust by listening attentively to what he says and showing respect for his concerns. Find a few minutes every so often to joke with him or talk with him about his interests. Help him begin the day on a positive note by making an upbeat comment or giving him a high five when he enters class. He is likely to make more appropriate choices if he feels that you support and accept him.

9. Monitor your students after a dangerous incident.

If your other students become aware that a classmate has brought a weapon to school, they may experience anxiety and fear. Be on the lookout for signs of distress. If you sense that a number of your students are troubled by what happened, you may want to talk with your class. You might have the principal, guidance counselor, or school psychologist join you. Listen to the students' concerns about the incident, but reassure them that the school has taken action that makes it very unlikely it will happen again. If students continue to be distressed after this discussion, arrange for them to talk with a school counselor individually.

10. After the incident, write down what happened. Do this as soon as possible when the details are freshest in your mind. Note with precision the time, location, sequence of events, individuals involved, and behavior of each. Give a copy to the principal and keep a copy for yourself.

11. Consider requesting the student's removal from your class. You may have concerns for your and your students' physical and emotional well-being if one of your students has brought a weapon to school. If so, request from your principal that the student be transferred out of your class on a permanent basis. Emphasize that your ability to teach will be compromised if you feel uncomfortable and unsafe in his presence and that your other students are likely to feel anxious and fearful as well. The principal may decide to move him to another class or seek to have him placed in a special education program where he can be supervised more closely.

See Also

Aggressive Behavior

Angry Outbursts

Bullying

Hitting or Threatening a Teacher

Whining

Few behaviors are more frustrating to teachers than whining. The student who constantly responds in a shrill, high-pitched voice when requesting help or complaining can exasperate the calmest of teachers. If you have a whiner in your class, your patience may wear thin and you may find that you are spending an inordinate amount of time responding to her. This attention may not only take time from your lesson but may actually reinforce her whining.

Children learn to whine because they have found it is more effective in getting their way or the attention of others than when they speak in a normal tone of voice. Having found that it works like a charm at home, they assume it will work similarly in school. And it often does. Whining can be so irritating to listen to that it may be hard for you to ignore. Although your attention may be negative, in the form of expressions of annoyance, this negative attention may be more valued to some students than no attention at all.

As with other immature behaviors, whining is a behavior that teachers can be successful in changing. Just as whining has been learned because of the reaction it elicits, it can be unlearned by modifying your response to it. In this way, you can help ensure that whining does not become an entrenched behavior.

What You Can Do

1. Establish a "no whining" rule.
As part of your discussion with your students about classroom rules, let them know that whining is not allowed because it is unpleasant to listen to and can disrupt a classroom lesson or activity. You may need to explain to your younger students what you mean by whining and perhaps give some examples of both appropriate and inappropriate ways of requesting help. Remind them of the "no whining" rule during the year if necessary. Tell them they can come to you with a concern, but they must express it in the proper way, namely in a pleasant, grown-up voice. Help them

understand that they are more likely to get a positive response if they use this voice rather than a whiny tone. Ask them what the class would sound like if everybody whined at the same time.

2. Gently correct a student who whines.
If this is one of the first times you have heard her whine, say in a matter-of-fact manner, "I have trouble understanding you when you speak in a whiny voice. I'll be glad to help you but only if you talk in a normal tone of voice." If in response to this comment she speaks normally, praise her and respond to her question or concern immediately. If she responds again with a whine, tell her that you know she can speak in a more clear, less whiny voice. With a younger child, you might model how to say it. With an older child who knows how to speak appropriately, you might then turn away without responding further to her.

3. After correcting a student for whining a couple of times, ignore this behavior.
You might say in a neutral manner, "Maria, you are whining," and then turn away without a further response, either positive or negative. Then return to what you were doing. Even expressions of annoyance can be reinforcing to a student seeking attention and may serve to maintain the behavior.

4. Praise the student immediately when she does not whine.
When she speaks in a pleasant, non-whiny manner, make an effort to respond to her as soon as you can, especially if this is a situation in which she would ordinarily whine. You might say, "I was pleased to hear you speak in a mature, grown-up way just now." Because your attention is likely very important to her, find other occasions to acknowledge appropriate behavior or academic accomplishments without making reference to her speaking voice.

5. Identify any factors that may give rise to the whining.
By observing the circumstances surrounding the student's whining, you may be able to anticipate when the behavior will occur and take preventive measures. It may be, for example, that she is more likely to whine when she is tired, hungry, or

frustrated academically. Also consider the possibility that her whining is due to a speech problem, namely a nasally voice. If you suspect this to be the case, talk with your school's speech-language specialist. She may want to observe the child or even do an evaluation.

6. Silently signal the student when she whines.

She may not recognize when she is using a whiny tone of voice. Give her a nonverbal signal that only the two of you understand to alert her when she is whining. You might, for example, put your finger on your lips, pull your ear, or raise your eyebrows. Or you might have her suggest the signal to you. You may have to call her name to get her to pay attention so you can signal her. The goal here is not to embarrass the student but to help her become more aware when she is whining so she can learn to monitor herself.

7. Teach the student proper communication skills.

She may whine because that is the best way she knows to get others' attention. If so, meet with her privately and teach her more appropriate ways to elicit attention, in particular, how to ask for what she wants or express a concern in a respectful, pleasant manner. You might role-play with her by giving her common school situations (for example, she wants to join a game classmates are playing during recess) and having her try out different responses while you give her feedback. Emphasize that she is more likely to get what she wants and less likely to annoy others if she learns to speak in a pleasant, clear, and grown-up manner.

8. Record the student's whining.

Consider taping her whining when she is not aware of it. Find some private time with her and play the tape so she understands what her whining sounds like. You might suggest a common school situation and ask her to respond in both a whiny and normal tone of voice to make sure she understands the difference. Or you might give her some sample responses and have her tell you which voice you are using. Let her know that you are not trying to embarrass her but to help her overcome a problem that can cause her classmates to avoid her.

See Also

For Further Information

Albert, L. *Cooperative Discipline.* Circle Pines, Minn.: American Guidance Service, 1996.

Canter, L., and Canter, M. *Assertive Discipline: Positive Behavior Management for Today's Classroom.* (3rd ed.) Santa Monica, Calif.: Lee Canter & Associates, 2002.

Canter, L., and Canter, M. *Succeeding with Difficult Students.* Santa Monica, Calif.: Lee Canter & Associates, 1993.

Charles, C. M. *Essential Elements of Effective Discipline.* Boston: Allyn & Bacon, 2001.

Curwin, R. L., and Mendler, A. N. *Discipline with Dignity.* (2nd ed.) Northbrook, Ill.: Association for Supervision & Curriculum Development, 1999.

Evertson, C., Emmer, E., Clements, B., and Worsham, M. *Classroom Discipline for Elementary Teachers.* (3rd ed.) Boston: Allyn & Bacon, 1994.

Flick, G. L. *ADD/ADHD Behavior-Change Resource Kit: Ready-to-Use Strategies & Activities for Helping Children with Attention Deficit Disorder.* Paramus, N.J.: Center for Applied Research in Education, 1998.

Garrity, C., Jens, K., Porter, W., Sager, N., and Short-Cammilli, C. *Bully-Proofing Your School: A Comprehensive Approach for Elementary Schools.* Longmont, Colo.: Sopris West, 1994.

Germinario, V., Cervalli, J., and Ogden, E. H. *All Children Successful: Real Answers for Helping At-Risk Elementary Students.* Lancaster, Penn.: Technomic, 1992.

Girard, K., and Koch, S. *Conflict Resolution in the Schools: A Manual for Educators.* San Francisco: Jossey-Bass, 1996.

Goldstein, S. *Understanding and Managing Children's Classroom Behavior.* New York: Wiley, 1995.

Gordon, S. B., and Asher, M. J. *Meeting the ADD Challenge: A Practical Guide for Teachers.* Champaign, Ill.: Research Press, 1994.

Jones, V., and Jones, L. *Comprehensive Classroom Management.* (4th ed.) Boston: Allyn & Bacon, 1995.

Karlin, M. S., and Berger, R. *Discipline and the Disruptive Child: A New, Expanded Practical Guide for Elementary Teachers.* Englewood Cliffs, N.J.: Parker Publishing, 1992.

Kazdin, A. *Behavior Modification in Applied Settings.* (5th ed.) Pacific Grove, Calif.: Brooks/Cole, 1994.

Kerr, M. M., and Nelson, C. M. *Strategies for Addressing Behavior Problems in the Classroom.* (4th ed.) Paramus, N.J.: Prentice Hall, 2001.

MacKenzie, R. J. *Setting Limits in the Classroom: How to Move Beyond the Classroom Dance of Discipline.* Rocklin, Calif.: Prima Publishing, 1996.

Metcalf, L. *Teaching Toward Solutions: Step-by-Step Strategies for Handling Academic, Behavior & Family Issues in the Classroom.* Paramus, N.J.: Center for Applied Research in Education, 1999.

Nelsen, J., Escobar, L., Ortolano, K., Duffy, R., and Owen-Sohocki, D. *Positive Discipline: A Teacher's A–Z Guide.* (2nd ed.) Rocklin, Calif.: Prima Publishing, 2001.

Porro, B., and Peaco, T. *Talk It Out: Conflict Resolution in the Elementary Classroom.* Northbrook, Ill.: Association for Supervision & Curriculum Development, 1996.

Rhode, G., Jenson, W. R., and Reavis, H. K. *The Tough Kid Book: Practical Classroom Management Strategies.* Longmont, Colo.: Sopris West, 1992.

Shore, K. *Special Kids Problem Solver: Ready-to-Use Interventions for Helping All Students with Academic, Behavioral & Physical Problems.* Paramus, N.J.: Prentice Hall, 1998.

Walker, H. M. *The Acting-Out Child: Coping with Classroom Disruption.* Longmont, Colo.: Sopris West, 1995.

Watson, G. *Classroom Discipline Problem Solver: Ready-to-Use Techniques & Materials for Managing All Kinds of Behavior Problems.* Paramus, N.J.: Center for Applied Research in Education, 1998.

Watson, G. *Teacher Smart! 125 Tested Techniques for Classroom Management & Control.* Paramus, N.J.: Center for Applied Research in Education, 1996.

Wolfgang, C. H. *Solving Discipline and Classroom Management Problems: Methods and Models for Today's Teachers.* (5th ed.) New York: Wiley, 2001.